Additional Praise for *Be the Dream*

"Here is the American dream fully realized—told by those who have been enabled to take part in its daily affirmation. Here are young witnesses to possibility become achievement—their voices, their memories and experiences, a mighty moral summons to a nation: that others be encouraged to follow their lead. Books come and go in our lives, but this collective testimony will earn a lasting place in our hearts and will stir readers to appreciative gratitude on behalf of their fellow citizens."

—Robert Coles, James Agee Professor of Social Ethics, Harvard University, and author, *Children of Crisis* and *The Inner Life of Children*

"Find a kid with a glint in her (or his) eye (or put one there); mix into that young person's life adults (parents or grandparents, usually; teachers often; some adults, somewhere) who both love that kid and push his mind and heart; provide that young adolescent with sensitive, sensible and safe schools; add money, in whatever quantities that may be needed; and ask her to dream: that is the recipe of Prep for Prep. It works. The stories here bear ample witness to that fact. May American policy makers ponder the recipe carefully—for all kids."

—Theodore R. Sizer, founder, Coalition of Essential Schools; Visiting Professor of Education, Harvard and Brandeis Universities; coauthor (with Nancy Sizer), *The Students Are Watching*; author, *Horace's Hope*

"The stories in this book brim with insight, wit and intelligence. They are powerful evidence of education in its essence—talents nurtured, intellects honed and lives transformed. Many people talk about the importance of searching out talented young people from every quarter and inspiring them to aim high and achieve the utmost standards of excellence. Prep for Prep has delivered on this promise for 25 years, and Harvard is proud to claim more than 100 of its graduates among our current students and alumni. Prep for Prep combines vision and effectiveness in a rare and potent way." —Lawrence H. Summers, President, Harvard University

"An inspiring collection of stories about the positive impact of experience and education. Each one drives home the importance of leveling the playing field of opportunity so that our society wholly benefits from the vital contributions of each of its members. A great read for anyone who believes in the power of possibility."

—Senator Bill Bradley

"Read this book and be inspired by the bright minds, eager hearts and glorious potential of some of the hundreds of gifted young minority group students Prep for Prep has prepared for the best schools in America. *Be the Dream* demonstrates that the Prep for Prep program works and, as a result, a new cadre of well-educated, talented young people are available to help our nation become the 'Shining City on a Hill' that it should be."
—Governor Mario M. Cuomo

"Prep for Prep has taken thousands of young people from inner-city communities and prepared them for success at some of the nation's top prep schools—putting many on the path to Ivy League educations and impressive professional careers. *Be the Dream* does much more, however, than document the achievements of this remarkable program. It literally puts us in the minds of the young people who have been so profoundly changed by Prep for Prep. To read their candid, passionate stories (of obstacles overcome, lives turned around, possibilities opened up) is to be inspired. It is also to be reminded that just as stereotypes and low expectations can destroy potential, faith and a nurturing environment can restore it. Sometimes all that separates those who succeed in life from those who are defeated by it is a door leading away from doom. *Be the Dream* invites you to walk through that door with people who truly understand what it means to be given a chance. It is a journey well worth taking."
—Ellis Cose, author,
The Envy of the World and *The Rage of a Privileged Class*;
Contributing Editor, *Newsweek*

"Here are stories as richly and optimistically American as any ever told—but these particular stories are more important than most. They show how it's possible for talented minority kids to make it. Let's celebrate their words and achievements by making sure millions of others follow in their footsteps."
—Robert B. Reich,
former Secretary of Labor and author, *The Work of Nations*

"*Be the Dream,* a rich collection of the experiences of Prep for Prep alumni, tells a very powerful story. Gary Simons celebrates the success of this program with thoughtful introductions and poignant narratives. Each offers tremendous insight into the development of young people and illustrates the importance of nurturing and challenging intellectually gifted African-American, Latino and Asian-American students. This book is a valuable resource for educators and other professionals working with adolescents."
—James P. Comer,
Maurice Falk Professor of Child Psychiatry,
Yale Child Study Center, and Associate Dean, Yale School of Medicine;
author, *Child by Child: The Comer Process for Change in Education*

"There is no more critical issue facing our society than providing a quality education for all students. Prep for Prep is truly an extraordinary organization. Its alumni have gone on to careers of achievement, commitment, service and integrity. Prep for Prep shows the power of believing in a vision and the hard work needed to make it come true. I hope this book will make it accessible to a wider audience as it celebrates its generation of accomplishments."

—Caroline Kennedy,
cofounder, Profiles in Courage Awards;
Chief Executive, Office of Strategic Partnerships,
New York City Department of Education

"This is more than an inspiring collection of stories about leaving poverty and achieving academic success. It is the American dream in flesh and blood—a chronicle of how to make things go right in this country."

—Jonathan Alter, Senior Editor, *Newsweek*;
NBC News Contributing Correspondent

"*Be the Dream* is a powerful book because it demonstrates what can be accomplished when resources and commitment are brought to bear and, as a result, young people are given a *real* chance to succeed. This collection of first-person accounts shatters the myth that kids from Harlem, Washington Heights, the South Bronx and similar communities around the country can't compete with the 'best and brightest' from far more affluent backgrounds. As these moving, heartfelt stories make clear, the road they travel is neither easy nor devoid of obstacles and difficult decisions. However, their reflections on their struggles and triumphs are not only inspirational, but also a reason for hope. The honesty, integrity and courage of these young leaders shine through each page."

—Congressman Charles B. Rangel

"Since 1978, 25 classes of Prep for Prep students have transformed the vision of the program's founder into the reality of names, faces and a stunning record of academic success. It has been heartening for all of us who care about the future of education in this country to see gifted students move to new levels of achievement because of the opportunities that Prep opens up for them. As a result, countless families, schools, colleges and universities have been enriched, and I am happy to say that Princeton has been a major beneficiary of these ripple effects. We have found that Prep students who apply to Princeton are extremely well prepared for our rigorous academic programs, and those we are fortunate enough to attract to the University have not only excelled academically but made their mark as student and alumni leaders."

—Shirley Tilghman, President, Princeton University

"Hurray! for the conjoining of high-quality pedagogical intervention with human ability, drive, spirit and determination. *Be the Dream* is a beautifully creative presentation of the story of Prep for Prep by the teaching and learning persons who have lived the experience. Rather than a story of how they did it, it is a collection of reflections on how they live it—the nurturance of academic ability and the achievement of intellective competence in a group of young people, many of whom would not otherwise have achieved it. Read and savor these testimonies to the depth, diversity and richness of human potential."

—Edmund W. Gordon, Richard March Hoe Emeritus
Professor of Psychology and Education, Teachers College, Columbia,
and John M. Musser Professor of Psychology, Emeritus, Yale University

"Prep for Prep students at Horace Mann School are at the center of activity—in Advanced Placement courses, student government and athletics. Strength in the classroom spills over into extracurriculars, where Prep students are confident leaders. For the past two years, Horace Mann's valedictorian has been a Prep student—elected by the senior class for having distinguished him or herself academically and in the community. Several Prep students over the years have served as student body president. My own son, who graduated from Horace Mann in 2002, counted Vinson Cunningham, Jose Leonor, Christopher Mizell, Ikechi Ogbonna and Andrew Patterson—all Prep students—as his closest friends. When he was an 11th-grader, he asked me, seriously, how he could join Prep. He loved the citywide camaraderie among the Prep students. I know that the active presence of Prep students has made Horace Mann a better school."

—Eileen Mullady, Head of School, Horace Mann School

"The stories told by these Prep for Prep alumni are both inspired and inspiring. They remind us of the power of education in the lives of young people, and they remind us, too, that programs such as this one deserve the best efforts of all of us who believe in promoting opportunity in America."

—William Bowen, President, Andrew W. Mellon Foundation;
former President, Princeton University;
coauthor (with Derek Bok), *The Shape of the River*

"Prep for Prep students have been an integral and valuable part of the Exeter community for more than 15 years. Students who come to us from the Prep for Prep program are thoroughly prepared for living and learning as part of the Exeter family. Their contributions far exceed their numbers."

—Tyler C. Tingley, Principal, Phillips Exeter Academy

(continued at back of book)

BE THE DREAM

Prep for Prep Graduates Share Their Stories

Compiled and Introduced by

GARY SIMONS

A Prep for Prep Press Book
ALGONQUIN BOOKS OF CHAPEL HILL

A PREP FOR PREP PRESS BOOK

Published by
Algonquin Books of Chapel Hill
Post Office Box 2225
Chapel Hill, North Carolina 27515-2225

a Division of Workman Publishing

Grateful acknowledgment is made for permission to reprint from *I've Been a Woman,*
edited by Sonia Sanchez, copyright 1967 by Sonia Sanchez,
reprinted by permission of Third World Pres, Inc., Chicago

Cataloging and publication information is available from the Library of Congress.

ISBN 1-5651-2416-2—ISBN 1-5651-2417-0 (pbk)

Cover photo by Anthony Loew

Printed in the United States of America
First printing May 2003

10 9 8 7 6 5 4 3 2

First Edition

To all the boys and girls who have found within themselves
the courage to embark on remarkable journeys
that give so many others hope for our country's future,

and

to all those many individuals whose financial support,
advocacy of our cause and direct work with our students
have helped to make the journeys of nearly
3,000 very special young people possible,

this book is dedicated.

FOREWORD

As you read the stories in this book, I hope you will be as impressed and inspired by this extraordinary group of young adults as I am. Admire their conscious, early decisions to be serious about their education and how they seized the rare opportunity they had been given to improve it. Their fierce determination as children is an example for all of us. Over and over you will see loving parents—mothers and fathers—reaching beyond the limitations of education, income or language to fight for opportunities to ensure the best possible future for their children. They disprove the notion that children in poor schools do poorly because their communities and families don't encourage them to value learning. *Brown v. Board of Education* came about because poor Black parents wanted a better education for their children, just as the families of these writers did.

These days we hear so much about the problems youths face and about "problem youths." We hear much too little about the many young people who are succeeding and helping others despite extraordinary obstacles. That's why the organization that I run, the Children's Defense Fund, began sponsoring Beat the Odds® celebrations in cities around the country to honor students who have overcome extraordinary adversity and who are excelling in school and in their communities. Their stories, like many of the ones in this book, are always a heartbreaking reminder of just how difficult many American children's lives are. But without fail, every one of these celebrations is ultimately joyful and inspiring. We marvel at the strength, resiliency, determination and vision our young winners have already demonstrated. And we rejoice as they affirm their determination to overcome obstacles they know lie ahead and to do and be as much as they can dream.

I thought often of these Beat the Odds® winners as I read the very moving stories in *Be the Dream*. Many of the authors in this book were blessed with at least one big advantage—a caring adult somewhere in their lives who strongly valued and emphasized education. But most began their childhoods facing steep odds, made more so by the common twin threats of poverty and a poor school system that was failing them. Their stories show us how each of them drew on their own remarkable inner strength and courage to navigate around the obstacles in their paths and discover what it means to "be the dream."

In the end, though, this book's most important testimonies are the accomplished, articulate, confident adults these writers have grown up to become. In our country, where a majority of American fourth-graders can't read or do math at a proficient level and 2,811 high school students drop out of school *every day*, these fine young people eloquently show how much our nation loses by tolerating an educational system that continues to leave millions of children behind.

In his introduction, Prep for Prep founder and vice chairman Gary Simons acknowledges the unresolved public policy debate about why a program like Prep for Prep is needed. My answer is that massive reform of public education to ensure all children a quality and equal educational opportunity is urgently needed. But until it is a reality, it is equally urgent to give as many children as possible—right now—a chance to succeed. Prep for Prep is not a substitute for good public schools. As we persistently work for a public school system where every child is expected and helped to achieve, I am glad Mr. Simons—and those who shared his vision—chose not to simply remain on the sidelines. They acted to make a difference, first for a few children, then for a classroomful, then for hundreds . . . and now for nearly three thousand. And the numbers continue to grow.

The Prep for Prep alumni who share their stories here are making a difference too, showing readers—as they have shown classmates at their preparatory schools and universities, as they have shown their colleagues in boardrooms and operating rooms and courtrooms, and as they have shown friends and family "back home"—that when given a chance, children whom many schools write off and leave behind can accomplish just as much or more than children whose excellent educations have been a lifelong gift. Please let this book inspire all of us in the richest nation on earth to work to ensure the right to a quality education every child needs so he or she can live out the dreams that come with it.

Marian Wright Edelman
President, Children's Defense Fund

TO INFINITY AND BEYOND

by DAMALI DRISKELL, *Age 11*

"Wheee!" I shouted as I raced around the room, a large beach towel tied around my neck, jumping and flapping my arms. "I can fly!"

"You can't fly," my brother said, grinning and shaking his head.

"I can fly!" I insisted as I screeched to a halt. "*You* can't."

"I did once," he said as if he always did.

"No, you did not," I insisted.

"Okay, so I didn't," he admitted. "But that's not the point. If you can prove to me that you can fly, you win a dollar and a victory over me."

That was all I needed to hear. Ready to show my skill through victory, I climbed to the top of the bunk. I wasn't nervous at all, so I looked up, sighed and jumped. It was a wonderful moment. I hit the ceiling as I went up. I had never done that before, and I felt good all over. I spread the towel, and it caught air. My being a bit skinny at that age, I was able to stay adrift. The towel served as a parachute, and I landed very slowly. I grinned at my brother and began to laugh. I had won the bet!

This autobiographical vignette, written in December 2001, is typical of those included in the placement folders of students when they apply to independent schools. Damali is currently a seventh-grader at Trinity School.

"You didn't win," my brother said. "You went up, drifted a bit and came down."

"So do some birds," I said.

Even though I was happier that I touched the ceiling that day, it loomed too high for me to reach in the usual way. But then I was ready to move on to bigger and better things.

INTRODUCTION

As an elementary school teacher in the South Bronx, I repeatedly encountered boys and girls who exhibited all the characteristics that most people would consider predictors of success: intelligence, a love of learning, a willingness to work hard, a sense of personal integrity and the ability to work well with others. Given the conditions in the local junior high school, however, it seemed to me unlikely that many of them would realize their potential. In fact, given so many signals that their efforts in school were an exercise in futility, it seemed extraordinary to me that these young people, at fifth or sixth grade, still retained the spirit, the enthusiasm for learning and the belief in the possible that made them stand out from the vast majority of their peers. I decided that if any group of youngsters deserved special intervention, I had happened upon some of them. These intellectually strong and motivated students were unlikely candidates for government intervention, since such programs tended to focus on children who were far behind. While affluent segments of society invested greatly in the personal and academic development of their ablest youngsters, the potentially highest achievers from less privileged groups—those that were already grossly underrepresented in the country's leadership pool—were rarely the recipients of special attention and access to experiences that would develop their talents and persuade them that it was legitimate to aim to be all you could be and to do all you could do in life.

For several years, I had been placing my ablest students in independent schools in Manhattan and Riverdale. Although these were students for whom I had developed a special curriculum and who had learned to work hard, their fortunes in independent school varied. Too many encountered problems that ought not to have become serious enough to be their undoing, yet often did lead to a student's withdrawal from independent school. I decided that playing Russian roulette with the lives of these youngsters was not something that made me comfortable. If I were to continue to advocate that such boys and girls follow a very different path than they otherwise would travel, it was incumbent upon me to develop a means that would make success the likely outcome. It was thinking along such lines that ultimately led me to develop a program that I dubbed "Prep for Prep"—preparation for college preparatory school.

Both the program and I have been lucky. Large numbers of people bought into the idea. Year by year, as students succeeded both in our Preparatory Component and in the independent schools into which we placed them, more independent schools committed scholarship places, more public schools nominated candidates and more donors offered financial support.

Prep for Prep is now a well-established program with a well-honed and long-tested methodology. Its structure has become more complicated as new components have been added, but the basic ethos has remained intact. Our numbers, however, have grown significantly. We admit about 215 children each year to our two Preparatory Components. There are currently well over 800 Prep for Prep students enrolled in independent day and boarding schools, and nearly 650 Prep alumni enrolled as college undergraduates. As of spring 2003, well over 1,000 alumni have already earned their undergraduate degrees, and many have gone on to earn advanced degrees in a wide range of fields. The Prep for Prep student and alumni community comprises about 2,800 intellectually gifted and highly motivated individuals. The overwhelming majority of our college graduates have earned their degrees from the 25 most selective colleges and universities in the country. A great many have developed into remarkable young adults.

The Prep Experience does not turn out to be successful for every student admitted to the program. Traditionally, about 75 percent of the children admitted each year have completed the 14-month Preparatory Component, although in recent years the statistic has risen to 80 percent. Once our students matriculate at independent school, about 90 percent stick it out and graduate. Of those who do not remain on our rosters until high school graduation, about one-third have left their schools simply because of family relocation rather than because of any difficulty they experienced at school. Virtually all of our high school graduates continue on to college.

I find it astonishing that we are now celebrating Prep for Prep's 25th anniversary. Where did the years go? Those of us fortunate enough to work at Prep have had the satisfaction of watching young children of great promise develop into young adults who are forging careers and striving to achieve often ambitious goals. We have been so caught up in what we've been doing that it is a fair indictment that we have done too little to share with others what has been accomplished. I say this notwithstanding the fact that Prep's success has given rise to nearly a dozen other programs that to varying degrees are modeled on Prep.

This anniversary year seems an appropriate time to share more widely some of what we have learned at Prep over the years. To that end I asked each of about 35 alumni to write a story that in some way illustrates how membership in Prep influenced their lives. I have long said that our students are the ablest and most eloquent spokespeople for the program. They make converts wherever they go. Some of the most committed members of our board of trustees came to Prep because their own children had become good friends with Prep students at their schools. Some of our most talented faculty members have come to our Preparatory Components because the Prep students they taught at their independent schools were among the most exciting students they had encountered in their teaching careers. In addition, Prep has always represented an *indirect* way of addressing many of the problems that plague our society. It is through the nurturing and development of the talents and ambitions and leadership potential of our students, and therefore ultimately through the work of our alumni in the various career fields they choose, that Prep will have its impact.

In their stories for this book, some of the alumni have focused on one particular moment or experience that is somehow illustrative of Prep's overall impact on them. Others have opted to write a series of vignettes that taken together illustrate a particular theme. Still others have responded with more encompassing narratives, either of a particular stage in their development or, in a few cases, with a more holistic story that suggests Prep's ongoing influence on their lives.

Several of those from whom I requested stories initially responded by saying, "If you think I can help, I'd love to do it, but my story is so cliché. Isn't it clear I wouldn't be where I am today—perhaps I wouldn't be *who* I am today—if I had not become part of Prep?" In each such instance, however, as we talked, the individuals in fact focused on particular ways in which Prep had influenced their development, with each of them emphasizing somewhat different elements of the Prep Experience. As a result of its comprehensive nature and long-term approach, the Prep Experience, it turns out, is so multilayered and multifaceted that there are numerous different ways in which membership has influenced various people—despite the more obvious commonalities.

The alumni represented here are for the most part either well along in their graduate or professional school programs or, in many cases, have already embarked upon their careers. They are individuals whose career fields are fairly clear, although, as we know, in today's economy people often do make career changes at various junctures in their lives. My point is simply that those from whom I asked for submissions have been out of college long enough to have a clear sense of direction and also perspective on their involvement with Prep. There are a couple of exceptions to this rule, individuals who completed their undergraduate studies only two years ago, but they are particularly strong-minded young women with a clear sense of what they want to do in life.

Some of the authors "went through the program" when Prep was in its earliest years. Others began their association with Prep at a point at which far more of the program's components had been developed and projects and services expanded. If a book of this sort were to be written 10 years from now, I am certain there would be far more references to Aspects of Leadership retreats, crucial intervention at critical moments by our Undergraduate Affairs Unit and formative experiences provided by our Alumni Professional Advancement Unit. When the authors of most of these stories were "in the program," not yet alumni, these and other elements of Prep's overall program simply did not yet exist.

Prep was founded on the belief that, ultimately, it is an individual's ability, drive, initiative, spirit and determination that renders success attainable. Notwithstanding this firm belief, however, the second pillar of Prep is the conviction that, as things now stand in our society, a great many children, including many of our nation's potentially ablest students, lack access to the types of experiences and opportunities that enable the best that is in a child to come to the fore. Programmatic intervention, whether by private, not-for-profit organizations or by publicly taken initiatives, has an important role to play in leveling the playing field so that social and economic circumstances and less than adequate educational opportunities do not continue to thwart the development of achievement-oriented, forward-looking, goal-focused behavior, even on the part of very able youngsters who just do not see life's possibilities or do not believe these possibilities are applicable to them.

Thus Prep for Prep has never been put forward as a substitute for broad reform of the current situation in which the gross inequalities of educational opportunity, whether in New York City or in our country as a whole, make a mockery of the American dream. Nevertheless, Prep still views the American dream as the essential element of our national political ideology, the one concept that has the most potential to hold this country together. Prep itself is a living, dynamic protest against inequality of educational opportunity. However, even in the midst of our country's obvious failure to honor the commitments implicit in the American dream, we ask our students to believe in the power of that concept and to envision ways in which *they* can put their education, their values and their leadership to work in the effort to realize the full potential of that unifying construct.

Prep for Prep and other programs that identify academically able students from underrepresented groups for placement in independent schools are often criticized from two different perspectives. One criticism is that by removing the ablest and most motivated youngsters from inner-city public school classrooms, we reduce the number of role models available to the other students. To this critique, we respond that as a nation we simply cannot afford the continued hemorrhaging of talent from segments of our population already grossly underrepresented in the upper echelons of government, business, academia and most other key sectors of American society. In addition, the potential "role models" far too often are overwhelmed by the social pressures to conform to the low academic expectations that are prevalent among their peers. My own experience in the South Bronx suggested this was not an infrequent result of allowing bright, highly academically motivated youngsters to remain in environments that negated who they were. Often the children who, at fourth or fifth or sixth grade, stood out as the ablest and most committed students were *not* those youngsters who several years later, as eighth-graders, were selected by A Better Chance (ABC) for placement in independent schools. It would appear that the most academically inclined students had had such a difficult time in the local junior high school that they either shut down, trimmed their sails or decided to conform to the expectations of their peers.

A second criticism of programs such as Prep centers on the difficulty students are assumed to experience when they "live in two worlds but belong to neither." Without denying that there are social challenges to be met, I regard this sort of criticism as an insult to the hundreds and hundreds of young people I know who have found the strength of self and personal integrity to overcome these hurdles, to get stronger and stronger year by year as they find or make a niche for themselves in their new school communities, and to emerge whole. I have watched a great many young people learn to develop multiple allegiances to their school communities, their ethnic communities, their church communities, and ultimately to those with whom they share professional ties. To believe that young people cannot be helped to do this is to consign American society to a truly bleak future.

In the widely acclaimed musical adaptation of *Les Misérables,* the doomed Fantine poignantly sings about the hopes she once had and ends with the chilling statement "Life has killed the dream I dreamed." I love the show and have seen it numerous times, but I still wince at that line. At Prep, we are committed to doing everything we humanly can do to empower and enable each of our students to BE THE DREAM.

Contents

IV. A PLACE TO BELONG · *115*

V. THE ME INSIDE OF ME · *147*

VI. NAVIGATING THE IDENTITY RAPIDS · *181*

VII. PREP FOR LIFE · *215*

VIII. JOURNEYS · *251*

IX. MAKING A DIFFERENCE · *295*

EPILOGUE · *339*

PROLOGUE

THE BANK OF TALL WINDOWS stretched the entire length of the classroom, each window reaching from the ceiling to about four feet from the floor. At that point, each windowsill was aligned with the top of one of the bookcases or cabinets that in similar fashion extended the entire length of the room. Only in the exact midpoint of the soldier-like lines of windows and wooden cabinets had a beam required that a two-foot-wide section of wall be allowed to interrupt the procession.

Had the expanse of glass provided a view of grassy fields or a patch of woods, I would have judged it by far the most appreciated element of the building's design. Instead, it was a constant reminder of where we were, displaying the littered streets, aging tenements and already run-down public housing projects of the South Bronx. For many years, if you stood in one corner of the room and twisted your neck a bit, you could see the tracks of the long-abandoned Third Avenue "el" still awaiting their promised removal.

He was perched atop one of the bookcases, oblivious to the

proximity of the windows. Various paperbacks were scattered around him. At least three official regulations had been broken, but this also went unnoticed by the boy and unremarked upon by me.

"I can't believe how many books we've read, and there's still four months left of the year!" A wide grin of self-amazement and self-congratulation spread across the boy's brown face. His dark eyes sparkled. "Yo, Kenny, we've read sixteen books already!" he called to one of the two other boys who were still helping to reorganize materials on the other side of the room. It was four o'clock. The rest of the class had left an hour ago.

And that was the moment I made my decision.

There ensued repeated pleas that I disclose the names of the books still to come as the spring unfolded, but I kept to my practice of letting each new book be a surprise, distributed with great fanfare to the 10 children who made up the advanced reading group in my class, officially designated an IGC, or Intellectually Gifted Class. The piles of paperbacks that had yet to fall into 20 eager hands were kept in a locked closet until each book's own time had arrived.

The boy perched on the bookcase was the most adamant about wanting to know what was still to come. His insistent questioning, however, only led to vague answers on my part, and his good nature prevented him from pressing beyond a certain carefully calibrated point. More importantly, he was still basking in the warmth of his own self-discovery, which he repeated to the other two boys as though there were any chance they had not already received and absorbed the astonishing news.

Over the course of the 10 years I had been teaching, I'd had more than my share of wonderful moments. Yet nothing quite like this had happened before; at least, nothing had engendered so strong a response from me. I had taken this particular class from fifth to sixth grade, and the boy with the wide grin and sparkling eyes had not been in the class the previous year. In fourth grade, the teacher who had the IGC ran it as an "open classroom," and at the end of that year the children who hadn't responded well to his approach had been removed from the class. At the end of fifth grade, I had insisted they be reinstated for the following year. I approached things in a much more structured way, and once I knew which students were truly capable of handling advanced work, I pushed them harder than they had ever imagined could be expected of them.

Under this regime, the boy with the wide grin and sparkling eyes had truly come alive. More than any of the other children, he was able to make a connection with ancient Greece and the Middle Ages, with characters and places that must have seemed to most of the children too abstract or absurd to feel or see. As the paperbacks I bought for the literature course followed a step behind the periods we covered in the world history series I had bought, I pressed the advanced group to make connections between history and literature. While they could all do it on an intellectual plane, only a few could truly transcend their immediate surroundings and imagine themselves in these remote places and distant ages. And none more so than the boy with the wide grin, who now wanted to know to what other realms we would be traveling in the months that remained of sixth grade.

And so it was, after six months of anguished deliberations, that I made my decision. Contrary to the wishes and advice of Dr. Abe Tannenbaum, my friend and mentor at Columbia University's Teachers College, I would *not* do my fieldwork in Albany and learn how the politics of gifted education played out in the commissioner's office. Contrary to what seemed to me to be good, commonsense advice, intended to advance my career and provide me with a network of contacts and exposure to how educational policy was made, I would instead insist that Dr. Tannenbaum sign off on a project that involved promoting the educational prospects for the ablest of the students I had come to know and care about in the South Bronx.

Thus Prep for Prep was announced to the world on Teachers College stationery. Dr. Tannenbaum had succeeded in obtaining a very large federal grant to establish the Graduate Leadership Education Project in Gifted Education (GLEP), with Teachers College as the flagship of a consortium of nine universities and himself as the project's director. Starting an experimental project with a small number of children from the South Bronx and Harlem was not what he had

had in mind for any of his Fellows, and I had enormous respect for Abe Tannenbaum.

I told myself, however, that Abe Tannenbaum was not in my classroom the afternoon that my decision was made. I had often heard him speak passionately on issues on which *he* felt strongly. I told myself that had he been in that classroom with me, he would have been pleased with my decision.

THE NEXT FEW MONTHS were a frenzy of activity. The various contacts I had made in exploring the feasibility of my program design all had to be cemented. Trinity School agreed to provide space for the program to conduct its classes and test sessions. Project Double Discovery, at Columbia University, agreed to pay for academic supplies and to provide vouchers that the students could use to purchase lunch at Teachers College. The Institute for Urban & Minority Education agreed to pay the summer session salaries of three teachers and three assistants. About 20 public schools in my own and two other districts allowed me to distribute information and to meet with interested parents in small meetings before or after classes. Somehow, by the end of June, we had a first contingent of 25 children recruited, tested, selected and ready to begin the program. They were to spend the next 14 months preparing for placement in independent schools.

The boy with the wide grin and sparkling eyes, straight black hair and a look that for some reason made him appear to me Mexican-American rather than Puerto Rican (although I knew he was extremely proud of his ethnicity), asked if he could spend the summer at my new program, even though he had already been admitted to an independent school for the seventh grade. I agreed to the proposal.

Then he asked if there were some way to obtain a huge roll of butcher-block paper, certain paints and a few other art supplies.

"For what purpose?" I asked.

"I'd like to make a big mural. It's for the new program."

The open classroom teacher had told me that the boy excelled in art projects, so I had had some of his work assessed by the staff of the

Artistic Talent Assessment Project that had been set up at Teachers College by another of the GLEP Fellows. They told me he really had the right stuff and advised me about possible programs in which he would have a chance to develop his talent. With preparations for the start of Prep for Prep taking every spare minute, however, I told myself we would look into these programs in the fall.

"What would the mural be about? I mean, do you already have an idea for it?"

"I can see the whole thing already. It's gonna be a boy holding the world in his hands—a globe, that is. And out of his head there's gonna be six or seven pictures of what he might be dreaming of becoming when he grows up. There's gonna be a judge, and a scientist, and a businessman, a doctor, an engineer building something like a bridge, an astronaut probably, maybe a teacher. Each dream is something you can only be if you get a good education and go to college. It's gonna have each of these people in kind of like clouds coming out of the boy's head, the way comic books have what the characters are saying in these clouds."

The idea intrigued me. And I was feeling a little bit guilty that I hadn't done anything much about looking into the art programs yet. So the boy got the commission.

He sketched out the basic design about a week before our summer classes actually started. By the time he was ready to start painting, we realized the only place to do it was on the third floor of the Lower School at Trinity, where Dr. Robin Lester, Trinity's headmaster, had given us the use of classrooms for the summer.

A lot of painting went on over the weekend before classes were set to begin. By opening day, the mural looked almost finished to me. It occupied a large section of the floor, but fortunately the floor area was wide enough at both ends of the hallway to allow for traffic. Each morning when the children arrived for classes, they first paid homage to the mural that still occupied its place on the floor.

Each day the young artist added further touches. He worked in the afternoons, when classes were over, and he worked during English class since he had already read all the books the children would be reading.

Much of another weekend was devoted to the mural. It was finished as far as I could see.

"It's time to hang it up on the wall," I announced.

"There's just a little bit more that I have to do."

"How much more?"

"Just a few little things."

Another week went by. The other children grew more intrigued each morning, often debating what had been added or changed since the previous day. Details of costume or facial expression sometimes became the focus of renewed efforts. A detail here, a detail there, a correction to the shape of South America on the globe, the lengthening of a cloud to allow additional props. I found myself asking, "Will it ever be finished?"

By the end of the second week of classes, when we finally hung the mural on the wall, I think it was still something of a compromise. I said we'd been lucky that nobody had stepped on the mural, but our luck might run out one of these days. Grudgingly, the boy pronounced the mural finished.

Hanging it up was quite a chore. It occupied a long section of the marble wall in the narrower part of the hallway. I don't recall that we ever actually measured it, but it must have been at least 20 feet by 15 feet.

"Does it have a name?" I inquired.

"*Be the Dream,*" Frankie answered.

The wide grin spread across his face, and that joy of self-amazement was again evident. He glowed with a quiet pride and a sense of achievement, something I was to see time and again on the faces of many of our students during the next 25 years.

"*Be the Dream,*" he repeated. "That's what the mural's about. That's the only name that makes sense for it."

Be the Dream it was.

And each day that first summer, it reminded us why we were there.

Gary Simons
January 10, 2003
New York City

I.
BEGINNINGS

NEARLY 25 YEARS AGO, I had a conversation with the father of a young girl who had just completed her first summer at Prep. He and his wife were struggling to raise eight children on his meager salary in a housing project located in a rather deteriorated section of the South Bronx. The family was quite religious, and I suspect that had a good deal to do with how strong a unit they were. Ruth had already shown herself to be an extremely able student, but it was evident that attending religious services three or four nights each week did not leave her enough time to stay on top of all her homework. Clearly, in September, matters would only get worse as she tried to balance her public school homework, Prep homework and religious obligations.

I remember the fear I harbored at the start of that conversation. Would we lose a child for whom the program could make a real difference? That fear turned out to be unwarranted, however, for at the end of our conversation Ruth's father proposed a solution. While the family would continue its normal schedule of religious observances, his daughter would join them only one evening each week. As he explained to me, "I think God must have intended for Ruth to go to college."

Seven years later, Ruth graduated from The Fieldston School, and four years after that she received her B.A. from Columbia—proving both God and her father quite right in their plans for her.

I am reminded again and again of the enormous investment of time and energy, of encouragement and belief, needed to raise a single child who is ready to take on the world. At Prep, we are not miracle workers. Determination, a sense of adventure and the ability to truly appreciate Prep as an opportunity are among the traits many ultimately successful students bring with them to the program. But what is so intriguing is that two children who have had seemingly similar life experiences may have processed them in entirely different ways, and this often has significant consequences in regard to how each child approaches Prep. Factors that are red flags weighing against the admission of one child can be precisely the factors that have provided another child with the inner strength needed to succeed at Prep.

My point is that much has already happened in the life of every child we admit long before anyone at Prep has laid eyes on the child. Even as its very existence is a recognition of the shortcomings of our educational system, Prep is also and more importantly a reaffirmation of the primacy of an individual's spirit and will to learn and grow and achieve. At Prep, many of a child's best qualities, often unrecognized in his or her public school and not infrequently viewed in that milieu as problematic, come to the fore and are given full rein. It is a little like watching invisible ink yield an exciting secret message.

AN OPEN LETTER TO FUTURE GENERATIONS OF STICKBALL PLAYERS AT 112 NAGLE AVENUE FROM A TRINITY SCHOOL EIGHTH-GRADER

by EZEQUIEL MINAYA

MAKE SURE YOUR MOTHER does not see you take her broom. If it's a weekday, she's probably at work, so the coast will be clear. But if it's the weekend, make sure your mother does not see you take her broom. If caught, you will be yelled at. You will be asked repeatedly (and bopped on the head if you answer), "Do you know how much brooms cost?"

Wait until she goes to visit a neighbor, to dip a roll in a *café con leche* and talk about did you hear about so-and-so's crazy kid, or so-and-so thinks she's *americana* with her bleached hair, or so-and-so is a fool if she thinks he's coming back. Your mother can and will be at this all day—think of it as her version of stickball. With her attention elsewhere, abscond with the broom. If she catches you slinking off with her wooden bristlehead in one hand and a tennis ball in the other, do not tell her you were going to sweep out the front of the building. Your mother, though she may or may not know English, is capable of astonishing feats of deductive reasoning. With a quick glance at your dirty hands and smudged face, for example, she can probably reconstruct, in detail, your actions for the last seven hours. Just give it up. Why compound a loss of seven innings of stickball with an ass-whuppin'?

Now, for those preparing for their Confirmation or First Communion, don't worry. Taking a broom for the purposes of making it a stickball bat is not a sin. For a broomstick, becoming a stickball bat is like becoming a doctor or lawyer or going to college. It's a broomstick's dream. Just as you become your favorite player when you're up at the plate, the broomstick will become a Louisville Slugger, blackened with tar (really black electrician's tape) and complete with a shaven handle. If guilt persists, mention at your next Confession the liberation of the broom from domestic bondage. At worst, the Father at Our Lady Queen of Martyrs will let you off with a rosary or two. Now you're ready to play ball.

Go down to the basement and walk through to the courtyard in the back. Be careful walking the passage. There's liable to be a fair amount of broken glass and garbage. If you fall and cut yourself, you will be yelled at. Your mom will say something along the lines of "I can't watch you all the time. I have to work!" In this situation, she may get emotional and start crying and hugging you tightly. If this happens, you'll be begging for the ass-whuppin'. The same goes for getting garbage on your clothing. If it's Sunday, this will have the doubly damning effect of ruining your finest attire and alerting your mom to your truancy from church. If this happens, you may never see the light of day again. It is okay, however, to pick up a discarded piece of wood, smear one end of it with dog feces and chase your friends with it. But let's remember why we are here, please, and be sure to use a responsible and restrained amount of dog doo.

The basement courtyard of 112 Nagle Avenue is not very big. It is about 70 feet long and 50 feet wide. Spend about 15 minutes kicking the scattered beer and liquor bottles to the side. You want them out of the way while you're playing. And when you're done, you can throw them off the roof at neighboring courtyards.

There are gates on three sides of the courtyard, separating it from the courtyards of adjacent buildings. It may seem odd to think the superintendents of these buildings went to all the trouble and expense of putting up iron-mesh gates, topped off with razor-sharp barbed wire, to stop stickball players. But they did. These gates serve no other purpose. They don't stop the burglars, drunks, junkies, bums, young couples and older kids who roam the alleys behind these buildings. Outside of hitting a smoking fastball, these gates pose a stickball player's greatest challenge. But more on that later.

On the side of the building you'll find a long, rectangular box with an X in its middle, joining all four corners. This is the strike zone. It has always been there. The super has painted over it a million times, and a million times it has reappeared. Keep a Magic Marker, a can of spray paint or a piece of chalk handy for those times when you come down and find that your super has performed his only apparent duty. A leak in the bathroom or a roach infestation will go unaddressed for months, but a stickball strike zone will be dispatched as soon as it is identified. A tip for the advanced or ambitious among you: carve the strike zone into the brick face with a rock or stray piece of metal. It will take the super weeks, instead of days, to get rid of it.

If you get caught by the super, he will tell your mother. Your mother will act surprised in front of the super and say something like "Are you sure it was *my* son?" but she knows it was you who defaced the building for perhaps the ten thousandth time. You will get an ass-whuppin'. Generally, the short duration and intensity of these ass-whuppin's are one of the benefits of not having a dad around. Not because your mom isn't strong enough to wear your ass out with a strip of hide. The lady on occasion has shown that she is more than up to the task. But since your mom spends so many hours at work, making shoes, shirts, dresses, dolls and belts, she'll either not be home or feel tired much of the time. So, let's get that strike zone up!!!

Now, this is important. You'll have to make friends with the one kid in the building who gets money from his mom on a regular basis. He's the one who will buy the balls. I know, I know, he's probably extremely annoying, can't really play and cries when you jokingly bean him with a pitch. But he'll save you the time and trouble of having to go around and collect bottles for recycling—in which case other kids will make fun of you and say things like "Your momma's on welfare"—which may or may not be true. Or having to sneak into your mother's purse, which besides being a fruitless venture most of the time, carries with it a stiff penalty if you are caught. That's right, the whuppin' of the ass. No, no. It's much better and easier to make friends with little Mr. Moneybags. Having him around won't be as bad as you think. You'll have balls when you need them, and somebody who can't beat you up to chase around with dog doo.

Now for the rules. A line drive that hits the far gate is a double. A ball that sails over the gate and hits the building next door from the second floor to the third floor is a triple. Fourth floor to the roof or beyond, and you touch them all.

Of course, triples and home runs are the most desirable of hits, but they pose a problem. You have to get over or around the gate to get the ball back. Now, the way the stickball court is shaped, all the high line drives go over to the courtyard of 114 Nagle Avenue. This is an odd building. All the supers on the block are Latino, except for the super of 114 Nagle Avenue. He's from Poland. We call him "the Russian." Most supers, though they'll complain heavily while they're doing it, will toss back a foul tip or errant ball. Not the Russian. He will snatch the ball off of his courtyard and refuse to entertain your entreaties. If you persist in asking for the balls he has stowed away (he must have thousands by now), he will get angry and, in his heavily accented English, call you and your group little roaches, little coils of dog shit, little bastards, little brown bastards, little sons of bitches, and so on.

Should the Russian not be in the courtyard when the ball goes over, race up to street level. There you'll find the entryway to 114. It is blocked by a large metal door with spikes across the top. The lightest of your group should get on the shoulder of the sturdiest and reach carefully over the spikes to unlatch the door. Then, using your best powers of persuasion, get Mr. Moneybags to run down and get the ball.

Now, if your mom should catch you playing after telling you not to, the jig is up. There is no use running. You'll get dragged up to your apartment, the door will slam behind you and, well, you know.

Crying and begging will not help. There is only one chance in a million of getting off. I repeat, you have only one chance. And here it is.

Sometimes, your mom will surprise you and your friends in the middle of a game. You won't hear her come down. You'll just look up and see her standing off to the side, watching you play. When you finally notice her and she has a weird look on her face and she smiles at you, then it's okay, play on.

EZEQUIEL MINAYA *is a member of Contingent V. Having grown up in Inwood in upper Manhattan, Zeke graduated from Trinity School in 1989 and received a B.A. in English from Guilford College in 1995. Pursuing a career in journalism, he worked as assistant editor of* Latina Magazine, *special assistant to the editor in chief of* El Diario/La Prensa *and intern reporter for the Hispanic Link News Service. As a freelance writer, his articles have appeared in* Hispanic Market Weekly *and* City Limits. *Subsequently, Zeke earned a master's in journalism from the University of California at Berkeley in 2001 and anticipates completion of a master's in Latin-American studies by May 2003. He has worked as a metro desk intern at the* Fresno Bee *and as a crime and enterprise reporter for the* Modesto Bee. *In October 2002, he was selected by the Tribune Company as a participant in the Minority Editorial Training Program and has been working as a reporter for the* Los Angeles Times.

THE SCENT OF SAWDUST

by THOMAS SZE LEONG YU

"HEY! GET YOUR ASS BACK OVER HERE!"

The metal deck groans once more under my weight before I quickly step back from the edge of the roof. A thin sheet of corrugated metal is all that is holding me up six tall stories above the ground. Chan, the construction foreman, waves me back closer to him with a thick, leathery arm. From my precarious perch overlooking the Lower East Side of Manhattan, I squint out at the sun, gazing at distant downtown skyscrapers shimmering with light. In their solemnity, they resemble silver crags of some imposing mountain chain, like summits of power in urban lore. The day is clear and hot, with not a cloud in the sky, the type of weather that makes men weary and slow. In just a few months, the construction crew has raised this structure six floors out of the ground, but now they need to break for a swig of tea to quench their afternoon thirst.

"So the roof has enough pitch for the rainwater to flow into the drains?" asks Vincent, the architect. He shifts his weight from one leg to the other and pats some dust off his shoulder. For an instant, the silver in his hair shines with the light of the afternoon sun.

Never a man to say more than he has to, Chan nods as his gaze takes in the sloping metal sheets from the edge of the roof to the point where they convene at the middle. The cigarette hanging from his lip glows with each breath, releasing smoke that curls around his tanned face.

"So how soon can we pour the concrete?" asks Vincent. He nudges the metal with his foot, making it bend slightly. "We need to pour soon."

I glance back at the skyscrapers off in the distance. Like stoic sentries, proud in height and firm in stance, they dwarf the tenement buildings I am accustomed to in Chinatown and the Lower East Side. Impressive as those skyscrapers are, each of their floors began with the same flimsy metal decks we have in the building we are working on. But pour some concrete on them, and in a short time the floors become steadfast and sturdy.

A family will live right here, I think. *Right below where I am standing.*

Chan takes a long drag from his cigarette before crushing it under his boot. "This week," replies Chan. "We'll pour this week."

Good, I think, *before the rains come.*

LISTENING TO HEAVY RAIN pelting a sheet of corrugated metal is like hearing rocks being thrown against a tin oil drum. Back in the Hong Kong squatter town where my family used to live, the pounding of the typhoon rains on the metal walls of our shack would drown out all conversation at the family table. We ate our dinner of rice and dried salted fish in silence as the storm roared outside, lashing relentlessly against the walls. My father would pause in his chewing and place his chopsticks down whenever a piece of our roof flew off and landed with a crash against the side of the neighbor's shack. On those dark nights after dinner, I would fall asleep to the rattling of raindrops on metal and the shouting of men outside in the rain as they picked up broken pieces of their homes.

THERE IS NO SHORTCUT TO LAYING FOUNDATIONS and underpinning buildings in lower Manhattan. The soil is loose, like sand, and digging into the earth is fraught with great danger. Dig too fast and you risk the walls of dirt collapsing in on you. But dig too slowly and you leave the foundation exposed to harsh elements. For the last week, Chan has hovered over the pits where his men have been hauling out buckets of loose soil dug up deep from the ground. As soon as the hole is big enough, the men will quickly pour concrete into the pit to give the earth a strength it did not have before.

Wai is the man deep in the pit right now, passing out buckets of soil to another fellow up at ground level. He is so far inside that his whole body is completely in the shadow of the hole, away from the scorching glare of the sun. The arch of his bare back is moist with sweat, and clumps of soil are stuck in thick patches on his shoulders. On a few spots his skin is raw, the color of beef jerky. Wai has been in the hole for almost an hour now, digging deeper and deeper into his own subterranean world.

I glance over at Chan and notice that the ash on his cigarette is hanging almost an inch long, ready to fall off and blow away in the wind. He is staring like a hawk at the dirt walls around Wai. I take a breath and blink for both of us.

"Ah, Wai! Get the fuck out. That should be enough now," says Chan in his hoarse Cantonese. He extends his hand into the pit to help pull Wai out.

"I can dig a little more," says Wai. He wipes the sweat from his eyes with a dirty bandanna tied around his wrist.

"That's deep enough," Chan grunts. "You're halfway to hell already. Just fill it in with concrete. I don't want a fucking cave-in."

Wai grabs Chan's hand to climb out of the hole and walks a few paces to a plastic gallon of water lying on the ground. After rinsing his mouth of sandy grit, he takes a long chug, letting the water spill down his chin onto his chest. A few drops land on the ground, darken the soil and then disappear as the earth in its bottomless thirst sucks the dirt dry.

At Chan's signal, two men lower a chute into the pit and start filling it with wet concrete. The concrete plops onto the ground below like a heap of oatmeal, and workers with long spades stir the gray batter around in rhythmic circles. I glance over at Chan, and his face is relaxed and puffy, no longer pulled taut with strict attention. Playing it safe, he will do no more holes today. He places another cigarette to his dry lips, lights it and looks up into the sky as he takes a drag. I, too, gaze up. A few pigeons are soaring overhead against a backdrop of clear azure.

When will the next rains come, I think. *Please let the concrete harden first.*

I ONCE FOUND A GIRL IN THE RAIN and lost her again in the sunlight. I was four, maybe five, and wandering the alleys between shacks near my house in Tai Hom village. The shantytown was almost empty, for most of the adults had left in search of work for the day in the city; only the feeble and those too young for labor had stayed behind. Mosquitoes buzzed a lazy drone around tall weeds, and cicadas muted their hum in the humid heat. Grandmothers sat outside fanning themselves, exchanging sharp neighborly gossip, while the old men cracked seeds between their last remaining molars and spat the shells out onto the dirt road. I ran around in search of discarded tin cans, hoping to find field toads hidden inside, and chased stray dogs that wandered through the village looking for scraps. As I played, I looked down and was careful not to cut my bare feet on broken glass hidden in the grass. It was such a calm day on the ground that the gray storm clouds of a Southeast Asian hurricane creeping up along the horizon loomed over our squatter town before any of us realized it.

The first thunderclaps roared down from the skies and echoed back from the distant mountains to the north. The pitter-patter of raindrops that began tiptoeing across the dirt streets rapidly turned into a stomping of the earth into puddles of mud. I ran back with the villagers stampeding toward their homes with soaked newspapers held over their heads. By the time I reached our shack and went inside, mud was caked to my ankles and my clothes were drenched. Gray water had started dripping down from the ceiling onto our wooden stools and table, and puddles collected in the depressions on the floor. The din from the rain hitting the roof was deafening, and I jumped in surprise when I discovered my mother had walked in behind me from outside.

"Sze Leong, did you see your father?" she asked. Her shirt clung to her wet shoulders like an oxen yoke, making her look thin and small.

I shook my head. Beads of water dripped down from mother's shiny black hair into her eyes. I listened to her breathe in short cadences as she peered up at the roof.

Suddenly, a burst of wind and rain slammed into the side of the shack, and the walls shook and screeched as metal plates rubbed violently against each other. When several tarpaulin mats from the roof slid down and fell with a crash to the ground, I ran to the window to peek outside. The mats had crumpled on the ground like grieving widows and sunk into the street of mud. I felt a sharp tug as my mother yanked me back by the shirt sleeve and dragged me with her to the door.

"We're not staying in here," she said. "We have to go somewhere safe."

I struggled to keep pace with my mother as we ran through the night. Some neighbors were still rushing back to their homes, slipping and sliding in the mud, while others were nailing wooden planks to their windows and walls. As I looked back, the damaged roof of our house faded further and further into the darkness. Water ran down my face into my eyes, but I did not bother to wipe it away. From a distance, I heard the crash of a shack collapsing in on itself, and my mother pulled us faster down the narrow road. The sounds of life in the night, like the cicadas' song and the chirping of caged birds, cowered into a glaring silence.

We stopped at a small, gray concrete shed standing several feet from the road. There was nothing inside, save a few farm tools, crates and bamboo baskets. No lightbulbs hung from the ceiling, and only when a burst of lightning flashed through the sky did I catch the glimmer of metal on the rakes and shovels. My mother breathed heavily, weighed down by the wet clothes hanging on her back.

Turning to me, she said, "Wait here, and don't go anywhere. I need to find your father."

I held on to her and began sobbing; the shadows in the room suddenly seemed to grow larger and more ominous. She wrested me off her arm and said, "Be good, I'll come get you in a bit." Grabbing a basket lid to hold over her head, she disappeared again into the night.

My cries echoed with a shrill ring inside the walls of the small shed. I looked out from the doorway for signs of my mother's return, but saw only sheets of rain spilling from the skies. I broke into rapid sobs, gasping for air in between, my tears mixing with rainwater down my face.

"Shhhh, stop crying," a voice behind me whispered.

I jumped. Turning around, I saw a young teenage girl sitting behind a few crates, her back against the wall.

"Crying only makes the thunder spirits angry," she said in a soft voice. Her eyes were wide and moist, and I could see the shiny blackness of her pupils in the shadows of the room. She brushed some sawdust from a piece of burlap on the ground and began using it to wipe her long, dark hair in slow, deliberate strokes. "What's your name, little brother?" she asked. "Your mother will be back soon. Don't be afraid."

I lingered by the doorway, wanting to run out into the rain in the direction my mother had taken. Seeing this, the girl dug her hand into her pocket and pulled out a thin pen flashlight. She clicked it on with a push of the switch, and a thin beam of yellow light broke through the darkness to the ceiling above me. I saw a thousand particles of illuminated dust floating through the air along the path of light, some floating, some swooping.

The girl panned the beam to light up the dark shapes in the corners of the room. "See, nothing scary in here," she said. "Come inside, away from the rain."

Fixing my eyes on my muddy feet, I shook my head and began scraping off the mud on one foot with the other, leaving little brown clumps on the floor. A gust of wind blew in from the doorway, and I shivered violently.

The girl gazed at me for a while. Her nose was small and pink, as if she were about to sneeze, and she sniffed every few minutes. She pointed her flashlight to the ceiling and then shut it off abruptly. I could still see where her eyes were in the blackness. They had a soft gleam to them, like the light from a full moon. From her eyes, I could tell she was smiling.

"Come inside," she said. She switched the flashlight on and off, and held it out to me. "I'll let you play with this if you sit down."

Another strong wind blew in from outside, spraying me with rain. Slowly, I walked to the back of the shed, feeling my way around the rough wooden edges of the crates. Taking the flashlight from her hand, I sat down next to her by the wall. The flashlight was warm to the touch, and a tiny button protruded like a wart on the side. I held it up to the girl, who turned it on and handed the flashlight back to me with a smile. I pointed the light up toward the ceiling. The girl made a shadow puppet with her hands and asked, "Doesn't that look like a dog?" I nodded. She made another animal, this time a bird with broad wings that flapped in the light.

"Tell me what animals you like," she said, "and I'll see if I can make them."

The girl made up a story for each new shadow puppet, and I watched the animals come to life on the ceiling as her hands seemed to fade away from view. "I used to have a cat," she said, "but he ran out of the house like this and never came back. Then I found a duck . . ." But after a few stories, the bulb began to flicker and shone amber, then dark orange. Soon, it went out completely.

We sat in the dark, listening to the rain outside. No sounds of other people could be heard for a great distance around. I began to think of my mother, and when she would come back for me. The cold air raised thousands of goose bumps on my arms, making my skin look like the brittle rind of a litchi fruit. Soon I was shivering again.

"Come closer," said the girl, motioning to me. Gladly, I climbed into her arms. Her body was fleshy and warm, and the skin on her neck was smooth as silk. Her hair had the faint smell of clean sawdust. "What's your name, little brother?" she whispered into my ear. "How old are you this year? I'm sure your mother will be here soon."

My thoughts drifted away to visions of shadow animals dancing along a wall. In my mind, they pranced flat against the wall until they reached the edge and peeled off to run away. And from the girl's hands would spring more animals, laughing and shouting as they came to life. I rested my head on her shoulder, listening to her breathe softly as she turned her head from time to time to look out at the rain.

To this day, I am not sure how I got home that night. When I ask my mother, she denies having any memory of my return or of a girl sitting against the wall inside the shed.

"Maybe you walked home even though I told you not to," my mother says. "It was far and you could have gotten lost. You're lucky nothing happened to you."

I just remember waking up in my house, lying in my parents' bed with my shirt dry and my feet all cleansed of mud. Outside in the bright morning sun, my father and our neighbor were standing on ladders, nailing new mats to the roof. There was no reminder of the girl from the night before, other than the faint scent of sawdust on my arms.

Life went back to normal after the typhoons, or as normal as life in a shantytown can be. Houses that fell down were repaired. Laundry blown off the clotheslines was picked up in the ditches. And eventually people put their wooden stools back outside in the streets to enjoy a smoke during the hot summer nights.

In the end, it was fire, not the typhoons, that destroyed Tai Hom village.

One night, as the village went to rest after a weary day, the sky was lit up this time from the ground. A house had caught fire, and soon the orange-red flames leapt from one roof to another. Within a matter of moments, most of the neighborhood was burning. I remember waking up coughing in a fog of smoke and hearing the roar of flames outside my window. Screams echoed through the alleys, and the wailing of men slowly merged into the cacophony of sirens from fire trucks rumbling through the narrow streets. My mother and father pulled my infant brother and me from our beds and carried us outside. When I think back now, that was the first time I saw what fear looked like on my father's face, and the first time I saw my mother close to tears.

I forget how long we lived in the homeless shelters. The people went to their factory jobs as usual during the day. But at night, in the heat and tight space of too many people in one place not meant for habitation, tempers flared and fights broke out. We grew tired of government promises to put us into new public housing. The Housing Authority postponed dealing with our problems because we had no deeds or utility bills left to prove our rights to the land. Men went to bureaucrats' offices and waved their fists in the air, only to shuffle back to the shelters with hunched shoulders that bent more and more each day. Some of the villagers were lucky; they moved into the new government projects being raised all over Hong Kong.

Finally, with nothing else to lose and everything possibly to gain, my family moved to America.

THE CONSTRUCTION INSPECTION is beginning to wrap up. Chan, the foreman, leads the way to the basement 15 feet underground. The glare from sun reflecting off the corrugated metal decks above remains in my eyes, making the descent dark and treacherous. I stand still for a moment until my vision adjusts, and gradually, through a gap in the back wall, I can make out the contours of an exposed earth wall. A styrofoam McDonald's carton, discarded over a decade ago, lies half buried in the soil. A few levels farther down, a classic Coke bottle sticks out of the earth like the helpless victim of a landslide.

Did she make it out that night?

SHELTERS WILL FOREVER CONJURE UP IMAGES of metal-framed bunk beds in my mind—rows and rows of bunk beds. I think of families draping blankets over the top bunk and letting them hang like curtains for privacy. Shelters are places where people who were once villagers become strangers scattered once more. My days in the shelters after the Tai Hom fire were spent peeking into the flaps of each bed, searching for the girl with the scent of sawdust.

Going back in time among the layers of Manhattan's past, I remind myself, *You never told her your name!* And then, as I contemplate the concrete and metal rising out of this ground into the sky, I want to shout, *It's Sze Leong! Do you see me now?*

THOMAS SZE LEONG YU *is a member of Contingent XII. Born in Hong Kong, Thomas immigrated to Manhattan's Lower East Side when he was five years old. He graduated from Poly Prep Country Day School in 1996 and received a B.A., cum laude, in government from Harvard University in 2000. At Harvard, Thomas served as co-president of the Harvard Chinese American Students Association and political programmer for the Harvard Asian American Association. He was formerly the Everett Foundation public service intern and is currently the planning and development project associate for Asian Americans for Equality. Among other responsibilities, he is involved in project management for the construction of affordable housing, which is why he was at the construction site depicted in this story. Thomas, who is also currently pursuing a master's degree in urban planning at New York University's Robert F. Wagner School of Public Service, has been a reporter for* Fortune *as well as a contributor to various journals and anthologies.*

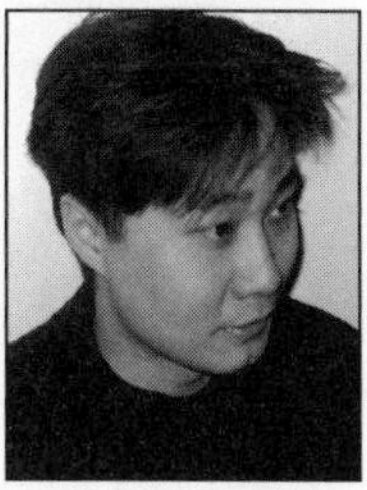

GOING HOME

by NICOLE ISAAC

LAST NIGHT I WENT HOME TO MY NEIGHBORHOOD, where the Jamaican beef patties are the best in the city and the jerk chicken brings reminders of a distant shore. I went home where trash lines the streets and neither I nor my brothers were allowed to stay outside too long because something was always happening in our section of the Bronx. I went home and walked up the stairs where the paint had been stripped four years ago because it was allegedly a fire hazard and the old gray cinder blocks darken the stairwell because it has never been repainted.

I went home to where my mother, a single Jamaican parent, had succeeded in raising three black men who "made it out" of the projects and was in the process of raising one more. Once inside my mother's apartment, the outside didn't matter as much, because the struggle for survival cannot consume you unless you allow it to. My beauty had always been reflected there, in the love of my mother and the courage of my four brothers. I went home because, although my path had been different, it began at home. My awareness of *struggle* began at Gunhill Road, and it began by watching my family and the people around us. More importantly, it began within.

My family was not rich, nor were we even well off, but my mother always reminded us that things could be worse and that conditions *were* worse in many other places. She reminded us that there were times in Jamaica when she had no food before school because her mom could not afford it. She told us that sometimes her older sister would boil a breadfruit from the tree in the yard and split the tender, sweet-potato-like fruit among five children. With those memories still very much alive in her mind, my mother insisted that we would always have food, and she would wake up sometimes two hours before going to work in order to boil cornmeal porridge for me and my older brothers on cold winter days. I remember wanting to make life better for all of us, and I tried concocting new inventions and ideas, hoping that one day . . .

The truth is, I believed I could do anything. Maybe it began with the stories I heard from Nanny, who like a grandmother told me of far-away places, of her home in St. Kitts and the whales that used to wash up on shore. Perhaps it began with Sunday school lessons, where the pictures were so vivid and marvelous, of apostolic individuals who had faith and accomplished all of their goals because they believed in something greater than themselves. This faith in something greater than myself could have begun the day I first saw mica, the shiny flecks in the concrete sidewalks, and excitedly exclaimed to my mom that I had found gold and we would all be okay. My mind continued to marvel past the concerns of an eight-year-old, and I was intent on helping to make my family's life better. My very first attempt was the Drowning Saver.

The Drowning Saver was my answer to the frequent reports of drownings on the television news. I was nine, but somehow I figured that fewer people would drown in pools if we did not have to rely on lifeguards. Conceptually, I thought that sensory mechanisms on the side of the pool could pick up either screams or pressure levels and trigger lifesavers on the ceiling that would fall, just in time, to rescue that drowning soul.

I turned this idea into a model, using a shoebox, a container, a few candy lifesavers, some twine and assorted other items. My teacher encouraged my effort and suggested I make a presentation to my class. When I presented my idea and my model, the students asked questions about how the sensory mechanisms would work, how the lifesavers would fall, how it would all happen. They didn't believe it was possible, but I didn't understand why my plan didn't make sense to them. Years later, I remember those moments with fondness and humor. I had always wanted to change the world.

The struggles, however, continued. Conditions in my neighborhood became worse, and although my oldest brother went off to college, my second-oldest brother turned 18 and the streets beckoned. My mother refused to surrender her child, and he was forced to choose between college and the military service. I was young, and I didn't understand why my brother couldn't stay home.

By the time I was accepted into Prep, I was ready. I even gave up a two-month summer vacation in Jamaica to remain in the sweltering humidity of New York City, living with my godmother. The only water I would see that summer was the water from the fire hydrants, sometimes directed at the yellow school bus that brought us to and from Manhattan, but that was okay with me. Although my understanding of the program's potential significance in my life's journey was rudimentary at best, I knew it presented me with a way to make things better for myself and for others. In fact, since my first day at Prep, my life has never been the same.

NICOLE ISAAC *is a member of Contingent XII. Born and raised in the Bronx, she graduated from The Fieldston School in 1996 and received a B.A. in English and African-American studies from Brown University in 2000. Having completed two years at the University of Pennsylvania Law School, Nicole is now attending Columbia University's School of International and Public Affairs. She anticipates receiving both a J.D. and a Master of International Affairs in May 2004. At Columbia, she is the assistant editor of the* Journal of International Affairs. *At the University of Pennsylvania, she served as associate editor of the* Journal of International Economic Law *and was awarded the law school's Certificate for Exemplary Public Service and an Equal Justice Fellowship. During the summer of 2001, she represented the International Commission of Jurists at the 53rd session of the United Nations Sub-Commission on the Promotion and Protection of Human Rights in Geneva, Switzerland.*

M'ETHANGATHA'S GIFT

by KARIMI GRACE MAILUTHA

IN THE SPAN OF THREE GENERATIONS, my family's life experiences have been dramatically altered. My parents were raised in Tigania, a rural village in Meru, Kenya, where poor families live in clusters of one-room homes made of thatched roofs and mud walls, without electricity and running water. My grandparents lived the traditional way, herding cows, growing their own food and using medicinal plants to treat their illnesses. Like most children in their village, they did not attend school because paying the school fees would make the difference between feeding only some or all of the family members. Despite ridicule from the other men, however, my grandfather, M'Ethangatha, over the years sold half his cows in order to give my mother an education. Today, I thank him for having had the foresight to challenge cultural norms. My mother, the fourth child in a family of 10 children, excelled in secondary school and was awarded scholarships to study at Nairobi University and later at American universities.

Only in his mid-twenties did my father finish sixth grade. His mother had died when he was nine years old, and he had to leave school to help raise his two younger brothers. When his father died years later, he continued to work to support his brothers and provide for their education until they reached college. Eventually, he graduated from high school and attended seminary school.

These life stories are so extraordinary because of the distance my mother and father traveled, from a village where they lived in poverty and where many of the members of their community were unable to overcome the economic hardships and lack of opportunity. I was two years old when we came to the United States, and these stories were part of my upbringing. As an immigrant family, we were constantly struggling to make ends meet, but my parents always praised America, and the freedoms and rights that the country afforded us. America protects the right of individuals to pursue an education and to attain the means to give back to their community and work toward improvements in the lives of others. I have been raised in the light of my family's work ethic and in the spiritual community of my church.

When I was a child, my parents worked temporary city jobs and often second jobs while attending graduate school. Yet no matter how busy they were, struggling to support my four siblings and me, they maintained our culture and traditions within the home. My father chose a job that would allow him to be at home with us after school. Throughout the years, my parents have urged me to value any opportunities that came my way and to study seriously, because education and hard work had been their saviors while growing up in Kenya. I remember the start of every summer, when my father would encourage us to join organized activities in the neighborhood. He enrolled us in the free summer activities at the local public school, in the karate classes sponsored by our building and in the Riverside Park Tennis Camp, which supported inner-city children. He always kept us engaged and entertained so that we would not spend those long and lazy summer days getting in trouble or hanging out on the corner.

Growing up on 121st Street between Amsterdam and Broadway, I had to find my place among my peers without losing a sense of myself or succumbing to the fatalism that friends from my neighborhood experienced. Harlem sharply and harshly contrasted with the abundance of opportunities at Columbia University, located in such close proximity.

Twelve years later, I still clearly remember the day that Mr. Bordonaro[1] came to my junior high school to talk with selected students about PREP 9. When my mother found the information sheets in my bookbag that evening, I told her that the program sounded even better than what was explained in the pages she was reading. For both of us, PREP 9 represented precisely the kind of opportunity that could be seized by families in America who had high aspirations for their children but lacked the financial means to secure a first-rate education on their own. For an immigrant family, it was the entry route into a stellar educational system that has traditionally been very exclusive. For many of my soon-to-be Prep friends and me, the program has been the means of leveling the playing field, allowing us to show what we were capable of achieving and how determined we were to reach our goals. For me, Prep has been the "golden key" that has unlocked the doors and provided access to opportunity through every phase of my education.

Armed with 14 months of PREP 9 classes, I had no problems competing academically with my peers at Choate Rosemary Hall. During our history and literature classes, we had engaged in impassioned and heady intellectual debates about the real and possibly hidden meanings in *The Adventures of Huckleberry Finn* and the significance of the rise and fall of imperialism. As juniors and seniors participating in Prep's Ethics of Leadership modules, we struggled valiantly and argued fiercely about how to balance individual rights and the Common Good. As I looked around the room, the faces that I gazed upon were intelligent and enthusiastic and came in every shade of brown imaginable, from Asian to Latin to Caribbean.

As a Choate student and a member of Prep, I sought out opportunities to grow. Among many other experiences, I learned to play field hockey, spent a semester abroad in France, volunteered in a kindergarten class while living and attending school on a Navajo reservation and participated in environmental research at NASA's Goddard Institute for Climate and Planets (ICP). Because of the

[1] Peter Bordonaro has been the director of PREP 9 for the past 15 years.

excitement of the discoveries that lay before me, I never feared leaving my family to go to boarding school or to participate in summer programs in distant places. Year by year, I was able to move forward with the wonderful support network and friendships that I formed within the Prep community encouraging me along with every new adventure and with the new friends I made along the way.

During my college years, I occasionally helped interview the new seventh-grade applicants to PREP 9. There was nothing more uplifting than listening to the 12-year-old students talk about their favorite books, their families, their future aspirations. I was enchanted by their charming combination of childhood innocence and budding intellectual maturity. While talking with the applicants, I realized how much of an impact Prep could potentially have on their lives. I wanted to select them all.

I am constantly moving between cultural spheres, each with its own set of rules. The first sphere is the traditional culture that I enjoy within my home and with my extended family in Kenya. Sometimes overlapping, at other times conflicting, is the sphere of mainstream American culture. It carries a set of rules of conduct in academics and social relationships with classmates, professors and mentors. Many of my classmates at Choate were children from some of the richest and most powerful families in the country. Far from home, I had to maintain my sense of direction and purpose without feeling intimidated or insecure; I dealt with ignorance, but I also made lasting friendships. Within American culture, there is also the particular sphere of African-American culture and experience that also carries roles and expectations.

As an immigrant American, I engage in all three spheres. I am constantly moving from sphere to sphere and negotiating my relationships as a member of each group. It can be very hard at times, because I feel torn between cultures, but it is also an infinite blessing that gives me a depth of understanding when relating to others. I will always retain the traditions and morals that my parents have provided, but being a part of each group contributes to shaping my identity, and it is my task to decide where and how I fit in. I learn more about myself and grow stronger by having to meld cultures that are so starkly different. I see myself as a member of an emerging group of educated young men and women of color who will continue to challenge and help shape American politics, culture and educational outcomes.

Unlike my cousins, I have the choice to go back to Kenya and then to return to America to access the opportunities that they cannot, to escape the harsh droughts and political instability that they live with each day. I am most at home in the fast pace and energy of city life, surrounded by people of racial and ethnic groups representing every part of the world. New York City is my home.

I understand the enormous expectations that I carry upon my shoulders. Each generation in my family, from my grandfather to my mother and father today, has sacrificed personal dreams and desires to put food on the table and to give me and each of my siblings a better chance to achieve. I am the youngest of five children and the first in my entire extended family to attend medical school. My mother calls me her "little mother" because I was named after my maternal grandmother. For my mom, I am the realization of everything she has worked so hard to achieve. She often tells me with encouragement and a wink, "The scripture says, 'The last shall be first and the first shall be last.'"

I have tremendous aspirations and a lasting sense of responsibility to my loved ones. While they would never ask for anything in return, I feel the deepest drive to make their sacrifices worthwhile, and I now live my life by their example.

KARIMI GRACE MAILUTHA *is a member of PREP 9's Contingent IV. Born in Kenya, she immigrated to the United States at the age of two and grew up in Manhattan and the Bronx. Karimi graduated from Choate Rosemary Hall in 1995 and received a B.S. in biology from Columbia University in 1999. She is currently a third-year student at Harvard Medical School and anticipates being awarded an M.D. degree in May 2004. During her undergraduate years, Karimi was a Kluge Research Fellow at Columbia College of Physicians and Surgeons, a summer fellow at the Yale University Minority Medical Education Program and a research fellow at NASA Goddard Institute for Space Studies. In 1999-2000, she served as an AmeriCorps fellow and health services coordinator for San Francisco's Promise. Since October 2000, Karimi has been a group leader with the Active Girls Initiative, sponsored by Soldiers of Health/Partners in Health, a non-profit organization working to improve health outcomes in Roxbury, Massachusetts. From May through August of 2001, she was a student researcher for the AMKENI Project, which works to improve the quality of integrated family planning, reproductive health, and neonatal child survival services in Kenya. In 2001, Karimi was also awarded a Paul & Daisy Soros Fellowship for New Americans.*

II.
THE CULTURE OF PREP

"I MOST ADMIRE NEIL ARMSTRONG for having the courage to get to the moon," wrote one of our students on his Prep for Prep application. "To me, that's brave, and it took nerve. He took the risk of not surviving the liftoff, but still he went ahead with his plans. Being an astronaut is a pretty scary job, but that didn't stop Neil Armstrong." A few months later, when Prep's Summer Session began, this 11-year-old got the chance to meet his own astronauts—only at Prep we call them advisors.

Quite apart from all the many specific duties that our advisors carry out each day, they are living proof that what may seem impossible actually can be done. They have been on the launching pad several times already and have, in the course of their individual journeys, reshaped their own lives. As they welcome new members into the Prep Community, they are living examples of our motto: "Excellence, Integrity, Commitment and Courage."

Nobody gets a free ride at Prep. We are quite explicit with the children that a lot depends on them and on the hope that they will live up to their potential. Prep is a community awash with traditions and symbols, a community that celebrates its past and its future. The bonding that begins in the Preparatory Component, characterized by high energy, good humor, excitement in the classroom and faith in the future, develops into the adolescent community of later years. At Prep, individual achievement and the sense of community go hand in hand. Beyond this, there is the sense that what we are involved in is part of something much larger than ourselves.

I remember one October evening when I was saying good night to students as they came out of their Wednesday classes. Unexpectedly, one girl gave me a hug and whispered, "Happy Halloween. I love Prep!" Given the fact that she was leaving with a ton of homework, she was remarkably upbeat. Every day at Prep was a challenge for her, yet she had come to understand that her success was a matter of real importance to a lot of other people—family, classmates and staff members alike. She reminded me once more of the fundamental truth on which our work is based: the job starts all over again with each and every child.

"¡ESOS MUCHACHOS!"

by ELBERT GARCIA

I WALKED INTO PREP'S OFFICES on West 91st Street for my interview with Karen Young, the newly appointed head of the Summer Advisory System, not knowing what to expect. While I had volunteered as a "grad" [1] the summer before, there was no conclusive evidence that linked the ability of a high school freshman to collate xerox copies with the ability to counsel the Preparatory Component's fifth- and sixth-graders. As I waited, my knee bounced up and down to a fast but erratic rhythm much the way it did that first afternoon when I was officially introduced to Prep for Prep in Trinity School's dining room three years earlier.

Back then, my nervous twitch probably had a lot to do with the dozens of cookies and doughnuts consumed by my brother, sister and me while waiting for the orientation meeting to begin. We had all traveled "downtown" with our mother on the subway, no small feat for youngsters who were rarely found farther than 50 yards from either school or home.

---

[1] A "grad" is a Prep student who has completed eighth grade in independent school and is chosen to work as a volunteer during the Summer Session, assisting with many types of clerical and logistical functions. Although these positions are unpaid, there is actually a great deal of competition for the 8 to 10 "grad" spots available each summer.

Exemplary behavior, constant nagging and an assortment of well-timed, high-pitched whines had convinced my parents that both my chronic asthma and I were up to the task at hand. It was just too hard to argue against the fact that all my high grades and awards had led up to what was our best opportunity to grasp our dreams.

After all, none of us was going to have fame, fortune or success handed to us. My sister, a jewel in Papi's eyes, was unlikely to enjoy the riches of any beauty crown. And while my brother was a terror on the base paths between the living room and the kitchen, there was little reason to believe that his natural abilities would translate into a starting job in any position for the New York Mets, no matter how Dominican he was. No, in my mind, I was a darker Luke Skywalker, my family's last hope at moving beyond Medicaid, plastic seat covers and hand-me-downs from an assortment of aunts and uncles into that two-floor house that Mami complained Papi could never get for her.

No sooner had I begun to explore the contents of my orientation packet than all the newly admitted students were whisked away from our parents by our "advisors," young adults at best, some no more than three or four years older than ourselves, who were to be our guides and role models through and beyond the summer maze. As we walked up to each advisory unit's meeting room, I marveled at what surrounded me. The walls were painted and decorated every color except the public school green that I was so used to seeing. More importantly, the colors also extended to my classmates, who were by all measures a sizable cross section of the city's youngest, finest minds. It was a scene that many would have expected to find in the dream of some long-dead civil rights activist rather than in a bunch of classrooms in a private school on the Upper West Side. Yet here we were, assembled in reality, united by a common set of talents and abilities that had also made us objects of ridicule at some point in the previous five years.

When my unit finally settled down, we were introduced to a set of games that would help us get to know each other. We interviewed each other, and then had to report back to the whole room our partners' names and where they were from, both geographically and in terms of their family's native country. As a unit it was important for us to know those things because, as we looked right and left, it was up to each of us to make sure that as many of us as possible made it all the way through the next 14 months.

As part of the last set of "getting to know you" exercises, we were each asked to tell the unit the one thing about ourselves that made us unique or special.

"But what if we can't come up with something?" whined the kid sitting on my right, a telltale sign that he would have problems the entire way through.

"Think hard. Really hard," barked the future Dr. Walker,[2] having not yet fully mastered his sparkling bedside manner.

By that point, I had already revealed in 10 minutes what it had taken my public school friends years to find out about me. But I thought hard to come up with an answer that was both true and would distinguish me from my fellow unit members.

"I am a writer," I said in a low but clear voice when my turn arrived.

I was and wanted to be known as a conveyor of stories, not only a voice for my own thoughts but also a voice for others. My dream hadn't recently arisen; I had been writing novellas and comic books for the last two summers. However, whenever I told people this, it was dismissed as idle talk. Next week I would want to be a fireman or a cop. Besides, who did I know in Washington Heights who was a writer?

Surprisingly, however, I didn't hear a snicker or a round of quiet laughter. Instead, somebody asked what I liked to write about, and somebody else inquired as to what were my favorite books. We continued to listen carefully to each other's qualities, finding things we had in common with one another. But all I could keep thinking about was how wonderful it was to be surrounded by the country's next wave of doctors, lawyers and great people. And how much I belonged.

I STILL REMEMBER EVERYONE RUNNING FOR THE HILLS after my first day of classes. Armed with an oversize backpack and focused on one simple goal, I went straight from the bus stop through

[2] Tyrone Walker of Contingent I became the first Prep alumnus to earn a medical degree.

my mother's arms to the kitchen table. I was going to tackle that infamous Prep workload and defeat it. Three hours? That was for the other jokers who had the misfortune of living in the outer boroughs and had to begin their homework after dinner.

Forced out of the kitchen briefly while my family ate a quick dinner, I managed to hustle the *arroz con pollo* down my throat without the need of too much water. As my mother did the dishes, I tried to resume my work on the sofa.

"Don't even think about it!" screamed my mother in Spanish without looking up from the kitchen sink.

"But I am not swimming," I pleaded.

"You have your head down," she insisted.

Though no child ever laid claim to seeing the book that contained the rule that prohibited any and all activities on a full stomach, I was sure there had to be some exemption for homework. Nevertheless, I proceeded to pick up *The Light in the Forest* and read standing up until I heard the last strokes of the mop finishing the post-meal cleanup. Then I raced back into the kitchen, careful not to slide all the way past the table, and plopped myself right back into my seat. I would show this program who was really the boss.

But just before eight I walked into my parents' room, hoping for a caress, a kind word—something that would help me finish my work. My dad was lying on the bed, resting his always ailing back, about an hour removed from a long day of polishing rings at work. Innocently asking what was wrong, his *"¿Qué pasa?"* was met with a torrent of emotions, of how this was hard, how this was different, how this was taking much longer than I had expected. Not lifting his head, he spoke, not offering a bit of sympathy:

"It's simple. If it's too hard, just don't go back."

"That's not the point," I protested. "It's only . . ."

"Just say the word, and we'll take you out," he continued.

That would be my father's response for the next 14 months. Maybe he was using reverse psychology. Maybe he just didn't want to be bothered with my whining. Regardless of his intention, I took it to mean that his shoulder would not be one that I could lean on.

"Ma!" I pleaded.

But it was too late. She was already sucked into the eight o'clock world of the Spanish *novela.* My dad could only stare back the same words he had uttered moments before. He knew. I knew. We all knew. Amidst dressing the kids, cooking and cleaning, going to work, washing and ironing, my mother asked for very few things in life. The only thing she ever insisted on was an hour every weekday from eight to nine to watch her favorite soap opera.

I didn't even try to step into the living room. I just went back to the kitchen table and resumed my work. A bit of a perfectionist, I had gotten past literature and writing, science, research skills and the highlighting that was the homework for history. Unfortunately, the math homework was keeping me up way past my bedtime. The adrenaline of the day was long gone, and the angle between my head and the loose-leaf denim notebook was getting increasingly smaller.

Having seen her show, said her prayers and almost readied herself for bed, my mother was surprised to find me still at the table. "I thought only the cockroaches hung out this late," she said with a wink. Sitting down across from me, she looked through the problem set and then at the work I had done up to that point. Although my father had spent more time in school than she had, Mami had always been the smarter one, or at least when it came to solving problems. But that night I caught her looking at the problems with a sadness that I had rarely seen. My heart still sinks a little, remembering her look of depressing wonder as she came face to face with a wall that her sixth-grade education and years of tenacious living could not climb.

She stroked my hand gently and looked me in the eye with a quiet smile. Maybe I just needed to rest. She would wake me up early the next morning and maybe, after spending some time away from the beast, I could get most of it done.

So we woke up the next day at the then-unthinkable hour of 5:30 A.M. It was early enough to see my dad shower; early enough to hear the garbage trucks rumble through the neighborhood; early enough to enjoy the sunrise. It was just not early enough to finish my homework, at least not with a certainty that all the answers were right.

There comes a point in every child's life when he realizes that his parents can't solve every problem for him. I had arrived at that moment of traumatic awareness.

"Do you want me to write a letter?" Mami asked, offering the one thing that always seemed to get any fifth-grader off the hook.

I gave her a fatalistic shrug and said no.

THE SUMMER WAS NOT STARTING OUT the way I expected. I still knew that I belonged among the city's finest. And after the first several days, seeing the same kids with the same bookbags complaining about the same things seemed to create a zone of comfort where I found some joy. But I couldn't help thinking that math would be my downfall. Three or four missed problems quickly became six or seven and led to a number of disastrous quizzes. By the time the first parent meeting came, I was afraid I might be on the verge of an "academic alert." Even more disturbing was the fact that I was still staying up far into the night, which also meant that the entire household wasn't getting enough sleep.

So Mami went to the second week's parent meeting with a mission of her own. After grabbing a predetermined amount of doughnuts and cookies, she and my sister hunted for answers from anyone and everyone. They came back home that night remarkably calm and relaxed.

"*¡Ese muchacho!*" All my mother kept talking about was *that boy*. How he understood what we were going through. How thoughtful he was for such a young man. How they both hoped I would learn a thing or two from him.

Had she met Jesus? No, she had just had a heart-to-heart talk with Frankie Cruz, then the head of the Summer Advisory System. Frankie was no more than 20 years old, but what he lacked in age and proper Spanish grammar, he more than made up for with his knowledge of the program. More importantly, he had told Mami to make sure I used my advisor and did not just keep all my difficulties and opinions to myself.

"You have to ask them for help," she told me.

"Ay, Mami, they are not supposed to be doing the work for me," I argued.

She threw up her hands in the air, more as a show of force than as an attempt to plead with an 11-year-old. "You need to talk to them," she said, letting it be known that there would be no further discussion of the matter.

What does it take for a child to learn? To not only memorize material but grow with it and apply it to new problems and unforeseen challenges? If you took the word of Frankie, through my mother, all you needed was one thing: love.

But this Frankie, he wasn't a Beatle. He was a Puerto Rican kid from the South Bronx. What did he know?

He knew either through personal or shared experiences that parents, like their kids, sometimes need reassurance of their value and their role. Despite the unknown words and unfamiliar math problems, my mother still had an important role to play in my education, even if it was just to stay up with me and make sure I didn't doze off or just to listen when I needed to vent.

Reinvigorated, my mother changed my routine. Starting that evening, she began to look more carefully at the order in which I did my homework assignments and even kept track that I was doing my time logs properly.[3] She enforced naps when I came home, and she arranged for the family to eat slightly later so I would have a little more energy. We even began taking weekly Sunday trips to the lakes along the Palisades so we could all have fun outside of the house and away from the business of school.

Most importantly, she stayed up with me every single night that first summer, scheduling a 15-minute break at 10 P.M. so we could share a *tazita* of black coffee. Just the two of us.

WHILE OUR FAMILIES DOMINATED THE HOME FRONT, our advisors seemed to be omnipresent from the very second we got on the yellow bus in the morning. The caretakers of our daytime world, they were as colorful as any of the characters on Mount Olympus.

[3] Time logs are used by the first-summer students to record how much time they spend doing each homework assignment; they are reviewed by the advisors to determine whether a student is spending too much or too little time on a particular subject or doing assignments in an order that is not working for that child. Grade logs (one for each subject) are forms on which first-summer students record each quiz, test, essay or lab report grade, so that they learn to keep track of their progress in each subject.

While some provided a gentle shoulder to lean on, others inspired perfect test scores and behavior by means of their serious dispositions, stern stares and the threat of supervised study during recreation time.

I had no problem speaking to my primary advisor, Cesar, who was my unit's assistant leader. He knew about my wacky family and always talked intensely about the previous night's Mets game. Then one day my difficulties in math seemed to surface as a blip not only on Cesar's radar, but on the screens of staff members I didn't even know. I would later learn that throughout a typical summer's day, the Prep system was set up to allow for a constant exchange of updated information among advisors, the guidance counselor, teachers and administrators. Advisors often shared what they observed about the kids in all sorts of environments, whether in the classroom, on the bus, during unit periods or recreation, and particularly during the daily one-on-one meetings they had with their advisees. Sometimes they struggled with what constituted a breach of trust or when an advisee's best interests required them to share things told in confidence. Usually, in these cases, they first explained to the advisee what they had to do and *why* they had to do it.

That day, however, when I was just 11 years old, only my vivid imagination could explain why my unit leader, Tyrone, came to see me for my pullout meeting instead of the assistant leader.

"But I didn't do nothing," I told Tyrone. He quickly reassured me that he was not there to rearrange my bones. He just wanted to find out what I was going to do about my math dilemma.

"Study harder," I said sheepishly.

"But isn't that what you've been doing? Have you talked to Mr. Carter about this?"

For all my so-called intelligence, I had never thought to go straight to my teacher. With math coming up next period, Tyrone was glad that I had the perfect opportunity to put his advice into action. I, on the other hand, was dreading another period with numbers. So as any rational 11-year-old would do, I went between periods to see if I could find some enlightenment in the bathroom.

The crowd soon dwindled as students rushed to find out who would win the "See, I got the first seat" contest held before each class. The only other person left in the bathroom was a boy about my size, hunched over the sink feverishly washing his already clean face. I just as feverishly washed my hands, hoping this would calm my anxiety, and we met at the towel dispenser.

"Do you do that every period?" I asked. I had noticed him arriving in class as if he'd just taken a bath and had shied away from sitting too close to him, thinking he might be afflicted by an inordinate amount of sweating.

"No," he said, acting as if I were the stupid one. "Only when I need to keep awake."

Clearly the result of a conversation with his advisor, I thought. Now see, here was some practical information that anyone could use.

"I'm also falling asleep, especially in the afternoon," I admitted.

"Then you should try it," he said.

I nodded. This kid was pretty popular. He even had some of the cute girls speaking to him. He was making sense, though.

My mother's extra-strong coffee at home and regular splashes of water with my new friend Freddy Godoy during the day helped me stay awake that first summer, an important prerequisite for dealing with any class. Actually, how to succeed in math wasn't so mysterious after I had a long talk with Mr. Carter, who suggested that many of my wrong answers were the result of careless errors and rushing through my work. I also began to take advantage of his policy of giving extra credit for resubmitting corrected versions of assignments and exams. The extra effort each day not only raised my average by several points, but also pounded important pre-algebraic theories into my head just long enough for me to ace the final. It was the hardest B+ I had earned up to that point, one that would continue to inspire me in times of academic trouble even in college.

More importantly, I learned that striving to do your best and reaching for your dreams didn't have to be a lonely burden or existence. Particularly during the school year, while we balanced public school and Prep's workload without the help of our advisors,[5] the members of my contingent learned to lean on one another for support. The impact of a quality education derives not only from the academic institutions that challenge you to think and to grow, but also from the people you meet and learn from along the way. The program had taken the phrase "I can't" out of my vocabulary and made the phrase *"Juntos podemos,"* "Together we can," a reality.

THERE WAS NEVER A DOUBT IN MY MIND that as an advisor my first job would be to help my students *help themselves* through the program. What I never imagined was how much I would continue to learn about myself through their academic and social trials and tribulations; how "America's future" would serve not only as a mirror to my own past, but also as a microscope through which to view and consider my present decisions. How could I tell them to push themselves to do their best, unless I was prepared to do the same thing? How could I expect them to control their tempers and treat everyone, even those whom they didn't like, with decency and respect, unless I set the example in how I treated them and how I interacted with the rest of the staff?

Thankfully, I would never have to look farther than my own colleagues, the other advisors, to know that what I was preaching to my kids wasn't just idealistic crap. Growing up each summer, surrounded by so many college-bound or college-enrolled students, would continually reaffirm the inevitability of my own success, however I chose to define it. Knowing that these future brilliant lawyers, scientists, businesspeople and dedicated artists believed enough in me to call me a colleague would entrench in my soul a belief that my own road, though still largely uncharted, promised the same rewards.

I do not know of many programs that respect their high school and college students enough to seriously consider their input in

[5] Soon after Elbert's contingent completed the Preparatory Component, Prep instituted the School Year Advisory Corps, a much smaller and limited version of the Summer Advisory System.

making decisions. Yet each summer I would witness the information gathered by advisors playing a critical role in the decision of the Preparatory Component administrators whether or not to retain a child in the program. This is what Prep has always been about—breaking stereotypes, defying expectations and demanding excellence at all levels.

Such profound observations were nowhere on my radar screen the day of my interview with Karen Young, but my feelings must have gotten across to her. Soon afterwards she called to tell me I would join the Summer Advisory System that year. A fierce but low-sounding screech turned into loud excitement as I told my mother and siblings about my appointment as an assistant unit leader.

"¿Qué's eso, qué's eso?" Papi inquired, wanting to know the cause of all the commotion.

"He's going to be a Frankie," my mother told him.

The job description crystallized in Papi's head as I helplessly shrugged at my mother's explanation. Such loose translation couldn't spoil the thrill of having climbed over another hurdle I once had thought impossible. Even if my pay was more valuable exchanged into Third World currency, the job was the opportunity to follow in my own advisors' footsteps. I thought of all that the program had done for me, all the people who had contributed to my success and how I wanted to do the exact same thing for other kids who would soon be feeling what I had felt.

But the greatest thing about it was that I didn't have to wait until I was older or wiser or wealthier to truly make a difference in someone else's life. None of us ever do.

Editor's note: Elbert served as an advisor for four years. Thereafter, during the summers of 1994–1997, he served as head of the Summer Advisory System. His four-year tenure represents the closest anyone has come to equaling the five-summer tenure of Frankie Cruz, the first head of the Summer Advisory System.

ELBERT GARCIA *is a member of Contingent IX. Born and raised in Washington Heights, he graduated from The Fieldston School in 1993 and received a B.A. in urban studies with a specialization in political science from Columbia University in 1997. At Columbia, Elbert cofounded the Dominican Student Organization (el Grupo Quisqueyano), was a columnist for the* Daily Spectator *and helped to design and implement the university's new Latino Studies Program. Pursuing a career in journalism, he has worked as interactive producer at WNBC/MSNBC, general manager and senior producer of The Latino News Network and overnight producer at The New York Times Digital. Over the past seven years, he has also devoted considerable time to his work as a freelance writer, with stories appearing in* Latingirl Magazine, Roots and Culture Magazine, The Source *and* Urban Latino Magazine. *Throughout his undergraduate years, Elbert served as head of the Summer Advisory System at Prep for Prep. Subsequently, he was assistant director of Leadership Development for Student Affairs for one year and has been coordinator and then a vice chair of Prep's Annual Alumni Giving Campaign for the past several years. He is the recipient of an American Political Science Association Fellowship, which is enabling him to work with Congressman Charles Rangel in Washington, D.C., and gain in-depth, practical knowledge about the daily workings of the U.S. Congress.*

PREP FOR PREP AND THE CONSTRUCTION OF MEANINGFUL DEMOCRACY

by JOSHUA DEMETRIUS BLOODWORTH

DURING MY SOPHOMORE YEAR AT HARVARD, two researchers associated with the university published *The Bell Curve.*[1] Behind the pseudo-research, skewed statistics and invented words like *inheritability* stood an age-old pernicious concept: the inferiority of black people. The book caused many of my fellow students with blood links to Africa to question themselves. Despite their achievements, they experienced an intense feeling of unworthiness. Stuck in the funk of internal mistrust, they lost interest in classes and extracurricular activities. One even considered transferring to a university "more appropriate" for his ability.

I did *not* suffer a crisis of tragic self-doubt. Neither did the president of the Harvard Black Students Association for the 1994-95 academic year. We recognized the polemical tract as simply a strategic assault in the psychological war on the value of people of color. Instead of sinking into a stagnant pool of personal uncertainty, we planned rallies, challenged the scurrilous scholarship during teach-ins and reminded our classmates that Harvard makes no mistakes when it comes to admissions. Looking back, the president and I

[1] *The Bell Curve: Intelligence and Class Structure in American Life,* Richard J. Herrnstein and Charles Murray, Free Press, 1994.

shared more than just a love of hip-hop and a desire to go to the Republic of South Africa. We were both Prep for Prep alumni. And we were both more than adequately prepared to withstand and oppose the racist miseducation embodied in the book.

As a poor black male from inner-city Brooklyn, I was a constant target of assaults on my identity and worth. The media, the government's massive deployment of domestic police forces, and store managers who shadowed me around their establishments all sought to instill one lesson: you are socially, intellectually and morally inferior. Into this obscene universe of esteem- and achievement-destroying rhetoric stepped Prep for Prep, a revolutionary organization whose counteroffensives against the forces of an oppressive status quo bring meaningful democracy to a larger segment of the American population.

There are many organizations that tell young people of color that we are just as smart, beautiful and worthy as any other people. What sets Prep for Prep apart, however, is the way it goes about proving that truth. For the 14 months of the Preparatory Component, students develop more than just the critical analytical skills that allow us to apply a striving for excellence to any and all endeavors. We are shown that the talents we exhibit are and have always been *within us*. That slight reorienting of emphasis has profound empowering effects.

I started the program two months after the other students in my contingent. Walking the halls of Trinity School that first day, I was astounded by the overwhelming aplomb with which they carried themselves. In the classrooms, the same self-assurance swirled in the air. My new peers posed and answered questions with skill. They looked to their own experiences, their own lives and situations, to decipher the multiple meanings of *Catcher in the Rye* and the influence of ancient Chinese government on western political organization. What I did not know on that first day was that the courage to risk being wrong in front of others, which undergirded the classroom discussions, was the natural result of Prep's approach to education and to its students.

Rather than reinforcing ideas that students are empty vessels or lost lambs waiting to be filled or saved by some outside authority,

Prep is an enabler of our achievement; it is not a benevolent tyrant dispensing goodies to beggars. Graduates of the Preparatory Component go off to independent day or boarding schools, where they are then able to test the theory of their prowess. In the classrooms of Phillips Exeter, I never felt less smart, less morally fit or less socially valuable than my peers. Around the Harkness table, I spoke when I had an insight that had escaped the notice of others. No fear of laughter or embarrassment about how to state my opinion dried my mouth and restrained my tongue. I felt entitled to participate in the discussions.

But Prep is about more than just achieving academic excellence. It stands for leadership and one's obligations to one's community. I remember well the moment I sat in my dorm's common room at Exeter, contemplating my plans to run for president of the Afro-Latino Exonian Society as well as president of the Student Council. A student asked me if I really believed I could capture either position, let alone both, but for me winning was not the most important question. The background discourse at Prep repeatedly stated that if you desire it, you can acquire it. My concerns pertained to whether I could do well in either or both positions. Did I honestly feel that I could make a positive contribution in these chosen capacities? Issues of integrity, an essential component of the Prep for Prep ideology, swirled around my mind. After pondering the situation and talking to my friends (many of whom were also Prep students), I decided to run and, in fact, was elected to both positions.

From the outset of my Exeter years, I felt I had a role to play in both groups; I saw no reason to have to choose between them. Multiple allegiances are a topic of much concern these days. For many who have experienced physical, emotional or social dislocation, deciding to which community they owe allegiance is a time-consuming endeavor. Luckily, I have been spared that Gordian knot of a dilemma. Prep's ideology neither limits us to seeking leadership positions in the neighborhoods of our birth or in communities defined by race or ethnicity, nor does it counsel us to remain aloof and detached from the larger community. The sword of advancement, in fact, lies in the program's assumption that committed people who apply the talents given to them can manage the complexity of belonging to and aiding several communities at the same time and can grow, as people and as leaders, while doing so. Ultimately, by example, we may be able to demonstrate to others as well that the false choices they often feel compelled to make can and should be resisted.

That same imperative of integrity colored my travels after I graduated from Harvard. From its inception, Prep has understood and taught that to live successfully and morally in the world, people must venture beyond the safe and known. To be of service to my community and country, I had to know about far more than just my own community and country. However, for me, going abroad just to learn what others knew, to take the resources others had, embodied many of the same deviant calculations that lead to the evil of colonialism. I chose therefore to go as a *teacher,* first to the United Kingdom and then to Japan. In that role, I was able not only to receive broader perspectives on the ills and virtues of those two societies, but also to share information I had gleaned from growing up in end-of-the-century America.

In the United Kingdom, I taught at a private secondary institution that tracked its students according to academic performance. Being the young, new guy, I instructed students who had been relegated to the C, D, E and unlettered classes, or put another way, the bottom three-fifths on the intellectual food chain. As a graduate of private institutions that expected all their students to display considerable intellectual prowess, I did not know I was supposed to treat my pupils as all-around inferior to their peers in the higher tracks. My expectations for them mirrored those I had for any of their schoolmates, and those I had had for myself at their age.

Of course, my students resisted. Time and again, they reminded me that they were the "thick" ones and that I was treating them as if they were clever; from their point of view, my expectations were unfair. I told them that while I harbored only slight suspicions that they might be closet Isaac Newtons, none of them reminded me of the poorly drawn Neanderthals in my seventh-grade biology textbook. I communicated my confidence in their ability just as the faculty of Prep had expressed its faith in me. On the first-term exams, many of them performed quite well, obtaining scores higher than those of their supposedly smarter age-mates. One was even elevated from the unlettered cohort to the C Group and told that he had miraculously undergone a transformation from an unlearned duckling into a brilliant swan. Instead of mysterious forces at work, however, I saw the wisdom of the Prep method. Though economically blessed and status privileged (there was the duke of this, princess of that and count of wherever), my students had been advised early on in life that they were just not smart. In the fashion of most kids, they internalized others' perceptions of them. Yet once confidence was instilled, all else followed.

On a recent visit to England, I found myself at an Orthodox Jewish wedding. People of many ethnicities and nationalities were present, but I was one of only three black people at the event, and the only black male. While standing in a corner nursing a Pims, I was approached by an older Scottish gentleman.

"You aren't uncomfortable?" he asked with a bright smile.

"No," I replied with much honesty.

"Then why aren't you in the middle of the room talking to everyone?"

"Because I do not wish to be."

"But how will you get to talk to people?"

"I am talking to you without being in the middle of the room."

Implicit in his questioning and reasoning was the idea that I could not be social or comfortable unless I drew attention to myself. He even assured me that *all* black people in the United Kingdom took center stage at parties and suggested that I follow their example.

I note this experience for an important reason. All of the aforementioned talk of presidencies, treasurerships and teaching positions might have given the mistaken impression that Prep's focus on leadership promotes extrovert showmanship over substantive contributions. Such a supposition could not be farther from the truth. Prep understands that it is usually the people you do *not* see who are making the real strides toward the beloved community. Through its commitment of resources, rhetoric and rewards, Prep for Prep demonstrates that the person who mentors or tutors students one on one is just as valuable as the musical prodigy or organization chair. Prep has shown me and many others that how one goes about paying one's debt to society is less important than actually paying one's debt—as long as it is done with excellence and integrity.

JOSHUA DEMETRIUS BLOODWORTH *is a member of PREP 9's Contingent II. Born and raised in Brooklyn, he graduated from Phillips Exeter Academy in 1993 and received a B.A. in history and African-American studies from Harvard University in 1997. Following graduation, Joshua taught history, math and ethics at the Stowe School in Buckinghamshire, England (1997-98), and served as an assistant English teacher for the Niigata City Board of Education in Japan (1998–2000). He returned to Japan as a summer fellow at the Japanese Civil Liberties Union in Tokyo in 2001. Joshua is currently a third-year student at Harvard Law School, where he has served as Community Service chair, co-chair of the Political Action Committee, president of the Harvard Black Law School Association (2002-03) and co-chair of the Asia Business Conference of the Harvard Asia Law Society. He has also served on the* Harvard Environmental Law Review. *In addition, he has been a teaching fellow for several Harvard undergraduate courses. During Summer Session 1994, Joshua was head advisor for PREP 9.*

THE TEST

by YU WONG

WHAT POSSESSED ME TO COME BACK? On the train in from Long Island, through the crush and furnace of Penn Station, up the Broadway express to 96th Street, the question wouldn't go away. What was I doing spending another summer in class? Here I was, the summer after my junior year in college, walking up 91st Street, past the Greystone Hotel and across Amsterdam Avenue toward Trinity School to take up my duties as a Prep English teaching assistant for the next two months.[1]

Yellow buses were double-parked along the north side of the block, the traditional face of the Upper West Side with its brownstones and the venerable church sprawling up toward the more modern institutional additions and luxury high-rises on Columbus. Hunkered on the south side, flat slabs of brown brick towers declared that mainstay of American urban planning: the housing project. If you saw me that morning, something like a horrified smile probably stared back at you.

Kids spilled out in front of me and broke into two contingents. There were clusters of children chatting and smiling, hugging each other and

[1] During the Preparatory Component's Summer Session, each English teacher has an undergraduate who works as his or her assistant, allowing the program to return papers very quickly to students and to have two people in the room during Writing Conference periods, so that there is adequate time to talk about each child's writing each day.

striding up the block as if they owned the neighborhood. The other class of slightly smaller kids gazed around, wide-eyed, carried by the flow. Were they wondering if they were on the right side of 91st Street?

Was I?

You can take the kid out of the projects, but does he want to go? Reluctantly, sometimes. The gravity of the life you hate can exceed the force of yearning for a way out. Even if you could realize the power of escape velocity, what potential exists still needs a spark.

SATURDAY MORNINGS WERE SACRED when I was growing up. While my parents slept late behind the closed doors of their bedroom, my brother Roger and I would get out of bed just before eight, raid the kitchen for Twinkies and potato chips or cold chicken left-overs, whatever we could find, and settle in front of the TV. We'd jockey for position on the big sofa that was part of a living room set my parents had bought in a dive off Delancey Street. They'd wanted something new, a fresh notion of this American life they found themselves embracing, so out went the ancient convertible couch inherited from my grandparents and in came this ensemble upholstered in blood-crimson polyester fur. All three pieces were delivered one morning in the dead of winter when I was seven. In our hospital-white, empty apartment on the 21st floor of Alphabet City's most recent housing project, they crouched like exotic animals—special delivery from Acme Co., courtesy of Bugs Bunny and friends. On chilly mornings, I would nest in heaps of thick comforters and pillows before the warm light of the TV. But as the weather warmed, Mother would dig out thick, transparent plastic covers, and throughout the summer and fall those seats were unbearable, our sweaty limbs sticking to the squeaky-smooth PVC.

Roger and I always started in sync with the Superfriends. We'd learned English decoding the boxy stories and bubbled dialogue of the Avengers, Superman and the Incredible Hulk. During our first year in America (I was five, my brother eight), interspersed in our awkward grammar and hit-or-miss idioms were gems like "You shall be utterly annihilated!" The Justice League welcomed us every weekend with a new supervillain who would be properly punished by the closing credits. At the other end of the Saturday morning spectrum were the Looney Tunes. In between, things could get dicey.

On a Saturday morning in late fall of 1982, Roger and I were wrestling on the rustling sofa, fighting for the remote control. Our racket was loud enough to bring my parents out of their bedroom and into our cartoon babble. As my mother tried to mediate, Roger piped: "He's not even supposed to be here. He's supposed to take that test!"

Father was furious. "This is true? Is this the day?"

"I forgot," I lied.

I'd hoped the matter had been forgotten. Weeks ago, Mr. Bowman, the bane of the fifth- and sixth-graders of P.S. 61 and my teacher that year, had told my mother, via Roger's translation, that he had recommended me as a candidate for a special program. All he had to say was "summer school" for me to realize just how much this man hated all children. The program accepted only a small number of those nominated, and the first step in the process was a long standardized test on a Saturday morning. I had vowed to keep quiet the whole day and so avoid exactly what was now happening.

"You forgot? How could you forget?" my father said.

Roger had faded into a Cheshire Cat smile in the background, his hands firmly locked on the remote. An undisputed victory! Silently, I swore I would pay him back somehow.

"Is it too late?" my father asked.

We were late, but he insisted on going anyway.

"This is an opportunity," he said. "Can't you see that?"

By the time we arrived at Trinity, the test had already begun. Someone told me to have a seat in the lobby while she tried to find a way to accommodate a latecomer. Father had calmed down after railing at the traffic on the FDR and every crosstown red light. He scanned the dim lobby with its hardwood benches and framed pictures on the walls. The smell of chlorine announced a pool somewhere in the near vicinity. Tense-looking mothers and fathers, black, Latino and Asian-American, crowded the seats or leaned against the walls, some trying to keep younger children entertained. Meanwhile, mostly white students, some in ties and jackets and others in sports uniforms, crossed in and out of the corridors.

For a 10-year-old, I'd been around town. Father's job took him to every inner-city neighborhood in the tri-state area. It seemed wherever there were tenements, government housing projects and crack houses, some enterprising Chinese immigrant would open a take-out restaurant. The economics were elementary. Mostly, customers went for the fast-food orders such as fried chicken wings and French fries, wonton soup and pork fried rice, dishes anyone could prepare with minimum training. Father would contract to outfit the restaurants, and inevitably Roger or I had to tag along as his translator or helper. Until that morning at Trinity, the Upper West Side was what we drove through to get from Harlem to Hell's Kitchen. There were a few landmarks I knew from school trips: the Museum of Natural History, for instance, and Lincoln Center. The rest was a foreign country. Trinity felt like something out of TV, an episode of *Diff'rent Strokes* or *The Facts of Life*.

"This looks like a nice school," Father said. He had to get to work. "You wait here. Take the test. Call your mom when you're done and go home."

He gave me money for pizza and the subway and left. I moved to an empty bench in the long hallway leading to the cafeteria, where other kids were already scribbling away on worksheets and filling in bubbles on answer sheets. I brooded. Summer school was for left-backs and flunkies. I was a top student. Why did I need more work? Why would I want to go to private school? You had to wear uniforms like the Catholic school kids and go to Bible class. I wanted to join my brother at I.S. 56 near Chinatown, where most of my friends would end up after sixth grade. I wanted to play in the marching band and hone my handball serve. Staring at the student art exhibits lining the walls of the long hallway, I realized a simple truth: No one could make me pass. I could score so low that there was no way any program would have me.

The idea had a rebellious ring to it. I was not a rebel. Getting yelled at in class for talking could release a flood of tears. And I had never flunked anything in my life. Scoring less than 100 percent, even on the smallest quiz, upset me for days. I was the guy who did the *extra* extra-credit problem for homework. It was a wonder I'd ever made it through grade school alive.

But there was nothing, no one, to stop me. Was it possible? Would I get away with it?

The woman who had told me to wait in the lobby tapped me on the shoulder and informed me there was no way to get me in today. I had to fight the urge to smile. Off the hook! Then she said: "I've scheduled you for next week. You can come back, can't you?"

No, I couldn't. What? Miss another Saturday morning of cartoons?

"Yes, I'll come back."

"Good. We'll see you next week. Be sure you're on time."

Outside Trinity I blinked in the gray glare of Saturday's ashes. The morning had been wasted, but the day was just starting. I decided two things. One, I'd tell my parents I had missed my chance to take the test, and that would be that. Two, I'd walk home, save the money my father had given me and buy myself a comic; that much I deserved. The longest walk I'd ever taken alone was from Chinatown to Alphabet City. This would be on another order. A quick calculation of how many blocks and avenues were involved and how long it took me to walk a block (about a minute, I figured) yielded an estimated two hours on the road. It would be an adventure, especially since I wouldn't be coming this way again.

I walked south and bore east in an errant pattern of steps back to the projects. Leaving the brownstones of the West Side, I crossed into Central Park, following the flow of bikers and joggers on the road before breaking away into the shadowed paths leading to the lake and boathouse. Eventually, I exited onto Fifth Avenue and kept going south, walking by the hansom cabs outside the Plaza, down to Rockefeller Center and St. Patrick's Cathedral. It was my personal tour of New York, gazing at the landmarks, watching shoppers on their whirlwind sprees, lingering on corners to wonder at the endless corridors of skyscrapers up and down the avenues. Somewhere around Grand Central, I wolfed down the most expensive pizza I'd ever eaten. That slice cost three times what they charged at Sal's on Avenue C. Vaguely, I regretted losing my comic-book money, yet I was too drunk on the city to care.

It took me four hours to get home. I staggered into the take-out restaurant my parents had opened two years before on Avenue B.

"What happened to you?" my mother asked. "I was about to call the police."

"I walked."

"You what?"

"Yeah, I walked."

She shook her head and laughed. "The entire way? You couldn't take the subway or a bus?"

There was no good way to answer that, so I just shrugged.

"And the test?"

"Too late," I said, and saw her face fall.

My father was the handyman who could fix anything. When he wasn't working, he was reading some technical manual or tinkering with machines other people had thrown out. When I had a math or science problem, I went to him. But Mother held it all together. It was she who schemed and prodded Father to open the take-out joint, a hole in the wall that had hijacked our lives in a way none of us had imagined. She opened the place every morning and didn't close up until long past midnight, unable to turn away stragglers. She took no holidays. The original plan had called for an all-in-the-family business, but Father didn't cut it as a chef. He was just not fast enough to fill orders during lunch or dinner rushes. Early on, he hung up his apron and returned to fixing refrigerators and installing the equipment for other people's restaurants. While my mother went through a succession of temperamental chefs, Roger and I practiced our math at the cash register for a couple of hours every night and afternoons on weekends. We quickly graduated to manning the deep fryers and ladling soup from the containers in the steam table. By his sixth grade, Roger could stir up a mean plate of shrimp fried rice or pepper steak with onions. I confined myself to preparing wonton soup.

Mother always hoped for better. She was the second of six children who grew up in the famine years of China's Great Leap Forward. The Cultural Revolution cut her education off at middle school. She survived a decade of violent chaos, all the while caring for a younger brother and three sisters, then Roger and me when Father went to Hong Kong to find work in the mid-seventies. She lobbied local officials incessantly to allow her entire family to immigrate to America and join her parents in New York when China finally opened its doors to the world in 1978. Then she persuaded my father to leave the life he had prepared for us in Hong Kong for the uncertainty of the United States, where she believed Roger and I would have a better chance.

Education was the cornerstone of my mother's faith. She didn't preach it, didn't monitor our schoolwork, or have to convince us of the importance of doing well in school. In her quiet way, she made sure I had time to go to the library every week. If we said we had homework to do, she sent us home from the restaurant with dinner and instructions not to stay up late. She assumed we wouldn't abuse her trust. Of course, we did so all the time. Saturday afternoon trips to the library sometimes involved long detours to the video arcade. We cited all sorts of "educational" purposes for toys we wanted our parents to buy. But in school both of us continued to excel. Our failures, academic and otherwise, reflected on her, and the bite of her disappointment hurt more than any of my father's disciplinary routines.

Looking at her that afternoon, I did something I've never been able to explain. "There's another test next week," I said. Now the words were out. "They told me to come back."

W*e were working our way through* A Midsummer Night's Dream, *one of Shakespeare's best-loved and most deceptively simple plays, when I realized I was in love.*

Every morning I would drag my feet up the stairs of Trinity's older wing, with its tall windows streaming light everywhere, to one of the gable-ceilinged classrooms on the top floor. Here, I would slouch in a chair, wondering how I was going to stay awake, where I would find the energy to get through the day.

Then the second-summer students would arrive, survivors of the most grueling 12 months of academic hell available for anyone their age. They had already been accepted into the most prestigious private schools in the city, where they would enroll in the fall. Two more months and they would return to being children, free to spend the summers as they wanted, masters of their Saturdays once again. I'd assumed they would be like second-semester seniors. They had flown high and crossed the Rockies; now they just needed to find a warm, comfortable current and ride it out.

Instead, they were like hungry dynamos, refusing anything less than my full attention to keep them spinning. Back in their public schools, they might have held back for fear of looking too smart or being called teacher's pets. Here, they pulled out all the stops, feeding off each other and getting stronger.

That energy was contagious. I was falling for these kids, every single hard-luck one of them.

Hard-luck? Someone had shown them a way out of the pit of despair, and they had gritted their teeth and started the climb. No one would cry for these underdogs, while many thousands of other bright kids still languished in unchallenging classes and underfunded schools. But who was I kidding? They had come up from the dust and were headed for the storm. They thought they had gotten through the worst of the worst, that being academically prepared would be enough. It wouldn't be the half of it. They were headed for the seventh and eighth grades at New York City's most elite private schools. There was no way really to prepare them for that. Now they were fortified walls of confidence, but later the cracks would start to show.

THE NEXT WEEK, Father got me there a half-hour early. He wasn't the only neurotic. The cafeteria was already full of kids sitting at long tables, squirming in their chairs, neatly arranging their No. 2 pencils in rows or just looking around. There must have been hundreds, yet an eerie silence stretched across the room. I was sticking to my original plan: Fill in the bubbles at random and spend the rest of my time doodling. I only hoped they wouldn't be stingy with the scratch paper.

I sat down with two others at a table intended for four, folding my hands in front of me. To my right, a pasty-faced boy with sandy-colored hair stretched out his hand.

"Hi, my name is Ben."

We shook hands as I introduced myself.

"That's an odd first name," said the moonfaced boy across from me. He had light brown skin, closed-cropped hair and big round glasses. "How do you spell it?"

"Without the O," I said. It was my stock answer.

"I'm Sean," he said, smiling and showing his dimples.

What? No "Hey, you" jokes? No "You got a pronoun for a name?" They had come to take the test, and they were all business. Ben's carrying case bulged with pencils. Sean had three No. 2s lined up in front of him and a sharpener at the ready. Usually that was how I was, too. But this was different. I'm not looking to ace this one, I wanted to say.

"You can borrow one of mine," Ben said, offering a pencil from his case, and Sean added that I could fall back on one of his if the point broke during the test. No thanks, I said, having spotted boxes of fresh pencils at the front of the room when I walked in.

"Want one of mine?" A fourth boy sat down at the table. He wore a knitted white skullcap and came armed to the teeth with pencils. He said his name was Abdul and then started talking about the test: how long it was; how hard it was said to be, particularly the math. "There's fractions, you know."

"I've done that," Ben said. Sean and I immediately said we had as well.

"Mixed fractions?"

"No sweat," Sean said.

"Well, I'm not worried, either," Abdul went on. "I scored the highest of my school in the reading *and* math tests last year."

Ben wasn't to be outdone. "I'm in the ninety-ninth percentile of scores *citywide* on the math and reading tests," he said.

"Do you know anyone who's ever scored a hundred?" I asked.

Abdul gave me a withering look. "You *can't* get a hundred. Ninety-nine's as high as you can go."

I was impressed. The highest I had ever scored was 95th percentile on the citywide math tests. In reading, I was still far down in the ranks. These guys were smart. Maybe they were *smarter* than me. Outrageous! For as long as I could remember, I had been the smartest kid at school, at least in my grade. There were *maybe* two others who came close in math now that I was in a combined fifth- and sixth-grade class, and others who were better in grammar and spelling. Overall, though, I had dominated my classmates academically since the second grade, and I had become an insufferable, arrogant nerd who only managed to avoid stitches or worse because I never refused to help anyone who asked.

I looked around the room. There were kids of every size and color from all over the city, and they were *all* smart.

"I'm gonna pass this, no problem," Abdul said.

"This is the easy part," said Ben. "You gotta pass two even harder tests after this."

Sean and I were both quiet. Then Sean smiled and shrugged. "Nothing to lose."

Nothing to lose? Everything to lose! Two summers and every Wednesday afternoon and Saturday for all of sixth grade! Doing homework while my friends were riding their bikes along the East River and working up to crossing over to Brooklyn? Missing all the pickup punchball and handball games, not to mention the morning game shows? And the reward was what, wearing a suit to go to school? No, that wasn't for me. Thanks very much, no.

"I don't really want to go," I said. They looked at me as if I'd said a four-letter word. "It's summer school!"

"So what?" Abdul said. "The smartest kids in the city will be there. Of course, most of you won't make it. It's a small program."

"You, who?" Now Sean was mad. "Who's not gonna make it? I'm gonna get in, no sweat."

Abdul rolled his eyes. "Not everyone can get in" was all he said.

Them's fightin' words. Who was this guy? I could pass if I wanted to. When the monitor came around offering pencils, I took three and borrowed Sean's sharpener. As the instructions were read aloud, I stared at the jagged line separating the wood and the lead, at the dull black tip waiting to make a mark, to fill in that first bubble on the answer sheet. That first oval is always the darkest. For three hours I barely touched the scratch paper.

I must have filled in enough of the right bubbles. A few months later, Prep called to schedule my IQ test.[2]

---

[2] About 20 percent of the children who sit for the First Level group-administered tests (fill in the "bubbles") do well enough to be advanced to Second Level, which involves the administration of an individual IQ test as well as an interview visit.

Fearless.

I watched and listened, bantered and joked with them. I wasn't their real teacher, so we could be on a first-name basis. I wasn't an advisor, so I knew little about their histories or their personal lives or whether someone was failing science. I was on the outskirts of authority but within the network of mentors. And I was one of them; they knew that.

"Contingent VI!" a student said on my first day. "You're old."

We were mirrors facing off, a prism of past and future, sometimes warped, reflections. Attitude permeated the room. I had to relearn how to read that mixture of defiance and determination.

We journeyed through the Odyssey *and read scenes from* A Midsummer Night's Dream. *I threw them the basics of deconstruction; they caught and ran with it and came back for more. It was humbling and exhilarating and maddening.*

Weren't they the slightest bit peeved by all this?

THE IQ TEST CAME in the middle of winter. I showed up at an office overlooking Washington Square Park[3] with every intention of being pronounced an imbecile. A young woman came in, and we began.

"This is not a very standard test," she explained. "There are no right answers for most of the exercises we're going to do, so don't try to figure out what I'm after. Just try your best."

Wait a minute. No right answers? What did that mean? It's a test. There's a score. If there were no right answers, how could I figure out the wrong way to answer the questions? Clearly she was trying to psyche me out. No problem, I could play that game.

It turned out to be a series of games. There were puzzles to put together, shapes to build, things to spot. Every now and then the woman jotted down something on her clipboard. She smiled here and there at some of the things I did, looked at her watch often, but otherwise gave no hint of how I was doing.

I was having fun. Each game started easy but became increasingly

[3] During Prep's early years, IQ testing was done at New York University, at the Testing Center associated with the Department of Educational Psychology, under the supervision of Dr. Gil Trachtman.

harder. By the time she got around to asking me factual questions, I was on a roll.

"How many pounds are in a ton?"

"Two thousand."

"Very good. Not many people know that."

Darn! I was blowing it. What was I doing? Giving her a stupid, aw-shucks smile, that's what. You're so arrogant, you can't play dumb! What's wrong with you?

And then it was over. We shook hands and I walked out into Washington Square, where I watched the chess players in the park for a little while. The speed games were the most fun: two going head to head, flicking their pieces around the board while slamming the clock like two guys playing the same drum. Sometimes they trash-talked each other, but mostly they were silently and psychotically bent against time.

Standing there, I knew I'd outsmarted myself.

We trooped down a sloping meadow, wading through the tall late-summer grass, then followed a narrow trail through the woods that opened onto the lake. It looked exactly as I remembered, down to the wide raft anchored beyond the pebbly beach in the sparkling water. The kids who could swim immediately made for the raft. The rest of us waded in to sit on the rocks or on low-lying branches of the huge trees that leaned out over the water.

Fourteen months of academic boot camp came down to these few days together at Hotchkiss[4] *before they would spread out again to the far corners of the city. The community these kids had formed—one of equal rivalry and merit, no questions asked—would fragment even though the program was by no means over. Counselors from Prep would circulate from school to school in the years ahead, keeping an eye on and lending a sympathetic ear to their tough charges. Prep would be around to organize tours of prospective colleges and give a second read to their application essays. In college, some long-lost*

---

[4] At the end of a contingent's second Summer Session, the students, advisors and many faculty members attend a four-day retreat on the campus of a boarding school, usually The Hotchkiss School in Lakeville, Connecticut, and sometimes The Taft School in Watertown, Connecticut.

summer companions would even find themselves in the same English class again.

This phase, however, was coming to an end. And that prospect, as Emily put it, was "really depressing."

"You think everything is depressing," Claire said.

"No, I don't! I just think it's sad that we won't be together anymore."

Weren't they glad it was over?

"No. I want to come back and be a 'grad'[5] *in two years."*

Why?

"You came back."

She had me there. There were all sorts of technical reasons for me to want to be in New York this summer, one of them being the need to get out of the suburbs where my parents had settled, fulfilling another condition of their American Dream. But New York was full of opportunities, things to do, matters of consequence to pursue. Why Prep?

I redirected the question. "Okay, but why do you *want to come back?" I pointed out that being a "grad" was no better than being a gofer, ordered around by the older advisors, teachers and various levels of assistants. You were always running one errand or another and getting little thanks for your efforts.*

"Yeah, but you get to be part of Prep again," Emily said.

What about having to work in the summer?

"So? What else have I got to do?" Emily shot back.

Was this the best game in town? What about having fun, staying out all day and not coming home until the summer sun set at nine in the evening? What about not having to do homework? What about . . . ?

So, there it was. I had been carrying it around with me for a decade. What a long time to be afraid of failure.

THE UPPER SCHOOL WING OF TRINITY looks as if it had been built to repel the perpetual threat of urban riot. I could relate to that. Most of the classrooms have no windows. On the second level, a few labs and other rooms have lateral slits set just below the high ceilings. There were about 12 of us staring up at the windows

[5] See footnote, page 41.

opening onto the high-rise condos sitting atop Trinity. With a little imagination, it wasn't hard to transform the cinder-block box into the dungeon of a tall castle. As we applied ourselves to another, much shorter math test and wrote a few paragraphs answering some odd questions, the guard would call us out one by one for more intensive interrogation.

This seemed the most mysterious part of the process. If I hit the right scores, what need was there for an interview? Would it be like the IQ test? Was this even a test? What were they looking for and how could I make sure they wouldn't get it from me? The written test seemed a joke. I breezed through it and was doodling when my name was finally called.

In an adjacent room, I met my interviewer, a tall, thin man with a ready smile and a soft, disarming voice. He had a stack of folders in front of him. We sat down facing each other.

"How are you doing?"

"Fine. Thank you."

"I hope the math test isn't too hard."

"Nope, I'm done."

"That's good. What do you think of the tests in general?"

Hmm. Trick question? "They were okay."

"Not too hard?"

"The first one was kinda long, but the IQ test was fun."

"Really? What was fun about it?"

"The puzzles and stuff."

"You like puzzles?"

"Yes."

"What else do you like? Any other kinds of games?"

"Chess. I play with my brother and my father."

And so it went, a normal-seeming conversation that flowed from one subject to the next. In no time, I had spilled my guts about my family, school, neighborhood. All useless information, I thought. When was he going to get around to the interview?

"So what do you think of the program?" he finally asked.

I hesitated. What would happen if I told him the truth, that I didn't want to have anything further to do with it?

"Let me put it another way. Do you think the program is right for you?"

"Right for me? Isn't that what you're supposed to decide?"

"Sure, but I want to know what you think. It's a big commitment. Your parents can't do it for you. Your teachers and friends will help, but in the end the question is: Can you handle it?"

What? "Of course I can!"

"You're sure? I saw you hesitate there," he said, raising one eyebrow.

"I can handle the work," I insisted.

"Excellent. We like to hear that."

Dolt!

And just like that, the interview was over. I went back to the other room, handed in my test and writing sample, and left.

A few months later, as the promise of summer ripened, my acceptance letter arrived. I cried. It was true what my brother said: I couldn't do anything right.

FROM MY PICKUP ON 13TH STREET and First Avenue, it was about 45 minutes on the Prep school bus to Trinity. I spent that first morning ride in silence, watching the cityscape flash by on the way uptown, fighting the urge to break down and cry again.

"I don't want to go," I had told my mother in tears a few weeks before.

"You've put so much time into this already. You've passed all the tests. Just go and try it. Do you know how many kids only wish for a chance like this?"

And here I was getting off the school bus, being herded to the cafeteria for more instructions, going to my homeroom.

"Yu! Hey, you made it!"

It was Abdul, giving me a huge smile. Did I detect relief? Yes, it was good to see a familiar face.

"Have you seen the others?" he asked.

What others?

Ben and Sean had been accepted as well, Abdul told me. "We all made it. Must have been a lucky table."

Yes, lucky for me, there had been enough fuel to go around that day.

Yu Wong *is a member of Contingent VI. Born in southern China, Yu immigrated to the United States at the age of five and grew up on Manhattan's Lower East Side. He graduated from The Dalton School in 1990 and received a Bachelor of Arts and Science in East Asian studies, magna cum laude with highest honors, from Harvard University in 1995. Yu spent the 1993-94 academic year at Fudan University in Shanghai, People's Republic of China, on a Harvard-Yenching Fellowship. Following graduation, he worked as a researcher in the Beijing bureau of the* New York Times *and subsequently joined the Beijing staff of the* Far Eastern Economic Review. *Over the next two years, he wrote features for the* Review *and also a weekly column about life in Beijing for the English-language* Hong Kong Standard, *while also freelancing for the* International Herald Tribune, *Christian Science Monitor Radio and National Public Radio. In 1997, Yu joined the* Asian Wall Street Journal *as a staff reporter, stationed in Hong Kong (1997-98) and in Taipei (1999). For the past three years, he has served as an editor for the international and domestic* Wall Street Journal *and recently joined the* Journal'*s on-line operations as a news writer. Yu lives in Brooklyn with his wife, Ilaria, and their two-year-old son, Matteo.*

III.
LESSONS LEARNED WELL AND EARLY

Having observed 25 contingents of students cope with the demands and complexities ofl our Preparatory Component, I believe it is a mistake to think of those initial 14 months at Prep as merely a rigorous academic program. In a typical year, 500 schools will have nominated candidates; a given contingent may contain students from 90 different schools. Some of the students who struggle the most are among those with the highest intellectual potential but happen to come from schools that have done a particularly poor job at providing them with basic skills. In other words, where a student ranks in his or her contingent may change drastically in the course of the 14 months. Some have had the experience of being students before, while others have merely attended school. It is a very uneven playing field when the starting bell rings. And since challenge leads necessarily to an examination of one's values, Prep students learn as much about *themselves* as they learn about American history or the rules of English grammar: How important is education to me? What am I willing to sacrifice? What are my priorities? What do I expect from myself? What *could* I expect?

Our students acquire study skills, time-management skills and organizational skills. They learn to speak up and defend their point of view in the classroom. But there is much else to learn as well. Taking responsibility for one's own work, knowing when and how to ask for help, setting realistic goals based on an understanding of one's strengths and weaknesses all come into play. Decision-making is a constant. Some students begin the Preparatory Component primarily because their parents want them at Prep, but it is a rare child indeed who can maintain the pace and find the stamina to persevere for the entire 14 months without at some point making a *personal* commitment: I am doing this for me, I am doing this because it is important, I am doing this because it is something I want to do. Students develop an awareness of their own values and an overall resolve to shape their own lives.

On the four-day trip that celebrates a contingent's completion of the Preparatory Component, interspersed among sports events, skit rehearsals, lake swims and other activities intended to be fun, are times set aside for serious reflection. At one session, I pose only a few questions; the students do most of the talking. I listen to child after child speak with unbelievable eloquence about what they've learned about themselves and how they found the strength not to give up. We can talk about school reform until we're all blue in the face, but in the end it's the chance for each child to learn what he or she is truly capable of doing that has to be the cornerstone in achieving equality of educational opportunity. By the end of the 14 months, Prep for Prep students understand this and carry it with them to their next challenge in life.

"I'M A BIDNESS MAN!"

by NNAMDI ORAKWUE

A GOOD FRIEND OF MINE was walking along a street in downtown Baltimore several years ago when he realized he was being followed by a group of small black children. Dressed in a dark pinstriped suit and briefcase in hand, he turned to look at the youngsters and realized they were heckling him. They were strutting down the street, chests stuck out like George Jefferson, proclaiming, "I'm a bidness man!"

When I think about my own progression from Prep for Prep to the budding businessman I am today, I'm struck by how much of me is represented in my friend's anecdote. Like those children in Baltimore, I had no idea what business was beyond what I saw on TV. And like my pinstriped friend, I chose a career in finance, a field dominated by white men in pursuit of economic profit. The heckling is the symbolic derision of history that views my foray as hopeless, the disapproval of some members of my own community who view my pursuit as selfish, and the nervous laughter inside my own proud mind as I promise myself that I'll prove them all wrong.

I learned three critical things as a member of the Prep community: to overcome fear of failure, to listen to and emulate those who are successful, and to accept and harness the personal thoughts and circumstances that truly motivate me to succeed. These behaviors were first ingrained in me during my days as a Preparatory Component student.

Many of the other students were from different cultural backgrounds and lived in different parts of the city. (If you grew up in Brooklyn, kids from Manhattan and the Bronx were virtual foreigners!) And I was no longer the smartest kid in the class. All the confidence I had from excelling socially and academically up to that point was gone. Fear set in. It wasn't as easy to raise my hand in class when half the room was as smart as me or even smarter. What if I gave the wrong answer or someone criticized my ideas? All of a sudden it was harder to tell a funny joke when my peers were so culturally diverse that I didn't know if they shared my sensibilities. What if nobody laughed?

If I was going to succeed in this highly competitive program, I would have to take risks and open myself up to the possibility of social or academic failure. This lesson, that success involves risk-taking and potential failure, has helped me immensely in my career. Even now, when I am faced with greater responsibility or difficult problems that stretch my abilities, I feel a twinge of anxiety. Yet it is followed by something akin to an immediate reflex as I draw on a long history of overcoming fear of failure. This history started during my days at Prep, and it propels me forward.

Taking risks also forced me to think through all the possible scenarios and outcomes in a situation, and this habit has been a terrific help in business. Mr. Roth was my teacher in an advanced history class. His Socratic method of teaching and sarcastic nature combined to make his classroom an intellectually threatening place. Whenever I took a position or made an argument, I thought about what his potential critiques might be and what weaknesses in my argument a classmate could exploit. In hindsight, what I did in Mr. Roth's class is no different than a memo I might write at work. I am just better at it today, because I starting honing these skills when I was 11 years old.

At Prep I also learned to listen. By *listen,* I mean that through the course of conversations with others, one should attempt to learn a little bit about who they are, what motivates them, *why* they believe *what* they believe—in sum, what makes them who they are. I found this an extremely difficult skill to learn. Even as an 11-year-old, so much of my self-esteem was built on a foundation of success and positive reinforcement that I had become cocky. I was reading children's books at age three and a half and was given "special projects" by my public school teachers because the regular work was too easy. My parents' friends would remark how bright I was. This went to my head. So it was tough to hold back, once I arrived at Prep, and patiently listen to someone else, to try to really understand what that *other* person was all about.

The other students at Prep so impressed me that I needed to learn what made them special. Their diverse experiences and thoughts could make *me* better. I was getting B's at Prep. If I wanted to get A's, I had to really listen and learn what Darko Dorsett was doing to get A's. This is a lesson I never forgot. When I'm in a business meeting, often the most important insights pertain to the demeanor, style, fears, interests and character of the other party.

After I listened and learned, I then had to emulate the behavior of those who were successful. Was Darko studying harder than I was? Was he studying differently? Was he studying by himself or in a group? Was he getting help after hours from the teacher? After figuring out the answers to these questions, I did what he did. This lesson stayed with me, and I apply it to my career today. Among my peers and my superiors, I try to take note of those who succeed in their careers, figure out how and why, and if what they do fits within my own style and ethics, I replicate their behaviors. I have sought out many business mentors, some of whom are Prep trustees, and I observe them and ask them the secrets of their success.

Perhaps the most crucial business lesson Prep taught me is the importance of understanding my own passion and how to channel it. Prep's focus on analysis of strong characters in great literature, from Odysseus to Atticus Finch, helped me think introspectively and critically. Who do I want to be? Why? What can I do with my career to move closer to the person I dream of becoming?

I am driven to succeed because I have been blessed with opportunities that few blacks in America get. It's like being in a bloody battle in which comrades are randomly being killed and wounded all around me, yet for some reason I emerge from the battle unscathed. There is a feeling almost akin to guilt that so much good fortune has been bestowed on me. Given my blessings, I have a responsibility to make the most of the opportunities I have had at Poly Prep Country Day, Harvard and Wharton business school.

I believe that of all the things I could choose as my life's work, my contributions will have the most impact on American society if I succeed in business. Social and economic advancement are indelibly linked with access to capital. This responsibility can be either an unbearable burden or an awesome motivator, depending on how I channel the energy. I believe I am among those fortunate enough to process this responsibility in a positive way, as a motivator to work as hard and as smart as I can, to go as far and as fast as I can. This is primarily because so many role models at Prep, through their own careers and guidance, have shown me how to ensure that the important things in life, starting with family and friends, are not overshadowed by an *obsession* with success.

NNAMDI ORAKWUE *is a member of Contingent VII. Born and raised in Brooklyn, he graduated from Poly Prep Country Day School in 1991 and received a B.A. in government, cum laude, from Harvard University in 1995. He subsequently earned an M.B.A. (major in finance) from The Wharton School of the University of Pennsylvania in 2001. At Wharton, Nnamdi was a Goldman Sachs Fellowship recipient and won first prize in the annual Whitney Young Business Plan Competition. Prior to attending Wharton, he worked as an investment banking financial analyst in the Consumer/Business Services Group of Alex. Brown & Sons and as an associate at Cornerstone Equity Investors, where he focused on middle-market LBOs in the consumer products and business services industries. Upon obtaining his M.B.A., Nnamdi joined IBM Corporation, first as a senior finance professional in Corporate Development—Mergers and Acquisitions and currently in its Treasury-Strategy unit.*

DOING THE RIGHT THING

by ORLANDO BISHOP

It's three o'clock in the morning. It's hot as hell. And I have no idea why the caged bird sings.[1] *To tell you the truth, at this point I really couldn't care less. It's my first summer of Prep for Prep, and I've never been through anything like this.*

BY THE TIME I GOT TO THE FIFTH GRADE at P.S. 92 in Brooklyn, a rough school full of tough kids, I had coasted to the top of the heap. I was a top student in the top class. It wasn't something I bragged about; in fact, I was much more proud of my scrapping. Win or lose, I would "throw 'em up."

But this was different. This "summer school" thing required a whole new brand of toughness. Wasn't the point of getting good grades that you *didn't* have to go to summer school? None of my boys got it, either. And as I walked past Alan, Hassan, Herbie, Dante, Dwayne and all my boys on Clarkson Avenue on my way home, sometimes they would stop what they were doing—playing football, messing with the hydrant to cool off, playing basketball in Waldbaum's lot—just long enough to ask in honest amazement, "Why you gotta go to extra school?"

---

[1] The reference is to *I Know Why the Caged Bird Sings* by Maya Angelou, which is among the many books Prep students read as part of our literature course.

I would mumble through some memorized bit about independent schools. The truth was that I really wanted to scream "Amen," throw that heavy-ass bookbag in the street and rejoin them in my place in the world, right there on my block. But I never did. I just grumbled, "See y'all later," and kept on walking. Besides, who had time to consider options when Mr. Clark's research homework was hanging over my head?

"Do you want to go to sleep and I'll get you up early?" Mommy's being comforting and supportive, but we both know it doesn't make any difference after a certain point. It is *early. And chances are, the sun will rise on me doing my homework—again. "I still have math and a lab report to do after this reading, and then I'll go to sleep." Doug (my advisor) was right. When I told him I was falling asleep on my reading, he suggested that I do my reading first when I got home. This is the first time I've ever needed a strategy to get my homework done.*

"I'M AFRAID OF TESTS." We were eighth-graders at Poly Prep, and K.B., my friend of a year and a half, was freaking out. We were preparing for midterms, and she didn't know whether she was coming or going. "It's just a piece of paper," I shot back. "Look, this is all we have to do . . ." I mapped out the week for her. "When are your exams?" "Which class do you have to study the longest time for?" "Which tests do you need to rock to pull up your grade for the semester?" It was as if a switch had flipped in my head, but it wasn't anything that dramatic. The fact was that I had learned how to organize study time, day after day, every time I sat in the Trinity stairwell with my advisor reviewing my homework logs.

Sure, I had my own tests to study for, but I was cool. As I had joked with some of my friends from Prep, the classes were the least of our problems when we got to our schools. The real "tests" were social. Prep doesn't have any classes on your first bar mitzvah. And it wouldn't matter if they did. No one can prepare you fully for "sweet sixteens" snatched out of fairy tales, when most of the weddings at your church have their receptions in the Community Hall. The point was not that either world was better . . . or worse. But I had to learn the language and customs of a New World, and that was possible because I hit the deck running in the classroom.

Most importantly, though, the time I spent on Student Government, Peer Leadership, varsity football, basketball and track, glee club, theater and the "buddy" program (to name just a few of my activities) allowed me to become a member of the Poly community. I most enjoyed the privilege of my membership in my junior year, when I joined with a group of Poly students to establish A.B.C., the Anti-Bias Coalition. At that time, the administration wanted to tell us what they had told others before us—that a group focused on issues of race and bias would do more damage than good to the Poly community—but we were different. We were *part* of the Poly community and, in most cases, leaders. We were members of the clubs and teams. We participated in school politics and activities. We were top students. Years later I would learn about the concept of social capital. The term was new to me, but the concept wasn't. My friends and I had pooled our capital to get the headmaster to take a chance on A.B.C.

I can't believe I'm still reading this book. Man, I'm sleepy. "Mother whispered, 'See, you don't have to think about doing the right thing. If you're for the right thing, then you do it without thinking.'"[2] *I better remember that for the quiz tomorrow. English . . . done.*

"WE CANNOT GIVE UP ON THIS KID."

Samona Joe, the assistant head of the Summer Advisory System and one no-nonsense woman, just tilted her head to the side a little. She had heard this tirade from me before. J.C. was like a little brother to me, so I took it very personally when it was suggested that he might be "dropped" in his second summer. What I loved about this kid (and when I say kid, please understand that I was only 16 years old at the time) was that he was the little engine that could. He was younger than a lot of the other kids. He was smaller than a lot of the other kids. And he didn't have the academic tools that most

[2] The quote is from the last page of Maya Angelou's *I Know Why the Caged Bird Sings.*

of the other kids had. But he never gave up. Never. He held on long after I would have thrown in the towel. And if he wasn't going to give up after a year of toiling, I wasn't giving up on him. I remember hugging him the day of the vote as he cried in Trinity's carpeted hallway. I told him not to worry and sent him back to class. I didn't tell him that I was plenty worried for the both of us.

I lobbied anyone who would listen, and as the day went by, it was getting tough to tell how the vote would go. I asked a friend to cover my bus for me. There was no way I could sleep that night if I didn't find out what had been decided. So I sat in the hallway outside the closed-door meeting and waited . . . and waited. Then the door opened. The first administrator out the door was a woman whom I had talked to death about J.C. She looked down at me and smiled. That was enough. I knew J.C. would graduate from the Preparatory Component and get to go to his independent school.

The end of the summer came, and we all headed off to Hotchkiss for the four-day trip that doubles as reward and retreat. When it came time to board the buses to go home, I went around to all the kids, saying good-bye. When I got to J.C., he simply gave me a hug. We didn't say anything. We didn't have to. Years later, I heard that he graduated from his independent school and went off to a top-tier college.[3] I knew he would.

I can see the detail in the brick of the building across the way. That means the sun is rising. I'm just going to have to finish my math on the bus. I have got to get some sleep. I lean into Mommy's room. "Mommy, wake me up at 6:45." "Okay." I can get ready in 20 minutes . . . if I hurry.

"NO FUCKING BAG!" I think that's what the Naples employee said.[4] He was screaming at Diahann, my classmate at Yale. Diahann and I had been friends since our first summer at Prep when we were 11 years old. And all she had done was ask for a bag to cover

[3] J.C. graduated from Wesleyan in 2000.

[4] The October 1990 incident dealt with in this section of Orlando's story is the same incident that is reported in Diahann Billings-Burford's story.

the pizza she had bought. So I yelled back the only thing that fully captured my feelings about the way the Naples guy was treating my friend. It went something like "No! Fuck you! Give her a bag!"

"The Naples Incident," as *The Yale Daily Press* called it, was big news. There was a boycott, mediation, the works. But none of that is what I take from the incident.

When the Yale police chose to question me, as opposed to interrogating the Naples employees who had now come onto Yale property, Diahann came to my defense. She was already inside, safe. She could have kept walking and left me to deal with the cops alone. In fact, I had told her to go. But she didn't. She marched back out of that entryway door and challenged the cops who had chosen to come after me, despite the fact that we were the ones who had been mistreated in the first place. She paid a hefty price for defending me. Yale took disciplinary action against her. The administration needed a sacrificial lamb, and they chose her. A few years later, when I told her how sorry I was that she'd been the scapegoat, that she'd gotten in trouble for defending me, she just said she didn't blame me and moved on. That was the last we ever spoke of it.

The Naples Incident caused both of us and a lot of other people a lot of pain, but I sometimes console myself with this thought: I had Diahann's back, and she had mine. Diahann and I have seen each other through a lot (Poly Prep, Yale, weddings, the deaths of parents), but every time I see "Wassup, Oz?" in my e-mail inbox, I know that somewhere at the core of our friendship are the 14 months we survived together in Prep.

"Orlando, get up." By the tone of Mommy's voice, I can tell that she's been calling me for a while. 6:58! Oh, no! I gotta get ready. The bus is gonna leave me.

I SAT IN A CHURCH PEW in absolute amazement as I watched Marvin Winans walk away. I was on tour with the Yale Gospel Choir, and I had just sung a solo in his church. To be honest, that would have been exciting enough for me. But he'd actually stopped as he walked past our pew, leaned in, smiled at me and said, "That's all right." It may not sound like much if you don't understand, but "That's all right" is up there with "Amen" and "You better sing" when it comes to gospel compliments.

When I was a kid, I had listened to The Winans. In fact, they had given me singing lessons. See, when your mother is raising two kids on a nurse's salary, you don't really think about things like singing lessons. At least I never did. I learned to sing by singing along with songs I liked. I had mimicked Marvin Winans (and Luther Vandross and Freddie Jackson and Lionel Richie and a bunch of other great singers) as I grew up. I didn't know whether I would ever be able to sing as well as them, but I learned a lot trying to do the things they did with their voices. I never dreamed that I would meet Marvin Winans . . . much less that *he* would like *my* singing. I was a long way from Flatbush.

At Yale, I learned that the world is a big place. Whether I was singing in Marvin Winans' church or at a Congressional Inauguration, I was seeing things I had never even dreamed I would see. Sometimes, when I was in Prep and heading off to Poly, I worried that I had abandoned my rightful place in the world. The people I met, the places I went and the events I witnessed at Yale convinced me that I hadn't yet even *found* my place in the world—and that I might enjoy the search.

It's 7:20 and here comes the cheese. The school bus pulls up and the door opens. I turn back for a second and know that in a couple of hours my boys are gonna be out here playing punchball. I get on the bus and brace myself to face another day.

"I WANNA DO THAT." I sat there in the dark with a bead of sweat trickling down my cheek as my heart raced. It was the summer of 1989. And it was the opening night of *Do the Right Thing*. At that point I didn't even know what "that" was, but I knew I had found what I was going to do with the rest of my life. Spike Lee was a brother from Brooklyn . . . just like me. And if he could do "that," I could do it, too. That night the revolution wasn't televised—it was brought to a theater near me. I was 16 and my life was forever changed.

"I do the right thing/so this boy n' the hood/could get straight outta Brooklyn/is that understood?" A few years later, sitting in a fifth-floor dorm room in Yale's Durfee Hall, I recited those lyrics over the beat we had laid down. We were odd musicians in that moment, though. Creating songs was fun, but it was simply our means to an end. We wanted to do music videos. It just so happened we had no music, so we had to make some. At that point, "we" consisted of Damani, Bill and I, three black kids from New York who wanted one simple thing—to create the baddest film production company the world ever did see. I had found my "right thing," and I never felt better than when I was doing it.

That was almost a decade ago, and Damani and I have teamed up with Kevin, our USC Film School classmate, to establish Black & Blue Entertainment, LLC. A dream that was born at Yale's Durfee Sweet Shoppe and nurtured through hours of movie talk at Commons has become a real-life, living, breathing thing. But for our little baby, "life ain't been no crystal stair."[5]

"They passed." Those are two words you do not want to hear when you're running a fledgling production company. We have heard them. Kevin, Damani and I have heard those words more than we would like. We have also heard "They wanted to go in a different direction." And, my personal favorite, "They loved you guys, but . . ."

But there have been the good moments, too. The times when Black & Blue Entertainment, LLC, has hit the bull's-eye. Selling a project to Fox. Appearing in *Variety*. Being chosen by Wesley Snipes to rewrite a script. When those things happen, I know in my heart that we're doing the right thing.

So whether an executive is telling us out of one side of his mouth how brilliant our script is or telling us we will essentially have to change everything out of the other, we just try to do the right thing. Whether we're chasing checks or cashing them, we just try to do the right thing. Whether we sell the project or we hear the dreaded "They loved you guys, but . . .," we just try to do the right thing.

---

[5] The quote is from "Mother to Son," a poem by Langston Hughes.

Whether we're up or down, every morning, I kiss my wife goodbye, get in my car and brace myself to face another day.

"*You don't have to think about doing the right thing. If you're for the right thing, then you do it without thinking.*" I read that once . . . one summer . . . when I was 11 years old.

ORLANDO BISHOP *is a member of Contingent VI. Born and raised in Brooklyn, he graduated from Poly Prep Country Day School in 1990 and received a B.A. in film studies and Afro-American studies from Yale University in 1994. Upon graduation, Orlando returned to his alma mater and taught English. He subsequently earned a Master of Fine Arts in motion picture producing from the University of Southern California School of Cinema-Television's Peter Stark Producing Program in 1999. While still a full-time student, he interned at Nelvana Communications, DreamWorks SKG Network TV and The Jacobson Company (associated with Disney). He was awarded the Stark Program's most heralded prize, the Robert S. Ferguson Marketing Award. In 1999, Orlando cofounded Black & Blue Entertainment, LLC, of which he is currently the managing member. Black & Blue Entertainment has worked with New Line Television and Big Ticket Television, has written scripts for Amen Ra Films (Wesley Snipes' production company) and Nickelodeon, and is in negotiation with major studios regarding other projects. Orlando also cowrote and will produce* One Love, *a hip-hop musical.*

"I AM THE MASTER OF MY FATE; I AM THE CAPTAIN OF MY SOUL"

by DAVID GONZALEZ

I DO NOT BELIEVE IN FATE. How could I? My life experience has taught me that through hard work, discipline and a positive attitude, one can overcome odds that surely tempt fate.

I grew up in a tiny two-bedroom apartment in Brooklyn. My father left before I was born, leaving my mother to support herself, my sister, my brother and me with welfare checks and odd jobs. Try to imagine a childhood without birthday gifts, steady meals or a winter coat, and you have come halfway to understanding mine. I did not meet my father until four years ago, and he died from AIDS four months later. My mother loved all of us dearly but turned to drugs and alcohol to ease her pain. I remember mornings when she emerged naked from her bedroom, rushing to the bathroom to vomit out her latest binge. By default, my sister—aged 10 at the time—raised my brother and me throughout our early childhood.

My mother yearned for a better life for her children. When I was a baby, she enrolled in Long Island University, hoping to fulfill her lifelong dream of becoming the first of her family to earn a college degree. The welfare system does not allow recipients to attend a four-year college, however, and she was forced out of school her sophomore year. When she was sober, my mother read avidly, and her habit rubbed off on me. I read everything I could: comic books, newspapers, magazines and novels. Before long, I began bringing home strings of A's on my elementary school report cards. My mother's dream was starting to materialize.

At age 11, I entered the Preparatory Component of Prep for Prep. Over 1,400[1] children were nominated to Prep my fifth-grade year; 140 were accepted, and fewer than 120 completed the program. For those 14 months, I was challenged to push the limits of my intellectual ability. I studied day in and day out, hoping to escape from Brooklyn. When I graduated from the Preparatory Component, I was awarded a scholarship to Hackley School, an elite private school in Westchester County.

At the end of the Prep commencement ceremony, each student's name is called out to receive a certificate. Onstage, he or she is also given an unlit candle and joins a semicircle facing the audience. After the entire contingent has been called, a student comes to the microphone and recites the poem "Invictus." Immediately following the recitation, the lights are dimmed and the students begin lighting one another's candles from both ends of the semicircle while singing "We've Only Just Begun."

The year of my commencement, I was the student selected to recite "Invictus." I committed the entire poem to memory, and two lines have remained with me to this day: "I am the master of my fate; I am the captain of my soul."

Throughout my academic career, I remained focused on my future by periodically returning to Brooklyn. For every step I took forward, my family took one step back. My older brother, Danny, dropped out of school in 10th grade, left home and sold drugs to support himself; when not running from his enemies, he was running from the police. Three years ago, he was arrested for selling drugs and sentenced to serve seven years in a maximum-security prison. When I was in eighth grade, Danny had informed me of his planned career as a drug dealer. I was horrified. I remember crying and begging him to reconsider. He argued that he was smarter than

---

[1] Over the years, the applicant pool has continued to grow. In a typical year now, about 3,000 candidates are actually tested for possible admission to Prep for Prep, and an additional 650 to 850 candidates are tested for admission to PREP 9.

other dealers and there was no way he would get caught. For Danny, dealing drugs was a means to obtain great things for himself and our family: expensive clothes, a VCR and maybe even a car. I could not dissuade him.

When I first heard the news of his arrest, I wanted to hop on the next plane to New York. My mother convinced me to stay calm and remain in Chicago. For the next six months, while his case unfolded, I rode an emotional roller coaster. I was overwhelmed with both fear for my brother's safety and guilt over my own failure to make him stop. For 22 years, Danny had protected me and, in many ways, provided the space I needed to focus on my studies. I could have done a better job convincing him to stop. I could have helped him get a legal job and given him money to help make ends meet. There are so many things I could have done.

I am elated whenever he calls me, and depressed for two days afterwards. Who decided that I should be able to carry on with my life while Danny spends his in prison? The answer is, he did, and I did. Many years ago, we shared the same dream of escaping Brooklyn. We chose different paths, but we both realized our dream. By our separate decisions, my brother and I have come to completely different stations in life. However, the fact still remains that he is there and I am here. Because of my brother's incarceration, I've learned to take an active role in protecting those I care about. Perhaps someday I'll also learn to forgive myself.

My sister, Lisa, also cut her academic career short by joining the navy after her freshman year of college. An extremely religious person, Lisa yearned for a "traditional" family. Perhaps settling too soon, she married a fellow navy enlistee and was divorced within a year. With nowhere else to go, she returned home to New York City, alone and broke. Desperately pursuing her dream of starting a family, she began dating a man she didn't love and became pregnant. My sister's relationship with the father of her child was doomed from the start, and Lisa is currently raising my niece, Alexa, by herself, on welfare.

It would be easy for me to blame my sister for her current situation and refuse to help, but how can I fail to support her dream when so many of my own dreams have already come true? Because I share the responsibility of bearing my sister's burden, the decision to walk away from a steady paycheck and pursue an M.B.A. degree was not an easy one. In the end, my family and I agreed that I should go, and somehow we would make ends meet like we always have.

I do not share my story often. It is not that I am embarrassed by it, just that I know many will not understand. The adversity I have overcome defines who I am. And, although this may sound strange, I would not trade my past for someone else's. Any problem I face today pales in comparison to those I have overcome, and I am stronger today because of it. I am currently enrolled in the Anderson School of Business at UCLA and will graduate with the class of 2004. I plan to continue my career in financial services, and I hope someday to manage my own business. The chapters of my life continue to unfold, and I am anxious to turn the next page.

DAVID GONZALEZ *is a member of Contingent X. Born in Manhattan and raised in Brooklyn, he graduated from Hackley School in Tarrytown, New York, in 1994 and received a B.A. in economics from Amherst College in 1998. David worked for four years at The Goldman Sachs Group, Inc. During his last two years at Goldman Sachs, he was a financial analyst in private wealth management, managing client relationships as part of a 12-member senior team and heading an Equity Capital Markets Strategy Group. David is currently pursuing an M.B.A. in finance and entrepreneurship at the Anderson School at the University of California at Los Angeles, where he is a Robert Toigo Fellow, coordinator of the Riordan Scholars Program and section representative for* The Exchange, *the Anderson School's weekly newspaper.*

ANOMALIES

by JAMEEL DENNIS

i.

"DON'T WALK WITH YOUR HEAD DOWN," my father always reminded me. "Keep your head up."

"But there's dog poop on the ground" was my usual response when we walked along Sedgwick Avenue.

One side of the avenue somehow had become the designated toilet for domestic and wild animals alike. Undoubtedly, the fact that no one lived on that side had something to do with it. It was the backyard of the Bronx Veterans Affairs Hospital.

Our neighbor, Tony, cared more than anyone else about Uncle Sam's yard. He must have realized that a two-way street could not really distance our homes from the filth accumulating on the property of our inconsiderate neighbor. Tony placed garbage cans by every other tree from one end of the block to the other. Despite the fines from the city to which he was subjected for having too many garbage cans for a single resident, he persistently collected the cans for the garbage men who also ignored the uninhabited area. Tony fought hard and alone. Eventually, defeated, he moved away, along with the rest of our white neighbors.

A patchwork of large apartment buildings and private homes of various sizes and conditions lined the residential side of Sedgwick Avenue. The distance from one traffic intersection to the next made it possible to divide the avenue into three separate communities. Most of the people living in the procession of apartment buildings closest to the corner of Kingsbridge Road were Hispanic, while those living in the large colonial homes near Bailey Avenue were rarely ever seen but were rumored to be white. Nestled in between were black people, with few exceptions. In the chaotic arrangement of the dwellings in this central district stood our small, two-level, red brick box house.

By nine A.M. on weekdays, the working-class community of Sedgwick Avenue was a ghost town. Life returned around three P.M., when the latchkey kids began to arrive home from school. All day, or so it seemed, Ms. Loretta sat in her second-floor apartment watching from her window facing the avenue.

She did not see me run away from home, however, because that summer evening I ran only as far as my brother's bedroom closet. There I sat, until the rumbling of my stomach became unbearable and I ventured down the narrow steps into the kitchen. As I returned with my delicious prize to evaluate my next move, the irresistible chatter of familiar voices prompted a quick peek. The entire neighborhood stood outside, recounting the events that had led to the broken window. I was spotted instantly and forced to apologize to the entire search party. The spanking that ensued was brief, yet the painful memory of distraught faces lit by flashlights and dozens of neighbors clad in bathrobes, head scarves and slippers haunts me still.

With the exception of that horrible night, summers were usually spent enjoying the outdoors with the other neighborhood children. Being small for my age, I did not fare well when it was time for sports. Not to mention, my interests did not motivate me to excel in athletics. In fact, I preferred to stay inside, reading a book or playing with my junior scientist microscope. But my parents would force me to go out and interact with my peers, and though I was reluctant to leave the house, I would often find myself begging for more time when summoned to come home. Despite the name-calling and occasional fights, these were my friends. Our parents were not just neighbors; they, too, were friends. In fact, our siblings were friends. We'd stay the night at each other's homes, walk to and from school together, have birthday parties and celebrate the holidays together. With so much in common, it was hard to understand why I felt so out of place.

After 14 months in Prep for Prep, where for the first time in my life I did *not* feel strange, I began to understand. Achieving academic success was just a part of the Prep experience. To survive the Preparatory Component, let alone six years at a demanding independent school, I had to become aware of my expectations of myself. I had to *believe* in myself. I had to work hard while my friends played games outside my bedroom window. I had to make sacrifices. Completing the required daily log of the time I spent working on homework assignments was one form of self-evaluation imposed by the program; the daily stress of deadlines, surprise quizzes, and learning study techniques and time management skills also required that I take inventory of myself. Without those challenges, I might never have come to understand myself well enough to feel anything but awkward in my own community or elsewhere. In addition, going through this formative period surrounded by children with similar interests, who shared this intense experience, gave me a sense of belonging when I needed it most.

ii.

THE BUS RIDE TO HORACE MANN took exactly 20 minutes. I'd board the overcrowded bus at the corner of Kingsbridge Road in front of the neighborhood deli. I'd travel down "suicide hill" and past my elementary school, which sat across from the Major Deegan Expressway. After the mass exodus of students attending the local public high school, the bus would continue its journey under the elevated train on Broadway. Just beyond the Stella Doro Bakery, free of the heavy canopy of the "el," I descended the steps of the bus onto 242nd Street. The playing fields of Van Cortlandt Park were on my right, and the hilly streets that climbed up to Riverdale beckoned on my left. I completed this last portion of my journey on foot. The school buses chartered by Horace Mann, filled with fellow students traveling from as far as New Jersey, would pass me as they made their way up the hill that disconnected our school from the city below.

The plush green fields and stoic architecture were a sharp contrast to Kingsbridge Road. The smell of fresh flowers around campus attracted butterflies in the spring. These were aspects of nature I had not experienced on Sedgwick Avenue despite all my efforts to cultivate a garden in the sandy, unfertile soil that posed as our front yard. Small, intimate classrooms without bars on the windows, and dozens of white children making their way from building to building, were the final demarcation from the past I had left behind 20 minutes earlier.

I immediately became aware of socioeconomics, not to mention the fact that I was poor, at least relatively speaking. Before Horace Mann, unsavory characters speeding through my neighborhood in their Nissan Maximas with pseudonyms engraved on the door panels were my idea of *rich.* After a few months in the posh Riverdale community, I was confronted with my ignorance of the world's finances. In response, I began to research the two microenvironments that I traversed daily and used my unique vantage point to formulate ideas about the "big picture."

The existing social order seemed to define *nearly* everything and everyone around me. What it failed to define or even hint at was the possible existence of my fellow Prep for Prep students and me. An anomaly? Maybe one, maybe a few, but hundreds of societal fence straddlers?

Fortunately, Prep had had the foresight to address society's apparent oversight. In addition to challenging us academically, guidance counselors like Angel Martinez[1] had stressed the necessity of knowing one's self and always being true to one's self in order to coexist in overtly paradoxical environments. Fairly heavy rhetoric for 12-year-old children to put into practice, but the circumstances made the import of the lesson clear. *Define yourself.*

---

[1] During a contingent's first summer in the Preparatory Component, each section meets two periods a week for Conclave with the guidance counselor. One class period each Saturday throughout the school-year trimesters is also devoted to Conclave. The Preparatory Component guidance counselor also works with children individually when a situation warrants it. Angel Martinez served as Preparatory Component guidance counselor for several years while pursuing his Ph.D. in clinical psychology. He now lives and practices in New Hampshire.

Typical adolescent self-doubt could not be avoided despite the sage advice. When confronted by my neighborhood friends about the frequency setting on my radio, I'd retreat in shame and quickly deny any connection between soft rock and me. But then, after the laughter had stopped and my friends had returned to their respective homes, I would feel a different kind of shame. *Why did I deny myself?* Acceptance, belonging, wanting to fit in had motivated me to become someone else. Not believing in myself had allowed me to give in. I would not make that mistake again. With clarity about my intentions, I reviewed my logic and recognized the difficulty associated with being who others wanted me to be. I forbade myself to suffer the humiliation of being defined by someone else out of fear of rejection. Mr. Martinez was right: I had to be true to myself, accepted or not. At that moment I embraced the possibility of solitude, and my confidence began to blossom.

Fortunately, my experience was not unique. Prep for Prep students around the city faced similar circumstances. Understanding our plight and working through it together strengthened our bond. While many who had faced the transition from public to private school in the past had been unsuccessful, the extraordinarily high incidence of success on the part of Prep students was in large part due to the support of fellow students. The resulting support network served as a family at school and at home. Like any family unit, we encouraged each other to explore our various environments with the assurance of a home to which we could always return.

iii.

"Head up!" shouted Coach Carlucci. "The key to success in wrestling is keeping your head up and your hips underneath you, especially when you're down." He'd explain it again: head up, back straight, knees bent, hands out. This position became as natural to me as breathing. I embraced the sport for its emphasis on the individual's contribution to the success of the whole. The physical and mental challenge produced an intoxicating rush. The primal nature of the sport helped me to recognize the basic humanity in others and myself.

"Wrestling is life" and "No one ever drowned in sweat" were two of the many yellowing quotes posted around the thickly padded wrestling room. The room also featured a Wall of Fame on which the names of former Horace Mann students who had excelled at the sport of wrestling were listed in chronological order. Two of the most recent inductees to "The Wall" were Luis Garzon and Carlton Jackson, both Prep alumni and both New York State private school wrestling champions.

Seeing their pictures among the collection of young white predecessors added a personal connection to the history of the school and its wrestling program. Racial and economic lines faded to the maroon and gray of my uniform and the uniforms of the young men on the wall.

iv.

AS I APPROACHED THE END of my high school career, Prep offered yet another opportunity for me to broaden my horizons. I traveled to Europe and spent several weeks living with a family in southern Italy.[2] Their home in the Italian equivalent of a suburb, complete with indoor trees, sunken living room, marble floors and fine leather furniture, had a comfortable elegance. Initially the deafening silence made it difficult to sleep, but soon I grew accustomed to the mild Mediterranean winds passing through the indigenous foliage surrounding the house.

By eight A.M. the townspeople were hard at work. At noon silence would fill the streets. *La riposa,* the communal naptime, lasted a few hours each day. Then it was back to work, followed by a light dinner and gatherings with friends. With the exception of language, the daily schedule and subtle cultural differences, life in Italy was surprisingly similar to that in New York.

One of the subtle cultural differences was the genuine belief that African-Americans were superior. I signed autographs. Children would touch my skin in awe. Beautiful young women would express

[2] Prep for Prep began a partnership with the U.S. Experiment in International Living. At first, only five or six Prep students went abroad, but in each of the several most recent years about 50 of Prep's high school students have spent three to five weeks of their summer in dozens of countries around the world.

their desire to be black like me. My efforts to dispel this notion of racial superiority and to promote the idea of equality met with a great deal of resistance, especially from my Italian father. Mr. Gargano owned a successful hair salon in the small town of Cosenza. His relaxed demeanor reminded me of Vito Corleone in the famed *Godfather* novels. Driving through the Italian countryside with unbelievable speed and accuracy had earned him the nickname Mario Andretti. Through our many-gestured conversations, he attempted to justify his claim that black men were gods. In his thick accent, he'd recite, "Michael Jordan, Louis Armstrong, Jesse Jackson, Michael Jackson, Martin Luther King." Then he'd raise his hands and shoulders in the universal gesture that means "Need I say more?"

It certainly felt strange trying to refute any correlation with divinity when I was being presented with such powerful examples of extraordinary achievement. Good, bad or otherwise, however, I refused to be defined by others.

"We are men, just like you," I repeated many times. A statement often used to challenge institutional racism had become my mantra.

Years of having routinely traveled between two distinct cultures, that of my section of Sedgwick Avenue and that of Horace Mann, had eased my transition to a foreign environment. However, it did not prepare me for the culture shock I experienced when I returned home. The streets I'd traveled so often had never seemed so crowded nor the people so aggressive. Gingerly walking through my neighborhood with my head up, I recognized the need to reacquaint myself with the quickened pace of the city.

Having temporarily stepped away from familiar faces and places, I could see that I had changed. My short life swiftly passing before my eyes, I reviewed the experiences that had modified my outlook on life and my place in it.

Then I remembered, "Define yourself," and I smiled. I continued to stroll but at my own pace through the bustling crowds on Kingsbridge Road.

JAMEEL DENNIS *is a member of Contingent VII. Born in Harlem and raised in the Bronx, he graduated from The Horace Mann School in 1991 and received a B.A. in philosophy from the University of Virginia in 1995. After interning at the Picower Institute for Medical Research and serving as a research technician at Northshore University Hospital Department of Surgery (Neurosurgery) Laboratory of Biomedical Science, Jameel returned to the University of Virginia, where he completed a Ph.D. in neuroscience in 2001. During graduate school, he was named an American Psychological Association fellow (1998–2001), served as a teaching assistant in genetics and taught English in an Upward Bound Program. Jameel is currently a postdoctoral fellow in the Genetics Department at Boys Town National Research Hospital in Omaha, Nebraska.*

FIFTY BUCKS IN YOUR POCKET

by RICHARD BERTEMATTI

Not speaking English, my mother could never say it correctly. "Pre too Pre" was her understanding of it. I'd often correct her, "Prep for Prep," but to no avail.

It didn't matter. My mother had a deeper understanding of what the program was and what it could accomplish than I did at first. I was a rather impressionable child, content to do anything if it meant learning something new, and I rarely questioned authority. I remember taking the subway downtown to take tests because I was told to. I passed the tests, and before I knew it, I was lugging a huge bookbag down to Trinity School every Wednesday afternoon and Saturday morning.

My mother always accompanied me to Trinity, and she became obsessed with the idea that I was destined to attend that particular prestigious private school upon completion of the Preparatory Component. When the time came to fill out applications, she would hear nothing about "safety schools." Only grudgingly, to appease the Prep administrators, did she send me off to a few other schools to interview. Just as her iron will had insisted, I was accepted at Trinity. My friends from public school, on the other hand, were all headed to the dreaded P.S. 165, where most of them were certain to stagnate, or drop out, or end up in worse straits.

By then I was growing in self-awareness and developing my individual identity. I realized that I worked hard not because I was told to or because it was expected of me. I did it because I wanted to succeed. Early on, my mother had considered me the family's personal messiah, the one who would raise them from ignobility. Had she not given me a Teutonic name meaning powerful, wealthy and mighty? Prep for Prep nurtured this desire to succeed, but it went much further than that by convincing me—through many long dark nights of the soul toiling over books and papers—that I should never give up.

In my younger and more vulnerable years, my father told me something I have never forgotten: "Your best friend is fifty bucks in your pocket."

Though not a font of wisdom and witticisms, my father occasionally impressed me with such statements, advice invariably revolving around the issue of money. His own life was characterized by constant work and thrift, and my earliest memories were of watching him come home at noon to eat soup before heading back out again. The work took its toll on him, and by the time of his death all the wealth he had carefully hoarded throughout his life had dwindled away into hospital coffers. Fortunately, one of his unintended bequests was his empty leather wallet. I immediately adopted it and exercised it diligently, feeling perhaps a mystical bond with its original owner, until only a few years ago when the aged threads that held it together fell apart. The wallet still retains a place of honor among all the knickknacks one keeps in a shoebox under the bed, things one no longer needs but cannot quite throw away.

As a child my allowance was a dollar a week, which I also carefully hoarded in imitation of my father, until by the age of 10 I had become a veritable bookie, lending out money to my profligate older sister *with interest*. I kept my tiny boon in a cigar box and loved to spend an afternoon counting every penny and making note of debits and credits in a small notebook. In those days, free from responsibility, I derived the greatest pleasure from my banking activities, greater than from play or sport as with other children. I could simply enjoy having money, touching it, counting it. When the need arose to *earn* money, however, I came to realize that life, like it or not, is a continual—and, in my father's case, deadly—quest for it. Those crinkly pieces of paper, decorated with obscure Latin, Masonic symbols and lithographs of dead presidents, I found to be man's primary tool in his Nietzschean struggle against oblivion.

Though born in humble circumstances, I never fell into such privation that I could share the sentiment of Albert Einstein, who claimed that hunger was his only constant companion as a youth; but I was without electricity at times, and many times without water. In this I could not entirely fault my father (whose only sin was excessive thrift) but rather the crummy buildings we lived in, scattered about the Upper West Side like whitewashed tombs. On the outside they still looked like grand 1920s-vintage edifices, but once you were inside there was little chance of escape from a marginal existence. The best way out, I decided, once Prep and Providence had made it possible for me to have such choices, was to study business.

My senior year at Trinity, I applied to six colleges—five of them with business programs. By a perhaps cruel trick of fate, the one school whose acceptance I could not turn down—Northwestern University in Evanston, Illinois—did *not* have an undergraduate business program. I had spent my time at Trinity participating actively in a film production club, heading it by the time I graduated. If I couldn't study business in college, I'd study filmmaking, an alternate and perhaps more enjoyable path to riches. Once I made a film or wrote a few screenplays, my future would be assured. But business still gnawed at the back of my mind, and I took several economics and accounting courses just in case I failed to become the next Spielberg.

Reality hit forcefully my senior year of college, when I realized that there were no "jobs" for filmmakers. Either you made it on your own, or you interned without salary somewhere, or you had a rich uncle who could finance your trip to L.A. In the hope that business was still a viable option, I interviewed with a number of financial companies, most of them investment banks, whose recruiters assured the masses of eager, desperate applicants that the best prospects were those who had *not* studied business (something about being more "well rounded"). Pickings became slimmer as graduation drew near, until I was left scraping for dubious corporate positions at supermarkets and department stores. No one hired me. After graduation, I remained in Chicago a few more months, working odd jobs—none of them related to business or filmmaking. In defeat, I left the Windy City, passing by Morris & Sons on the way to Union Station to catch my train home for the last time. *Someday I'd be able to afford that expertly tailored, double-breasted, 100% wool herringbone suit that's looking condescendingly at me from behind the window.*

My first real job was with the New York Public Library as a clerk in a clinical, shiny-tiled office from which emanated only the sounds of earnest typing on mainframe keyboards. After a few lateral moves within the organization, I knew I had to do something drastic to fulfill my ambitions. I had to find some entry into the business world—without a business degree, without a lot of money and without any viable contacts.

One day, I risked poverty and simply resigned. Living again with my mother, I could not bear to tell her I was unemployed. So I dressed every morning, packed my lunch and headed to a local library, which I made my job-hunting headquarters. Utilizing the free computers, employment resources and pay phones, I spent months trying to insinuate myself into the business world. Finally my chance came. I was hired as a stockbroker trainee by a newly opened brokerage firm.

It was exhilarating to walk into brand-new offices, phones ringing, with dozens of brokers plying their trade, busy watching red and green symbols on a wall-length ticker. An incredible, pulsating real-world power emanated from the trading floor like heat off a red-hot coal. I was given a desk and a phone. My job: to open accounts. During my daily commute I self-importantly read the financial papers, feeling like I had to keep my fingers on the pulse of my new career.

My enthusiasm quickly dissipated after I found myself calling and subsequently being cursed at by absolute strangers for 12 hours a day. This age-old process is known as "cold-calling," although I'm not sure if it was named for the act itself or the cold response one receives more often than not. The principals of the firm, I later came to realize, were shysters who made their money scamming people in the boom-boom eighties and were now further stretching their unscrupulous tentacles by operating one of the many "boiler rooms" that sprang up around town in the mid- and late nineties. By the end of each day I was ready to quit, but only until the nightly sales meetings when the principals would strut in in their $800 suits and cajole us with visions of fast cars and loose women. That supplied my sagging spirits with just enough energy to get up the next day and go at it again.

My departure three months later from this firm proved fortuitous, for it was soon afterward shut down by the SEC for fraud. But my time there was not entirely a waste; I had managed to obtain my securities license, which meant I could pretty much work anywhere I wanted on Wall Street. I'd heard it said that the world may be big but the Street is very small, and I found this to be true as I landed in firms up and down it, often seeing many of the people I had bumped into previously. The avalanche of wealth still had not come crashing around my ears, but I felt I was getting closer. Eventually I found a good home in brokerage administration and compliance. Money became much less of a concern, but something still bothered me. I still did not feel like a success. I remembered something John D. Rockefeller once said: "The only way to make a great deal of money is to start a business of your own." I was pondering his words one day as the new millennium approached, gazing at boats plying the East River from my window on the 32nd floor, when my musings were interrupted by a phone call.

The person on the other end of the line was Mr. N, one of my supervisors at a previous pit stop through my tortuous traversal of Wall Street. I remembered him as a stickler on details and an annoying perfectionist, but he was the only boss who had ever given me a Christmas bonus six months *after* I quit working for him. He told me he was no longer with the same company, and I asked him where he was working now.

"I can't tell you that," he said mysteriously. "But can we meet?"

Hoping that Mr. N wanted to give me another Christmas bonus (Thanksgiving was a week away), I agreed. The next day I walked over to a building near the ancient Trinity Church at the head of Wall Street. Mr. N appeared with another man. They both looked a little jumpy, so I followed them cautiously into a small conference room.

Mr. N began to explain why he had called me, while his companion, a stocky Israeli who looked like he could be a Mossad agent, watched me with a calculated smile. Mr. N was now CEO of a new venture: an online brokerage that was to revolutionize the Internet, nay the World. The name of the company? It was constructed with the name of a very big animal appended to a suffix that would make it sound unmistakably like a cutting-edge, dot-com concern.

"Why that particular animal?" I asked Mr. N's companion.

"Because it makes you think of Big," he said with a thick accent that sounded more Russian than anything else.

It was then that I realized, looking up at a sign on the wall, that I was actually in the offices of a well-known Wall Street behemoth. Mr. N's venture was apparently being financed by this deep-pocketed firm. The marketing budget alone for the coming year was to be $50 million, I was told, and there were plans to advertise during the Super Bowl. They had also arranged to have a string of their namesake beasts march down Wall Street; Mr. N's friend assured me that I could even ride on one of them.

Mr. N had not yet discussed compensation, and I was already salivating. Then lights exploded all around me, and I could hear the dulcet rhythms of a cherubic choir as the words came out of Mr. N's mouth:

"Rich, you are going to be rich."

He chuckled at his own play on words and proceeded to give me a quick breakdown of my potential ownership in the company. The calculations in my head perhaps missed some zeros, but I realized that the stock options he was offering me would turn me into a bona-fide multimillionaire.

I left the meeting in a daze. I had not felt this elated since the day I walked into my first Wall Street job in my one and only suit, impressionable and distracted by the dancing dollar signs that circled my head. But this time I could see the future more clearly. I could practically taste it. This was the dot-com era, the age of stock options and quick riches. Didn't one fellow become a billionaire by designing a Web site for Pez (yes, the candy) enthusiasts? And another by founding a company that delivered movies to your door for more than it would cost to just go rent it yourself? I decided the first thing I would do, once I became a multimillionaire, was take a weekend jaunt to Chicago, to Morris & Sons, and buy myself more than one of those 100 percent wool herringbone suits.

I immediately resigned from my job and reported to my new employer at an office in midtown Manhattan, adjacent to an African mission protected by Uzi-toting black guards. The company had several offices, but this was the command center, the nexus from which the Internet was to be revolutionized. There, like an initiate into a secret order, I was made privy to all the secret handshakes and met the founders of the company of which Mr. N's start-up was to be a subsidiary. They were two twin brothers: Mr. D, bespectacled, was the "nice" one. Mr. R, whose sallow complexion made him look like he was always hungry, was the "mean" one. I use those terms loosely, but I can safely say that I do not recall ever witnessing Mr. R smiling. I swiftly came under the impression that these two, "The Boys," as Mr. N called them, were brilliant entrepreneurs. Young, tall and well-dressed, they certainly *looked* like brilliant entrepreneurs.

Within a few weeks, I moved to my permanent station, a vast, unfinished office space in central New Jersey. Mr. N's team was completed with the addition of a young Orthodox Jew who could eat nothing but cakes from the kosher Entenmann's store across the street, and a Chicagoan in his early thirties who could have been air-dropped into a college frat house without disturbing anyone. I was undaunted by the fact that we had space (approximately 31,000 square feet of it) and nothing else: no desks, computers or even door knobs. We shared the building with a cosmetics company and were obligated to raid its defunct cafeteria for tables and soiled chairs. We were an Internet company without Internet access, so we had to rely on a few phone lines rigged up by our network guru and a dial-up service and a printer Mr. N had purchased at J&R Music World. We were also without heat. It was February, and the air-conditioning was still going full blast. Between the cold and the electrical wires hanging from the ceilings, I began to wonder which was better, freezing to death or getting electrocuted. The bathroom was so far away that I controlled my nature calls carefully so as to make no unnecessary trips. At some point, someone mentioned that the furniture had been ordered. Someone else then issued a correction: The Boys in New York had not yet authorized payment for any furniture. As a matter of fact, The Boys were late with so many bills that it was a wonder any vendors at all were still servicing us.

Of Mr. N we saw less and less. It may have been because he had the corner office all the way at the end of the floor, and it was simply too far for me to visit him on a regular basis. Then one day, Mr. N vanished. The Boys crossed the Hudson to grace us with their presence. They ushered everyone into a room with a nice but borrowed conference table and spoke as if they had graduated magna cum laude from the Tony Robbins School of Persuasive Oratory. Everything was going to be all right, they cooed. Mr. N had left for personal reasons. Someone asked about our stock options. The Boys assured him that they would soon straighten all that out.

Over the next few days, we were visited by officers from the parent company. The compliance director came first. Our punishment was to watch this 300-pound man with facial hair eat a sandwich slathered with mayonnaise. Then came Mr. J, the parent company's chief operating officer. Though stationed in yet another office in New Hampshire, he was now responsible for our fledgling company. He came into our office, corralled a couple of workers, went on a shopping spree at a nearby Costco and returned with $700 worth of junk food: soda, pretzels, Animal Crackers, Twizzlers, trail mix and peanuts galore. If that was not the way to win the hearts of a handful of discouraged employees, I don't know what is (although, in the short run, door knobs would probably have served us better).

Mr. J, a childhood friend of The Boys, had headed a company founded on the brilliant idea of linking credit cards with data from state motor vehicle offices so that store clerks could call up a purchaser's photo and other confidential information for verification. The company, not surprisingly, ran afoul of the law and civil libertarians and was forced to close down. Mr. J came, in his own words, "to shine a light in the black box," meaning, we guessed in our proletarian ignorance, to keep us New Jersey exiles abreast of developments. With him came his technology guru, another refugee from his failed company, and another crony who had run a day trading firm in his prior incarnation. And yes, that company had failed, too.

It was now four months since I had left a secure job for a dot-com start-up. I had been living the dream of a select few caught up in the euphoria of the Internet bubble. Just knowing that millions were awaiting me, and that after cashing in I would never have to worry about anything again, had made my entire existence at that time almost surreal. I slept and ate well. My demeanor was always jovial. Daily cares simply rolled off me. For the first time in my adult life, I felt like I had finally achieved real success.

But after four months, we were not even in business.

When we were down to our last few bags of Costco trail mix, The Boys announced a change in strategic focus and assured us that the venture capitalists would be investing any day now. I looked out at the empty office space, tempted to bring in my soccer ball to kick around while waiting for the money. My stab at riches had evidently pricked the Internet bubble. It all began to crash around my ears. The cherubic hymns turned into a plaintive dirge. Employees started quitting. I shut my knobless door for the last time one afternoon and joined the ranks of the victims of the dot-com implosion.

I am consoled, if any value can be placed on reminiscence, by the idea that I was taken up in the *Zeitgeist* of two different decades, and vicariously of a third, for I cannot watch the movie *Wall Street* without feeling as if I had relived the eighties life of Bud Fox and bumped into more than one Gordon Gecko.

I had tried and failed, yet again, to become successful by my own vaunted definition. My obsession, I realized, had not been with money at all, but with the idea of *not* needing it. That was precisely what my father had meant by his pithy anecdote. Only those who have enough money enjoy true freedom in this world, for they are liberated from the incessant, life-wasting struggle to acquire it.

Of all the American presidents, I have always reserved my greatest admiration for Abraham Lincoln, and now I realized the reason. He failed and failed and failed, that is, until he succeeded. As I write, I am yet again on the threshold of another venture, with the potential to dwarf anything I have attempted thus far. Following Rockefeller's advice, I have started my own business. Whether I'll be successful, only time will tell. But I have felt it appropriate to adopt as my personal credo a verse of a popular song nowadays: "I am invincible as long as I'm alive."

My graduation from Trinity School took place at the historic Trinity Church, located in lower Manhattan. Wall Street runs from there to the East River, giving rise to the old quip: "Wall Street is a street with a river at one end and a graveyard at the other." After the ceremony, we all went out to that graveyard behind the church to take pictures near monuments and faded headstones.

My mother was there, at the end of my high school journey, just as she had been at the beginning, believing that Trinity Church was somehow affiliated with the school (it was, long ago) and proud of me and everything related to Trinity. For her, "Pre too Pre" had accomplished its goal, and now I was on my way to even greater things as I prepared to matriculate at college. She became a little worried that I was going so far away, out of the range of her watchful care. She told me I should not let women, or drink, or the cares of life distract me from accomplishing my goals.

I smiled, because by that time I had become immune to such thinking.

RICHARD BERTEMATTI *is a member of Contingent V. Born and raised in Manhattan, Richard graduated from Trinity School in 1989 and received a B.S. in communications from Northwestern University in 1993. He earned an M.B.A. from Baruch College in 2000, while simultaneously working full-time at a series of financial services firms. He is currently the managing member of a hedge fund specializing in short-term trading. Richard also served as a photojournalist in the U.S. Army Reserve (1994–2002) and is the author of* Project Death: A Tito Rico Mystery, *published in 1997.*

IV.
A PLACE TO BELONG

ADOLESCENCE ISN'T EASY. Even if you have everything going for you, a nice home, great parents, lots of friends, a good school and a safe environment, there will be those moments. For most of our students, the conditions are not so ideal. As they begin to come to terms with how much is really expected of them both academically and in terms of extracurricular activities and leadership positions, they are also becoming much more aware of the class lines and racial divisions that still plague our society. For these students, it is not simply a matter of coming to terms with how they see themselves; it also means learning how to respond to the expectations that society-at-large projects.

In training our counselors, an important consideration is to help them distinguish between typical adolescent issues, issues that truly relate to class or race, and individual, serious issues of an emotional or psychological nature that require professional help. One type of issue so often masquerades as another.

At any given time, most of our students are doing quite well.

Over a period of four or six years, however, at one time or another, a considerable number of them will experience problems that have the potential to distract them enough from the business at hand—doing well at school—and jeopardize all that they have worked for up to that point.

Apart from attending good schools, our kids have another enormous advantage. They have each other. Most often when adults talk about peer pressure, they assume it is a negative force: somebody else's son or daughter is going to lead my kid astray. At Prep, far more often, peer pressure is a positive influence. Students who have gone through a great deal together, surviving the 14-month academic "boot camp" followed by the adjustment to attending schools that are overwhelmingly white and affluent, are poised to share insights, advice, coping mechanisms and support.

While dramas may be playing out in the background, students are captaining teams, establishing new student organizations, enrolling in multiple A.P. courses, and being elected class and student government presidents. College applications loom on the horizon, and students are trying to picture who and what they want to be 10 years down the road, even if they are not absolutely sure who they want to be next week.

It is a confusing time. It is a time when almost more than anything else, a youngster needs a place to belong.

WHO'S THAT SMILING THROUGH MY FACE?

by DERRICK BINEY-AMISSAH

THERE IS A PHOTOGRAPH of me with my friends Nandalal Lutchmansingh and Gary Simons, taken in early June of 1990 on the night of the Lilac Ball in the grand ballroom of the Waldorf-Astoria. The event celebrates the college acceptances of each year's senior class, so Nandalal and I are in our tuxedos, standing on either side of Mr. Simons with big smiles on our faces, and we are proudly brandishing our Prep for Prep Certificates of Achievement. Each of us still has a copy of that photograph, and each of us has a story by which to measure the moment it was taken. For me, that night brought a tremendous relief because it marked the end of a four-year-long chapter in my life that was filled with difficult times. I was glad to be able to enjoy that milestone on such a high note. The boyish grin on my face in that photo hid a massive struggle just to get to that point.

Three weeks before the start of my freshman year at Trinity School, my mother had disappeared. She would not return for another seven years, and for what it was worth at the time, my older sister and I did not know if we would *ever* see her again. Between that fall and the time of the Lilac Ball photograph, I lived in three different boroughs and shifted legal guardians four times. My sister and I lost virtually everything we owned. The only constants during those years were the love and support of my sister, the activities I was involved in at Trinity and my strong affiliation with Prep for Prep.

Of my first summer in the program, I remember generally staying up past two in the morning to complete homework assignments that at times made it seem as if I were studying several foreign languages all at once. It was the first time I'd had a different teacher for each subject, which added a whole new dimension of pressure to do well. Suddenly I was accountable to six people rather than one. There were also the ominous specters of being *unprepared, on probation* and *asked to leave the program*. No one wanted those words to be associated with them, but there were constant rumors as to whose status in the program was in what degree of jeopardy. I promised myself early on that I would not be one of the casualties of those first seven weeks. I might quit later, I told myself, but not that summer.

The fact that all of us were going through the same tough academic drill was a source of encouragement and provided for a unique bond amongst us. Many of my most enduring friendships began that summer. Over the weeks, something else also happened: I grew more committed to the type and caliber of the education we were getting. My own success, as well as the success of my contingent mates, became personally important. "I might quit later" gave way to "I'll be damned if I'm going to get left behind and miss what's on the other side of this, our journey."

Some of the strongest impressions of the fall, winter and spring trimesters were made during Mr. Simons' occasional and not-so-impromptu gatherings in the hallways of Trinity. These meetings would occur after our last class period on Wednesday and Saturday evenings. The first time we had one, I was struck by the accessibility of the program's director. There would be the 75 or so of us, all packed up and ready to go home, and Mr. Simons, equally ready, with some last-minute food for thought to impart to us. He would talk about the new Prep for Prep enrollment numbers at Horace Mann or Dalton, or inform us that so-and-so would soon be the first Prep student at Town School. He would then discuss the significance of those facts in terms of what our predecessors were doing at those schools, and furthermore, what their examples meant we should expect of ourselves. There was a camaraderie in these gatherings, and it really came across that *our* fight was *his* fight.

What I also came to appreciate about those corridor lectures and conversations was that they fed into a culture at Prep for Prep. Even as we struggled with the rigors of being Prep students, we knew that we were part of something larger than our contingent. We knew that our success was tied to a continuum that both preceded us and would proceed from us. This continuum would extend not only through the broader Prep community, but eventually into society in general.

So when everything seemed to fall apart for me in 1986, my life became very simple, very quickly. There were a precious few things of which I was certain: that what I had started at Prep for Prep and then continued at Trinity School would end with a bachelor's degree; that sticking to the plan despite my mother's absence was both within my power as a student as well as the best way I could help my family; and that, although my expectation of better times often seemed mocked by my then present circumstances, I knew I had a resource in Prep, because Prep, and Mr. Simons, had those same expectations for me.

During those four years of high school, I lived with various relatives, each stay ranging from six months to a year and a half. More of my time was spent keeping busy at Trinity and at Prep for Prep's brownstone office than at any one of those homes. I got involved in a number of opportunities to share my own experiences with up-and-coming contingents. Two of those opportunities of which I am particularly proud were working on the Prep for Prep *Telegraph,* which Nandalal and I edited for two years, and being an advisor to the younger students who were then experiencing their own 14-month-long trial by fire. Along the way, I came back in contact with classmates from my own contingent, as well as members of younger and older contingents, who were generally doing the same thing I was: giving back.

The friendships made then are still strong, and sometimes I'm surprised by the age range within that group. I've known Nandalal since that first summer at Prep when we were in the same homeroom section and were nicknamed "the Twins." Every time I see Chris McLeod, Joey Pabon and Himi Khan, all of whom were my advisees and years later, when they themselves had become advisors, my colleagues, I know something of who they are beyond their careers, beyond the adults they have become. I was honored to have Maisha Gilyard, Dorothy Kim, Bo Tan and Ganya Alvarado attend my MFA thesis show at Pratt a few years ago. Some of those dozens of friends are anywhere from seven years younger to five years older, but whenever we meet, we remember each other in the context of experiences we shared at Prep and it's like seeing a sibling or cousin. No amount of time seems to lessen the sense of familiarity.

Whenever I look at that Lilac Ball photograph, I weigh my circumstances at the time against the image and almost begin to think it's someone else in the picture who is smiling, using my face as a vehicle to express his own joy. Then I think about the resonance of 14 months, a community, and all the decisions that had brought me to that point—that point of achievement—and I am grateful for the options that were available to me in a time of crisis. The sum of all the experiences embodied in that captured moment is a balance in which the strength of friendships, of accomplishments and victories, provided the wherewithal to cope with the challenges and upheavals that occur in life. It is this tested understanding that allows me now to recognize and appreciate the good times and acknowledge them with a smile that I know is mine.

DERRICK BINEY-AMISSAH *is a member of Contingent VI. Born in New York, he spent most of his first six years in Ghana and returned to the United States in 1978. He graduated from Trinity School in 1990 and received a B.A. in philosophy and fine arts from Georgetown University in 1995. Pursuing a career as a painter and graphic designer, Derrick earned a Master of Fine Arts degree in painting from Pratt Institute in 2000. He is currently a visiting instructor and assistant chairperson of media arts at Pratt Institute .*

QUESTIONS AND ANSWERS

by Shana M. Harris

I REALLY DID IT because I wanted to get out of the house. But what kind of answer is that? It is certainly not an answer that family friends and relatives sit on the edge of their seats to discover. And it most definitely is not the response that student reporters want to use to open their stories in the school paper. When people ask why you chose to go to boarding school, you had better come up with something better than that. Admissions officers, public school teachers, adults from the neighborhood, even some classmates all asked why, but they didn't really want to know. They wanted to hear an affirmation of their own fantasies about why I, at age 13, wanted to go away to school. They wanted an answer to flow from my lips as beautiful as the picture they had painted in their own minds.

So, naturally, I gave them what they wanted. "Well, I want to go to boarding school because there is a certain educational opportunity, a chance for personal growth and independence that only the boarding school experience has to offer," I would say, nodding my head to accentuate the serious thought I would put into my unconventional decision. Then I would continue: "I guess I'm most excited about being part of a larger community of achievement, you know, where all the kids are serious and the teachers really know you.

The teachers actually live in your dorm and coach your sports, and are there for you all the time." And finally, still nodding, but now with my eyebrows raised and a smile: "I'll learn to be a more responsible person since I'll have to make choices on my own." That was the clincher, no more questions.

No matter with whom I had this little dialogue (and I had it countless times that year), if I offered up those answers, they approved. If I was talking to another kid, "Wow," and then silence. A teacher would give me a pat on the back and a hearty "Good for you! I'm sure you'll do well." A relative like my grandfather, or even one of my uncles, would give me some cash. In fact, sharing my desire to be responsible was just about as close as I felt I could safely come to sharing my main reason for wanting to attend boarding school. There was really no way I could let people know that I was using this great opportunity for such a selfish purpose. I needed to make everyone think that going away to school was nothing more than an educational opportunity I could not refuse. As the smart kid of my family, of my neighborhood, of my race, I was responsible for other people's dreams and expectations. My reasons for choosing boarding school had to make these people proud and reinforce their idea that I was somehow as extraordinary as they regarded the choice itself. I guess I didn't tell the entire truth because I felt that no one would understand. I'm sure someone must have known, but no one ever really pressed or probed too hard.

At the beginning of my eighth-grade year, two of my mother's younger sisters and their three children moved out of my grandparents' home into our one-bedroom apartment. The landlord had sold their South Bronx property, and no one else could, or would, take them in. The place was complete mayhem. The seven of us shared one bathroom, three beds and a convertible sofa. The television in the living room was always on, and we were all miserable.

I hated being there, so instead I spent as much time as possible away from home. Each day since the sixth grade, I had taken the city bus between my Harlem magnet school and my home in Washington Heights. In the eighth grade, I started staying late at school, up to an hour after we were dismissed, reasoning with my teachers and guidance counselor that I preferred taking the bus once the after-school crowds had dissipated. When daylight saving time ended, I would go to one or another friend's apartment to complete home-work assignments and hang out until her parents came home. Sometimes, along with a friend who I only now realize was also avoiding home, I dallied in the local McDonald's over fries and a vanilla milk shake. I'd go to the local public library, wander through the stores on 181st Street or sit with the neighborhood kids on the stoop of a building down the block. I tried my best to keep as much of my life as normal as possible. The more unbearable home became, however, the more I wanted to get away, so I began to study maniacally.

The bright spot of that fall was actually visiting boarding schools. I took the bus with my PREP 9 classmates to Delaware, Connecticut, Massachusetts, New Hampshire and New Jersey. A couple of those states I had never been to before. All the schools were in somewhat rural areas, surrounded by woods, fields and livestock. As the buses wound down the curving roads and struggled up the rolling hills, I began to appreciate just how far away from home I was going. I bristled with fear and excitement. On each campus, the pictures I had seen in the school brochures came to life. Students, observing various rules of school and societal dress codes, strode down the paths, headed for classes, sports or the dining hall. They were rushing and sauntering, laughing and shouting, and they were everywhere. The leaves on the trees were turning shades of gold, crimson, purple and orange. Each school was its own beautiful planet, and my visits filled me with anticipation. What new world would I enter? Which place would be mine?

Those trips were my escape. With each I could see the possibilities, more options for the new life I was planning for myself. But even though the schools were wonderful places and offered everything I had dreamed of, the places all seemed wrong. None of them felt like that place that I wanted to make my new *home*. None of them, that is, until I arrived on a campus in southern New Hampshire at the pitch-black hour of five P.M. The moment I stepped onto Phillips Exeter Academy's campus, I knew that *it* would be the new home I sought. I felt it when we went to have dinner as a group in the dining hall and all the students stopped and stared at us, only briefly, and then went back to business as usual. I felt it an hour later in the steam heat that greeted me when I walked into the admissions office to meet my host. This was the one.

Alison Palmer was an identical twin from Georgia. She and her sister, Angie, had just come to Exeter as ninth-graders a couple of months before. Along the paths we took on our way to her dorm, many of the girls and boys we passed greeted Alison. She was obviously well liked and displayed an ease in these brief interactions that I accepted as maturity and the norm among Exeter students. As we walked down the hall to her single in Amon, I noticed the construction paper signs on each door that listed the occupant's name. The girls had hung dry erase boards on their doors, and each board was riddled with notes from friends who had stopped by to visit, telephone messages from home, and silly drawings and inside jokes from dorm mates. As I slept on the reclining chair that was my bed in Alison's room that night and listened to the sounds from the hallway and from outside, I wondered how I could already have such a strong feeling about this place. I resolved to calm down and wait until the next day to see if I really liked it as much as I thought I did.

The next day we skipped breakfast and went straight to Junior Studies, a required class for all freshmen. The instructor, Mr. Tremolo, a husky, short man in his fifties with a receding hairline and stark white hair cropped close, looked more like my idea of a weathered sailor than a teacher. He welcomed me with a wink and thanked me for joining the class, then pushed the 11 students, head first, into conversation about the previous night's reading. I'd never seen anything like this. Mr. Tremalo opened with a question, and I'm not sure if he ever spoke again, but the students all took the bait; it was as if he'd actually thrown his question into the middle of the oval table we sat around, and everyone clambered to grab it and give the answer. Using real-life examples and reading from the text, the class launched into something that was halfway between an argument and a conversation. Students disagreed with each other and tried to prove their individual points. Some supported their classmates' assertions but added their own opinions. Everyone listened and responded, but rarely did two students overlap in speaking and never did one student interrupt another. Each had the opportunity to get his or her point across, and no one could hide. It was all so slick, and fast, that I was having a little trouble keeping up.

When it was over, Mr. Tremalo asked me, "How'd you like that?"

I looked at him and smiled. Still reeling from what I had just seen and heard, I managed to say, "Incredible."

"Ha!" he laughed, and threw his book down on the table.

Later that morning, after a psychology class, I sat at the end of a very long table in the school café and met some black and Latino students. They hailed from New York, Ohio and Washington, D.C., and seemed even more mature and adult than Alison had the evening before. A couple of the guys were seniors and bragged that they would be "Audi 5000" the next year, but if I were to attend the Academy, they assured me, I would be in good hands with the other students.

"Do you like it here? I mean, are you happy you came?" I mustered the nerve to ask the entire table the questions that I wanted the answers to the most.

"Well, it was difficult at first," a junior from D.C. started off. "When the work gets harder, you begin to wonder if you made the right decision. Basically anything that goes wrong, you think, 'This wouldn't happen if I were at home,' but soon you realize, that's life! You make friends, and then you start to find your place here."

"I'm happy I came here," added one freshman boy. "It's funny, though, because I'm from the Bronx, and this is *real* far from the Bronx. But I do think about what it would be like if I were still at home. I miss it."

"Especially the food," chimed in another freshman.

"Word!" the entire table agreed.

Everything about my 20 hours on Exeter's campus proved that it was the place for me to make my new home, the place where I would begin to find the person I was so desperate to one day become. The campus layout and the buildings, the administrators, the students who encouraged me to come the following year and the classes I attended all enveloped me in a feeling of belonging. I could see myself walking down the paths, eating at Elm Street dining hall, sitting around the oval Harkness tables or in my own single room in a dormitory. I needed Exeter to help me define my life, my goals and expectations. I needed to be there. It was the only school that would bring me the safety, peace, quiet and stability that I wanted.

By the time I boarded the bus to return to New York after lunch, I knew I couldn't go back to that other life. When you so clearly see your future, you change, and I had seen flashes of it on that visit. In the way that only a 13-year-old can believe, I was sure that, despite all the hard work I had done and the continued commitment I would display over the coming months, hoping and praying would truly ensure my spot. So I hoped and I prayed every day until March, when my letter of acceptance arrived.

THE FIRST FEW WEEKS OF BOARDING SCHOOL are much like the beginning of college. New students spend the majority of their time together. In class, at meals, during free time and in the dorms, they travel in groups and appear as one. Returning students rejoice in the familiar; they reunite with friends after the summer spent apart. Girls hug and kiss in the dormitory halls. They scream, whisper or snicker at the changes that they and their peers have made to their appearance: the contact lenses, lost pounds, nose jobs and haircuts. The new students quietly unpack their bags and boxes, look for their classrooms and search for familiar faces in the crowds at assembly or in the dining halls. Secretly they hope that one day, they too will have a group of close friends, but fear that that day is very far away.

For a new kid, I was lucky. I already knew five other freshmen that year. Altogether six PREP 9 students enrolled at Exeter in the fall of 1988. Three girls and three boys, from Manhattan, Brooklyn and the Bronx, we came specially prepared with each other. One of the girls, Gloriana (or Glory, as everyone came to call her), was an identical twin. Her sister was also in PREP 9, but she attended Choate Rosemary Hall in Connecticut. During the first few days of school Glory was sick from the separation, but she did her best to hide it. We all spent a fair amount of time with each other in the beginning, and our relationships were very supportive, but we also realized the importance of branching out and making new friends.

Before enrolling at Exeter, I had envisioned a high school social experience that strayed from the cliques of junior high. I had vowed not to spend any more time with kids in whom I was not interested, and I was particularly against befriending others just because they were black. Though it would eventually cost me some relationships, I refused to believe that race necessitated friendship. Though we were all black, we did not all need to be friends with one another. I needed more than race to forge bonds; what I needed was mutual respect, and common interests, things that the students of color, I'm sorry to say, did not always afford each other. I decided to be friendly only to those I liked, while still being nice to all the others. But at Exeter, this was a difficult stance to take.

The faculty and the older students were all invested in creating a visible community of color to help students feel supported and have a sense of belonging. By the end of the second week, I knew just about every other black student on campus. Almost every social event that I attended was centered on the Afro-Latino Exonian Society, the student group focused on black issues. At the Afro, the room in the student center where the society met, I could listen to the music I listened to at home, hang out with people who already understood my culture and be just another black girl in a group of black girls and boys. But this course of action became trying after a while. The Afro was too small, the faces too familiar, the conversations and actions too predictable. The anonymity I had initially found liberating became increasingly stifling, unacceptable at a place in which I was supposed to grow. How would I learn anything new if I spent all my time surrounded by what I already knew? Though some of my closest friends at Exeter were the young women and men whom I got to know through our interactions in the Afro-Exonian Society, my best friends today are those I did not cling to because of race but stayed close with because of mutual admiration and pure affection. If anything, the Afro taught me that my decision to focus beyond race while searching for the new family I would build from friends and faculty on Exeter's campus was the right choice for me.

During my first year, older girls like Alison and her sister took me under their wing. In Dunbar, my dorm, my close friends included a Korean-American girl from California, the two other black Dunbar freshmen, a white junior from Washington State and her roommate, a black sophomore from Michigan. I remained close with Glory and Crystal, the other girl from PREP 9, as well as the three PREP 9 boys. I also counted a Puerto Rican sophomore boy from the Bronx as one of my close friends that year. These people were the family I had gathered in my new home. Over my four years at Exeter, the family would grow and shrink, shift and change, as its members disappeared and then resurfaced, graduated or moved closer to others, but every one of our relationships was important to me. Together we felt the fear and euphoria of breaking rules and then not getting caught. We pulled "all-nighters" to study for tests or finish 10-page English papers. We had passionate screaming matches in the quads and ignored one another for weeks. I cried with and for each of them.

My strongest bonds were with the girls from my dorm. Tamara, Roxanne and I gravitated to each other during the first nights after check-in. Though we had very different upbringings and were from very different places, Roxanne from Wisconsin, Tamara from Tennessee, as the three black freshman in the largest single dorm on campus we always ended up together those first few weeks. Eventually we spent time together outside the dorm as well. I had a single, so my room was the default meeting place during study hours and otherwise. The time we spent studying, procrastinating and pontificating drew us close as we shared stories and ideas, helped each other with assignments and considered the latest Afro, campus and dorm drama, in that order.

I have one favorite memory of Tamara and Roxanne. It's from a Friday night during our first spring trimester, just as the weather began to turn mild. Exeter had Saturday classes most weekends during the academic year, but students usually had only two classes on those days, so the homework load was light on Friday nights. We had finished our assignments fairly early, and by 10 o'clock we were essentially bored stiff. We made the usual rounds, dropping in on freshman girls and a few upperclassmen, making small talk, listening to gossip, eating food and drinking soda. By one in the morning, when most everyone was asleep, we were hopped up on caffeine and sugar. Needing some excitement, we came up with a series of pranks that ran the gamut from pure silly to completely annoying. We taped heavy-duty black garbage bags around bedroom door frames. We took soda cans from the recycling bins and stacked them against doors from floor to ceiling. Roxanne thought to stretch the plastic from dry-cleaning deliveries over the toilets to create covers that would render them unusable. We put Vaseline on doorknobs and switched name tags in the halls.

Tamara's contribution, from which we definitely drew the most pleasure, included fireworks. Back then, small fireworks called poppers were pretty popular among teenagers. They looked like innocent wads of paper, but they would explode if you threw them on the ground, making a noise much like a cap gun or pinched bubble wrap. Kids would put poppers on the floor and step on them as unsuspecting people walked by. Tamara decided that we should put them under the toilet seats. When a girl sat down, *pow!*

At seven-thirty A.M., as girls started to shower and get ready for class, we sat still and listened. Aluminum crashed as empty soda cans collided with the floor. There were whimpers as girls opened their doors to a wall of pitch-blackness and loud screams as they sat on covered or exploding toilets. Nobody got hurt, and we got to make fun of them all. In the world of the dorm, where the youngest students always answered the phones or climbed countless flights of stairs to announce male visitors, we were queens for a day. No one ever discovered that we were responsible; actually, I doubt we were even suspected. Our dorm head, Mr. Bergofsky, who was also a math instructor and the boys' lacrosse coach, mentioned it at the next dorm meeting and admonished those responsible for making such a mess. After a few seconds of blank stares and silence, he went on to introduce the following year's student proctors.

That April night is my favorite memory of Tamara and Roxanne because it is about being together, against everyone else. That night was about the itch we all felt as the weather transitioned from freezing darkness to warmth and light. I remember that the next day Roxanne fell asleep in English class as we watched a tape of *Macbeth;* fortunately, our instructor, Mr. Boland, didn't notice. I do not recall ever talking about that night afterwards with either of the girls. By the next spring, the three of us rarely did anything together. And the ways each of us dealt with boredom and spring fever were much less innocent after that.

ACADEMICS ALWAYS CAME FIRST and foremost at Exeter. By Thanksgiving of my freshman year, a black student named Steve had already been dismissed due to his poor performance. Though he was extremely smart and prepared for Exeter, he was unhappy. His misery consumed everything else in his life. He came late to classes, avoided his assignments and missed sports regularly. I felt very sorry for Steve as I watched him stumble and misstep through the lessons in our Spanish class. He seemed to have worked so hard to get to Exeter and now all he wanted to do was go back home. The faculty saw how unhappy he was, so the dean of students suggested that he not return from Thanksgiving vacation. Steve was also from New York, and he told me about his dismissal on the bus ride to the city. He was more relaxed than I had ever seen him at school. I hugged him before we exited the bus and wished him luck.

"I hope you come back," I said as I stepped out of the embrace.

"I doubt it," he replied. "Bye."

I thought about Steve throughout my high school career, especially whenever I was struggling with a course. He represented just how easily an Exeter career could end. He also had shown me that to truly succeed, a person must be happy. Returning to campus after that first break, I vowed to give a clear impression to all my instructors and the other faculty that I wanted to stay at Exeter until graduation.

My sophomore year, I struggled tremendously in biology and geometry. I had avoided taking biology during my first year, thinking I would do better in it after having a year of Exeter under my belt. But I foundered in the course. The more I read, the more confused I became. The other students in my class were also lost from time to time, so we always helped one another and I emerged from the course slightly bruised but better for the wear. Geometry was the same. I got help from my dorm mates and spent extra time with my teachers on assignments and problem solving. I put forth a strong effort but was unable to earn better than C's that year. I had never gotten C's before, but I understood my grades and came to appreciate the advantages of hard work.

Trigonometry and chemistry flat out beat me my junior year. I had never worked so hard in my life before I took those courses. The harder I worked, the fewer positive results I got, and then the teachers stepped in. I had wonderful instructors who were always willing to help and spend more time with me. Trigonometry would mark the end of my mathematics career, but not because of my teacher. Mr. Parris was patient; when I doubted myself, he encouraged me. I always wished I was a better math student, just to show him what a great teacher he was. It was Mr. Parris who helped me to recognize that trying is as important as achieving in the classroom and elsewhere.

Chemistry was another story. Though I didn't fail the course in any of the three trimesters, my grades were the worst I had ever earned and I actually began to question my intelligence. Finally my teacher, Ms. Pasterzyck, came to my rescue. After countless study sessions, after allowing me to take two tests without time restrictions, and after hours of crying (me, not her), she said, "Shana, maybe you're just not a good chemistry student right now. Perhaps you should try again later."

I hugged her and kissed her on the cheek. "Thank you!" I screamed. "Thank you! Thank you!"

I was so relieved. She had just confirmed that I wasn't losing my intelligence. Even better, she had revealed the possibility, which I had never considered, that I was just not ready to learn the subject.

I was traumatized by my math and science grades for some time. What made it most difficult for me was the disparity between these grades and those in all of my other classes. My grades in English, Spanish, history, psychology, religion and art were all B's and A's;

I earned honors most terms, and occasionally had high and highest honors. My friends were supportive, assuring me that some people were better at certain types of subjects and that my high grades in the humanities proved I was a "right brain" person. In the end, I remained unhappy with my performance in math and science, but I was secure in the knowledge that I had worked hard and was learning from my failures. I was not throwing away my opportunity. I was not like Steve; I wanted to be at Exeter. I was happy. I wouldn't be asked to leave.

Each spring, Exeter produced its own dance concert. I was a choreographer and dancer, and my contribution to dance at the school was to incorporate popular urban music and dance into the performances, which had previously been limited to modern, ballet, jazz and tap. Several black girls, including Tamara and Glory, also participated in the concert each year, since many of us either did not play team sports at all or were not on teams for the spring season. After our sophomore year, when we choreographed pieces to Madonna and various rap and freestyle artists, the concert became very popular among the students and staff who had not been fans of more traditional dance.

It was very difficult for me to learn to dance. Although I would go on to direct a dance company in college and teach dance in middle school, back then I had trouble translating counts to the beats in the music. My junior year was the first time I had to dance in a piece that I hadn't choreographed (the music was Janet Jackson's "Rhythm Nation"), and in rehearsals I was always a few steps behind the others. Only in the final week did everything start to come together.

My mother and her boyfriend were supposed to arrive in the early afternoon on the opening Saturday so we might spend some time together before the concert. Three o'clock came and went. At four-thirty, I sat and waited in the TV room near the front entrance to my dorm. At five-thirty, I went to grab a sandwich from the dining hall. I got back to Dunbar just before six and found a sophomore girl I knew fairly well.

"Polly, are you going to be here for a while?" I asked.

"Yeah, what's up?"

"I have to be in the theater in like two minutes. When my mother shows up, would you please let her know where I am and that I'll save her two seats near the front?"

"Sure, no problem," she reassured me. "That's easy."

"Thanks, I really appreciate it," I responded, turning to walk down the path toward the theater.

"You know, Shana," Polly added with a tremor in her voice.

"What?" I turned back around.

"I know this is stupid," she said, "but I never thought of you as having parents. You know what I mean?"

"Yeah. Thanks for the favor, Polly."

"See you later, Shana." Her voice cracked. "Break a leg!"

I shook my head as I walked down the path. Polly had never thought of my parents in part because parents just don't exist at boarding school. Except for the times when they visit, parents can seem like ghosts. But the way I related to my parents also informed Polly's perception. Unlike many of the other girls, I never cried to or screamed at them over either of Dunbar's two public pay phones. My conversations with my parents were short and discreet. In addition, I did not talk about my parents in passing, and they never came to visit. My paternal grandmother was the only person who sent me care packages. I seemed parentless in many ways, and perhaps in some aspects I was. My parents were not a presence in my life. Indeed, I had decided to go to boarding school to start a new life and create a new family. Apparently, I had been a success.

My mother didn't show up until 15 minutes after the show had begun. She missed the Janet Jackson number. That night, for the first time ever, I performed the piece completely in time, without missing a mark or a step.

AS A TEENAGER, when you're in the middle of just about anything, you can become consumed. Perhaps there is a biological component to the self-centeredness of adolescence that we can blame, but like an individual with a personality disorder, a teenager can be completely unaware of what's happening right outside her door. Living completely and absolutely in the moment, there is no future, only the present, with its chemistry tests, study sessions, English papers and Saturday night dates. The rest of the world is on hold and the future is far away. At Exeter, we did spend time discussing the devastation of Hurricane Andrew, the Milli Vanilli recording scandal, the Gulf War, Mike Tyson, police brutality against Rodney King, the L.A. riots and AIDS. These were realities that could not be overlooked, so we incorporated them into our world. Only two things snapped me back to earth, down from planet Shana. The first was my paternal grandmother dying of ovarian cancer at the start of my senior year. The second was the college application process.

Prep school prepares you for college, that is an inalienable truth, but while it's preparing you, you're not necessarily paying much attention. Though many consider Exeter to be a "conveyor belt to the Ivy League," as I recently heard a colleague say, I hadn't thought seriously about college until my junior year. For as long as I could remember, college had been part of the Master Plan. After the eighth grade I would attend high school, then go to college, then get a job. The Master Plan had no specifics, but relied on the general instead, like one day you're born, one day you'll die, that sort of thing. I did know some freshmen who freaked out over any grade below A— because they thought it might keep them out of college, but I thought they were crazy, just like the kids who said they wouldn't smoke marijuana because they hoped to be president someday, little did they know. Apart from these paranoid cases, true college mania did not start for most Exeter students until junior year, and by senior year it was in full swing.

Far from the confidence I'd had when applying to boarding schools in the winter of eighth grade, I was mystified by colleges in the fall of my senior year. The possibilities were endless. There were different countries, different regions of the United States, different types of schools of all different sizes. There was funding to consider and a major to declare. I was completely overwhelmed by the selection process, and I wished someone could make the decision for me. Well, that's what I *thought* I wanted, until someone actually tried to tell me where to apply to college.

Over Thanksgiving break, I received a letter from my college counselor in which she suggested that my proposed application list (Oberlin, Penn, Vassar, Wesleyan and a couple of other small liberal arts colleges) was too ambitious. She wanted me to add Syracuse to my list, as well as a few other less competitive colleges. I was outraged. I understood that my chemistry and trigonometry grades would not help my applications, but I still had a very strong record and a high grade-point average. My list was not, as she said, full of "reaches," the term college counselors use for schools to which a student would be extremely lucky (but unlikely) to gain admission. In fact, it contained mostly schools to which I believed I would definitely gain admission. And how dare she ambush me at home? She could have called me into her office before vacation or after we returned the following week. I knew her game. She'd written me at home so my parents would get scared and make me apply to her crummy list.

I needed to talk to someone, so I made an appointment with Peter Bordonaro, the director of PREP 9. Mr. Bordonaro was the one adult I could always depend on to tell me the truth; he was available and brutally honest. If he said I should apply to Syracuse, then I would, but I thought I had a good idea of where he would come down on that issue. We met at his office the Tuesday before Thanksgiving.

"So, Miss Harris, what's the problem?" He looked at me over his reading glasses.

"This!" I held out the letter. "My college counselor is insane!"

"I see." He took the letter from my hands and read it all the way through.

"I'm not doing it," I said. "I refuse."

"I think that's wise," he said.

"I'm sorry, but I didn't go to Exeter in order to attend Syracuse. I'm not trying to be elitist or anything, but really, I could have stayed at home for that."

He laughed. We talked for about an hour, discussing the applications that I would have to complete by the end of December. We agreed that I would not add any colleges to my list, and that I would explain my decision to my college counselor at my next meeting with her. I would not apply to any school that I would not even consider attending, and her list only had colleges that I did not want to attend.

"Thanks for listening," I said, standing up to leave. "This really helped."

"Can I ask you one question, though?" Mr. Bordonaro asked.

"Sure."

"Why isn't Yale on your list?" Mr. Bordonaro knew how much I liked Yale. In fact, I had visited the university several times. He also knew me very well. Though I saw him only on breaks from school, he was the adult who best knew my ambitions and goals. And he knew that Yale was the place for me.

"But I'll never get into Yale!"

"Well, of course," he said, deadpan. "If you don't apply, you definitely won't get in."

He put on his glasses and went back to the papers on his desk, signaling that the conversation was over. I walked down the stairs from his office, and the November air slapped my face when I reached the street. On my way to the subway, I thought about his question and tried to decipher the real answer.

Finding my next place in the world was not as important as when I was applying to boarding school. I was happy where I was. In fact, it would have been perfect if I could have stayed at Exeter; I truly felt that the school had become my home. Though I understood that the time for me to move on was near, I was trying my best to cling to the *now*. Perhaps I believed by then that hoping and praying would not get me anything anymore. Or maybe I could no longer put so much hope in any one thing. I was scared, and it was dangerous.

I went back to school after Thanksgiving and handed my final list to my college counselor. She never said a thing. I worked on my applications during my winter break and took them to the post office on December 30, the day before the deadline for mailing them. I spent the winter trimester in a program at a local language school in Cuernavaca, Mexico, and returned to campus in March, two weeks before college acceptance letters were expected to arrive.

When I received my letter from Yale, I opened it with tremendous regret. The envelope was thin, and though I didn't think I had been rejected, I believed my application must have been incomplete. I must have forgotten something, like a teacher's recommendation or my SAT scores. I took out the letter, read it and returned it to the envelope. Heather, a younger PREP 9 student, walked into the post office.

"What's wrong?" she asked.

"Um . . . I don't know."

Heather scowled and snatched the letter from my hand. After scanning the page, she screamed and began jumping up and down. I took back my letter and walked to my next class.

That night I wrote to Mr. Bordonaro. I told him about Mexico and thanked him for the advice he had given me that winter. I told him about spring semester and how much I was looking forward to graduation. Then I signed my name and added a postscript:

"By the way, I got into Yale."

Three days later, he sent me a telegram. To this day, it's the only one I have ever received.

SHANA M. HARRIS *is a member of PREP 9's Contingent I. Born in Harlem and raised in the Bronx and Washington Heights, Shana graduated from Phillips Exeter Academy in 1992 and received a B.A. in Latin-American studies from Yale University in 1996. Following graduation, she worked for two years at* Boston Magazine, *initially as a research assistant but soon promoted to research editor. In June 1998, Shana was recruited by Prep and named assistant director of the Network for Undergraduate Affairs & Professional Advancement. In July 1999, she was appointed director of Undergraduate Affairs, a position she has held for the past four years. As director, she supervises a six-person unit and accesses the assistance of additional shared resource personnel when appropriate. Shana lives with her husband in Brooklyn, New York.*

GOLDEN BOY

by LIONEL ARCHILLE

I SAT ACROSS FROM THE CFO of a Fortune 500 company and began to make my recommendations for how he could restructure his business in order to create shareholder value. Everyone at the meeting perked up as I went through my presentation, impressed by my explanation of the complex transaction and my ability to handle the client's questions. When the meeting ended, I smiled to myself and wondered if this distinguished executive and his colleagues knew who I was and the long journey that had enabled me to sit across from him in the executive conference room. It is difficult to believe that Fate simply intended me to arrive at such a point given the way my life began.

I had grown up in the Polo Grounds Houses, which were built on the former site of the stadium that had housed the New York Giants baseball team as well as the New York Yankees and the New York Mets. I lived there throughout my childhood and adolescence and will always carry a vivid image in my mind of the various towers that make up that particular development. Just over a decade old, the buildings already suffered from neglect as elevators and trash chutes routinely broke down, but the neighborhood itself was very dynamic. During the day and on into the evening, people spent much time on the sidewalk talking and watching passersby; mostly friendly and only occasionally intimidating, they provided a sense of comfort and familiarity. Late at night, however, when few people were outside, the neighborhood could become a terrifying place.

During the early 1990s, the Polo Grounds Houses were notorious in New York City. In fact, as an adolescent, I would occasionally meet people from some of the toughest neighborhoods in the Bronx and Brooklyn who would shudder when I told them where I lived. Observing their reactions was always a strange experience for me. As a child, I had had no ill-perceived notions about my neighborhood. Since I had lived there my entire life, and most of my friends and relatives lived in similar circumstances, I never thought there was anything abnormal about my living situation. For my childhood friends and me, the Polo Grounds Houses were home, and for many they had been home for more than one generation. Parents who were unable to realize their dreams would pass them on to their children with the hope that they would make these dreams come true. As I think back now on those years, there was nothing more wonderful than watching the joy on the parents' faces as they talked about their children's bright futures, and there was nothing as sad as when they began to realize that these bright futures would not become realities.

When I was younger, I did not know many "successful" people. I'm not sure if I even had an idea of what "success" would mean to me. My admission to Prep for Prep at the end of my fifth-grade school year was an introduction to a whole new world. It was not until I started attending private school that I began to get a sense of the limitless possibilities that life could hold for me.

For me, the transition to private school was a smooth one. I adapted to the new environment quickly and performed well academically, bouncing back and forth between my elite private school and my inner-city neighborhood. Every day after leaving school, I wore a baseball cap and replaced my penny loafers with some Nike sneakers. During the fall and winter, I would wear a jacket over my shirt and tie uniform. My change in wardrobe made me feel more comfortable as I moved back and forth between school and home. At the time, I did not give much thought to the need to change my image and "identity" to fit my surroundings. I wanted to belong to both of those worlds. I loved the benefits that private school provided me in the form of increased security, a far more engaging academic program and improved facilities vis-à-vis public school, yet I also loved the energy and familiarity of my neighborhood.

However, as time passed, the gap between my school and my neighborhood widened, and it became more difficult to reconcile the different sets of expectations. My neighborhood friends became less understanding of the challenges that I encountered at my school, particularly as the focus increasingly centered upon the college admission process. At this point, I remember feeling a sense of loneliness as many of my childhood friends did not understand my "preoccupation" with college admissions. While sympathetic, not many of my school friends could relate to the issues of poverty and race with which I dealt. In response to a growing sense of isolation, I began building "walls" that kept a distance between me and those who were supposed to be close to me. I found ways to deal with issues such as not having access to a computer for my assignments, and I found solace in discovering that I could manage on my own.

By my sophomore year, I had reached a crossroads between where I came from and where I was expected to go. I began the school year during a difficult time for New York City. The economic recession of the early 1990s had hit New York hard, and crime was out of control. Every day the headline news would begin with details of the latest gruesome offense, most likely having occurred in a neighborhood just like mine. As the chasm widened between my two worlds, the pressures of thinking ahead about college, career and life began to weigh heavily on my mind. My grades were respectable but the lowest to date. To make matters worse, my goal of making the basketball team evaporated after a series of embarrassing performances during tryouts. The end result of all these problems, and of being an adolescent, was that I became more distant with family, friends and other influential people in my life. I remember a conversation with my Prep counselor during the winter trimester in which he tried to talk about the source of the change in my attitude and academic performance. I didn't tell him that I was afraid I couldn't handle the challenges that lay ahead of me. Constantly frustrated, I hid my disappointments and fears from everyone and continued going along with the rules of the game—trying to keep up with the growing expectations of teachers, parents and Prep for Prep.

A few weeks after I met with my counselor, I headed home on the subway—reading from *Macbeth* for my English literature class. As I came out on the street and started walking, a man stopped me and demanded that I give him the new sneakers my parents had bought me for basketball season. I remember thinking for a brief moment about resisting or escaping, but as his two accomplices emerged from the dark, I realized that there really were no options left for me. He grabbed me by the neck, and I ended up on the sidewalk. In a quick moment, my sneakers were taken; luckily, my life was not.

Afterwards, I stood up and assessed the situation. I wasn't particularly embarrassed by the prospect of walking home in late winter in my gym socks. What preoccupied me was how to tell my family. I wondered if they would perceive my having been mugged as a personal failure, and if their perception of me as some sort of "golden boy" would be tarnished. I was confronted by the horrifying truth regarding my own personal limitations and the realization that I was not invincible. I did not want to share this reality with people who were close to me, so I lingered for some time, wondering if I should go to a friend's house to borrow some shoes.

Finally, I decided to bring an end to the day and just go home. My sister saw me as I walked in the door and immediately guessed that my sneakers had been stolen. My family asked me if I was hurt and quickly got me out of the now-filthy socks. I had been trying to pretend to take care of myself for so long that I forgot how much I needed the support of other people. In being welcomed home, I realized that I had underestimated the unconditional love my family had for me. Later I would realize that I had also placed too much value on being the model citizen and on achievements, such as playing for the basketball team, that really were not that important to anyone—including me.

Still, at school the next day, I did not talk to any of my classmates about the mugging. In fact, several days passed before I told anyone besides my family. At a meeting of JAMAA, an organization for students of color at Collegiate, one of my Prep classmates made an offhand reference to being hassled in his neighborhood, and his remark resonated deeply with me because he was able to say so easily what I had tried to hide. After the meeting, we packed up and headed home on the subway, and I talked to him and another classmate about my own mugging. Their reply was something along the line of "Who hasn't been? That's just the world we live in." I wondered how many of my own trials and tribulations were shared by my peers. Was I just oblivious to other people's problems?

I had missed the companionship of many of my classmates; after my disappointment about the basketball team, I had spent less time with my friends. My desire to reconnect with my friends led me to the track team. Many of the older Prep students were on the team, and that spring turned into a great opportunity for me to get to know the guys who had probably already been through everything I had experienced, and more. I spent time asking the Prep seniors about their approach to the college admission process and about some obstacles they had faced along the way, and I was able to learn a lot from their achievements as well as their mistakes.

Another important change was that I began to take Collegiate's community service requirement more seriously, and for the first time in my life I viewed myself as a role model—someone who could have a positive impact on the lives of others. My history teacher, Ivan Hageman, was heavily involved with Exodus House, an afterschool program in East Harlem that would later become a private school, and had set up a volunteer program for Collegiate students to help out there. I would visit the school in the afternoon to help the students with their homework and supervise the sports activities. Working with the gifted kids at Exodus House, I saw younger versions of myself and realized how much I had been helped by others to achieve my goals. I also began to feel less anxious as I focused less on myself and my own problems.

Ironically, having felt so vulnerable during and after my mugging ultimately led me to unload some of the burdens and pressures that I had been carrying around. Through conversations with friends and classmates about *their* hopes and dreams, and from trying new activities that would challenge me, I found an invaluable support network. I also reconnected with many of my Prep friends in various other independent schools and with the Prep organization itself to get guidance about summer jobs and college choices. In a strange way, my negative experience had reawakened my desire to see how far I could go, and I was able to refocus myself and salvage the remaining part of my sophomore year. I dedicated myself to doing well in school, and the strong grades that I earned over the next two years told me I was heading in the right direction.

The day I moved into my residence hall at Princeton was the first time I had lived anywhere outside of the Polo Grounds Houses. After we had moved all my stuff into my dorm room, I walked with my parents to the Dinky train station, where a shuttle train departs from the Princeton campus. I remember waving good-bye to my father and my crying mother as they took their seats in the train, and I waited until the train pulled away from the station before I ran back to my dorm.

I sat outside on the lawn and stared at the Gothic structures that were just as sturdy as the Polo Grounds towers I had left a couple of hours earlier. The similarities between the two sets of buildings ended there, however, and I couldn't help wondering what the future held for me. It was the end of an era in many ways, and the start of a new life for me. My four years at Princeton would prepare me eventually to meet with executives all over the world and allow me to see that world through lenses of knowledge and imagination I did not even know existed.

Sitting on the lawn that day, I did not know these things, but I was confident that I would have real choices and that I would be able to make the best decisions for me.

LIONEL ARCHILLE *is a member of Contingent X. Born and raised in Harlem, Lionel graduated from Saint David's School in 1990 and from Collegiate School in 1994. He received a B.A. in economics from Princeton University in 1998 and an M.B.A. from Harvard Business School in 2002. Prior to business school, Lionel worked for two years as an analyst at Citigroup and as a summer associate at Warburg Pincus. He is currently an associate at JPMorgan.*

V.
THE ME INSIDE OF ME

AS THEY LEAVE THE PREPARATORY COMPONENT, I urge our students to focus on the things about themselves and on the other people that helped them make it through those 14 months. Most say that during those months they grew and changed a lot. Knowing the identity battles are just around the corner, I ask them to try and determine what it really is that makes each of them the person he or she is. Hold on to that, I suggest, and in other ways allow yourselves to continue to grow, to change, to get stronger, with each new experience and opportunity. I am proud of them for finding the strength and courage to do so.

For many of our students, the task is to allow the person they truly are *to emerge.* This often means taking the road less traveled. Particularly for students who have already expended considerable energy in hiding or denying their real selves, fearing to have the appellation of "nerd" or "geek" or "weird" applied to them, the Preparatory Component is a liberating experience. For many, it represents the first time they have been able to be open about themselves, to share themselves with others, to discover they are not *alone* facing a hostile world.

In adolescence, the urge to conform is strong, but our students are also apt to feel a contradictory urge to define themselves individually. By leaving their neighborhood schools, they have escaped the trap that by doing well academically they are "acting white." But they must decide which elements of the prevailing culture in their independent schools provide them with a level of comfort. In fact, if they are courageous enough, they can be eclectic, and in that way each one can become that unique individual he or she had the potential to be.

Environments have a way of limiting people. Multiple environments suggest the possibilities of greater choice. In the course of becoming who one wants to be, rather than learning to conform to codes of behavior and expected interests, many of our students over the years have said that they have been able to become the person they already were, the person who was sometimes invisible even to themselves. Others have put it differently and talked of the opportunity and the encouragement to explore new interests, to be honest with themselves about the things they liked and did not like, to create a self. In either case, they have learned the meaning of freedom and, as a result, hopefully will champion the freedom of others.

HEROES AND SAVIORS NEED NOT APPLY

by DONNELL BUTLER

I WAS BORN LATE ONE MORNING IN MAY OF 1973. I'm told that I went directly from the hospital to my grandmother's apartment. My parents had been recently married and would divorce two years later. Soon after, I would leave the Bronx and live in seven different homes on two continents until November 1983, when I returned to where it had all begun, my grandmother's apartment at 1165 Fulton Avenue in the Morissania section of the South Bronx. I was in the fifth grade and would be attending my fourth elementary school.

Luckily, as a result of moving so often, I had developed a chameleon-like personality that allowed me to make new friends quickly. I would soon learn, however, that I had another characteristic, one that set me very much apart from my classmates. This quality would make this the most difficult transition I have ever made before or since in my life.

After the principal of P.S. 132 met with me, she assigned me to 5-2, the normal-track fifth grade class. She commented that I would probably end up in 5-1, the advanced-track class, but she would leave that decision up to the teachers. The decision took one day. The next morning, I was introduced to the 5-1 teacher, Mr. Harris, and my new classmates.

I quickly made a name for myself around school. I was so bored that I was constantly being told to stop talking to students in class because I was disrupting their progress. I had to be given extra assignments and a seat in the front row to calm me down. Then we got the results from the standardized reading and math tests that all the upper-level public elementary school students in the state take every year. My school and district were notorious for having large percentages of students scoring below grade level. I didn't know anything about this at the time I took the tests, but I soon would. When the results came back, I had obtained not only the highest reading and math scores in school history for fifth grade, but also higher scores than any of the current sixth-graders. I was reading at a 10th-grade level, and I had the maximum score possible in mathematics.

I was heralded around school and in my community as the local genius. Let me tell you something about genius. Genius is relative. Genius is what people label you when you stand out from everyone else. Furthermore, don't let anyone tell you that it is innate. Someone might have a natural talent for the piano. But if they never see a piano, then how could that person ever be labeled a genius as a pianist? My genius was simply a matter of having acquired in the course of my travels significantly more academic knowledge than any of my peers at P.S. 132.

My intelligence, in fact, was borne of a mixture of loneliness and wanting to be loved. My mother and stepfather worked constantly and didn't have much time to spend with me. So they bought me books—lots of books of all genres and on all subjects. I was lonely and bored, so I read, and read, and read. I began to have subjects that I could discuss with my parents. Our time together seemed to have more quality attached to it now that I was actually interacting with them. In addition, it felt as if they were prouder of me and even liked me more as a person. I figured I had hit on a good thing, so for birthdays and holidays I would always ask for more books.

By the time I was in third grade, I was able to talk intelligently with adults on a wide range of topics. People often used the words *precocious* and *inquisitive* to describe me. I appreciated the attention from my baby-sitters and other adults who actually seemed to enjoy talking to me. As my reading increased, so did the number of topics that I could discuss maturely. My modus operandi was to learn as much as I could about a subject and then ask an adult for clarification, simplification or examples. I learned early in life that adults love to be teachers, and I loved being a student.

As you can see, the so-called local genius wasn't that different from everyone else. I simply had chosen a path to obtain love and attention that happened also to lead to the acquisition of the type of knowledge necessary to succeed in school. This path also led to greater interaction with adults and the development of the cultural tools necessary to give the impression of being an exceptional student. Alas, however, it was an unfortunate circumstance that led me back to my birthplace and to a school in which most students did not have the amount of academic knowledge and cultural capital that I had acquired.

I had come to like the attention that I received from other adults, but that quickly changed when I returned to the Bronx. I was fine talking to family members, baby-sitters and teachers, but I felt very uncomfortable when neighbors and strangers wanted to speak to me, especially since many of them did not have as much academic knowledge as I did. Some of the male adults in my neighborhood became unusually aggressive around me. Some of the female adults in my neighborhood were unusually affectionate toward me. Soon, I found myself feeling uncomfortable every day walking home from school.

When I was accepted into Prep for Prep, I saw it as a way to get out of the house during the summer without having to hang around my building or my neighborhood. Also, I knew I would be bored at home all summer because my grandmother couldn't afford to buy me books, and I was much too young to get a job. For me, going to Prep for Prep was going to be like going to summer camp.

Needless to say, Prep wasn't exactly a summer camp. I had always loved reading, but I had never been challenged before. My teachers had always asked questions that required nothing more than a regurgitation of what I had read. At Prep, the first book we read in the

English course was Conrad Richter's *The Light in the Forest,*[1] in which a white boy is captured by Native Americans and raised in their culture, only to later find himself reunited with his white family—people he doesn't even know. I was expecting the usual: What is the name of the main character? What is the story about? and so forth. I didn't get the usual. The teacher pressed me to relate the story to my own life, to discuss not just what I liked about the book but what I *didn't* like. The teacher wanted me to consider whether certain figures and characters represented something more than what was obviously presented. Ultimately, was the identity of True Son, the main character, determined by his birth (as a white infant) or his rearing (as a Native American)?

This was very new. The teachers were asking me to *think*. No one had ever really asked me to think before; I was always just asked to *do.* In fact, an old adage that I grew up hearing was "Don't think, just do." Prior to Prep, a book report meant rewriting the story in two pages. Now it meant recognizing not only the main story, but also subsidiary plots and, more importantly, the theme and subthemes of the book. In the old days, I took quizzes and tests. Now, at Prep, I was being asked to write essays, short papers and memorandums.

Some habits die hard. I was still talking excessively to other students during class. It got so bad that I was put on "social probation," which meant that if things didn't improve, I would be asked to leave the program. This time, however, I wasn't distracting the other students because I was bored. It was the exact opposite. I was excited about being around other kids who didn't expect me to always know the answer; in fact, at times I could even blend in, which was quite relaxing in comparison to always being onstage. And I was excited about learning for the sake of learning. I was no longer reading to garner attention from adults. I was reading because it allowed me to develop my own knowledge and ideas. I really liked some of those ideas. I looked forward to new assignments because I wanted to see

[1] The first summer literature course is focused on the theme of identity and provides students the opportunity to explore different aspects of the topic. The reading list includes *The Light in the Forest, Shadow of the Bull, The Secret Life of Walter Mitty, A Raisin in the Sun, The Diary of Anne Frank, The House on Mango Street* and *Black Boy.*

what new and original ideas I would have in response to what I read.

The first summer of Prep ended, but the challenges continued. I was at P.S. 132 weekdays and at Prep on Wednesday evenings and all day on Saturdays. Most of my P.S. 132 classmates thought I was a fool. And sometimes I did, too, because I wasn't so sure that going to a "good school" would make all that much difference in my life. I went to Prep because it relieved my daily academic boredom, excited an intellectual and social side in me and kept me out of trouble.

Trouble soon found me nonetheless. Once again the standardized reading and math tests were given, and this time I went from local genius to something otherworldly. The school was all abuzz when the results were announced. Once again I had the highest reading and math scores in school history. Moreover, I had the highest *possible* reading and math scores that one could obtain on those particular tests. Somehow there was a ceiling, and I had hit it. In my school I was awarded prizes and certificates, and news of my academic heroics even spread to the local junior high and high schools.

One day during recess, my classmates and I were playing on the concrete playground when someone ran up to me and told me I needed to get out of there. Before I could assess the situation, I was knocked to the concrete and was being pummeled. I remember only three things from the incident: 1) unfamiliar voices yelling things like "You're not so smart now," 2) the voices of my classmates screaming for help, and 3) my feelings of pure rage.

As the story was later relayed to me, the students from I.S. 148, the junior high school down the street, had had about enough of hearing about how this sixth-grader was twice as smart as all of them. And at some point during the pummeling, I had leaped up and begun furiously to attack anyone who was near me. Apparently, it took some minutes and a number of teachers to finally restrain me. Moreover, from what I was later told, after being restrained I unleashed a profanity-laden verbal assault on every teacher I saw from the concrete recess area all the way into the building.

By the time I had calmed down, it was far too late to regain my former image among the teachers. My classmates and even the I.S. 148 kids (who, by the way, never bothered me again) were actually impressed by the outburst. Suddenly, I was "cool" for having fought back against junior high school kids and unabashedly cursing out teachers. The teachers and local community, however, actually worried that I might have a screw loose and viewed my outburst as highly disrespectful and dangerous. Frankly, I was proud of myself for fighting back when in the past I would have just taken a beating from the bullies.

Mr. Spicer, the science teacher who had talked me into applying for Prep, told me that my actions had cost me numerous awards on graduation day. The school was obligated to give me the awards for highest reading and math scores, but it was unlikely that I would win anything else. It was in that moment that something very important dawned on me. I needed to start liking myself for me, my ideas, my accomplishments. I told Mr. Spicer that regardless of what anyone else thought, I was proud of myself, because before that day I had never liked myself enough to stand up for myself.

All my life up until then, I had wanted to please adults and win their love in an effort to relieve my loneliness. I only liked myself when I was entertaining or engaging others. At Prep, the process of relating readings to my own life and developing my own ideas had begun to give me a sense of pride and personal validation. Sure, there were mathematics, science, foreign languages and all those other courses, but what really changed my life was literature. I remember reading works like *Death Be Not Proud, I Know Why the Caged Bird Sings* and *The Diary of Anne Frank.* These books highlighted characters who excelled and rose above their obstacles, and I began to understand that obstacles are just a part of life. Obstacles could be overcome. I had been through a lot in my life, and if I had gotten this far, then maybe I could do anything. More than that, I learned about *character* both from these literary works and from my Prep classmates. I was surrounded by real and fictional characters who every day faced obstacles, just as I did, and somehow managed to overcome them. I was surrounded by real and fictional characters who made mistakes, but when they did, they learned from them. I discovered that as long as I do my best, when I get knocked down, I can and will get back up.

When I talk to young people today, so many of couraged about themselves. They doubt their capabilities tion their opportunities. They seem always to be looking for a someone else to define who they are or could be. In my day it was "Be Like Mike." Today they're running around saying "I am Tiger Woods." There are so many inquisitive young men and women out there like me. Many of them, like me, have suffered loss, face obstacles and just need an opportunity. They don't need a hero or a savior. They need a chance to prove to themselves that they are good enough, a chance to show the world that they can compete when given a level playing field, a chance to find the hero inside of themselves. Prep for Prep gave me that chance.

DONNELL BUTLER *is a member of Contingent VII. Born in the Bronx, Donnell graduated from The Horace Mann School in 1991 and received a B.A. in sociology and in business administration (accounting), magna cum laude, from Franklin and Marshall College in 1995. He worked for several years at Ernst & Young LLP as a senior assurance and advisory business services professional. Subsequently he earned a master's degree in sociology from Princeton University in 2001 and is currently a full-time Ph.D. candidate, anticipating the completion of degree requirements in June 2004. At Princeton, he is a teaching assistant in the sociology department; he served for two years as departmental representative to the graduate student government and is currently treasurer of that organization. He is the recipient of a National Science Foundation Graduate Fellowship Award and a Princeton Woodrow Wilson Scholars Fellowship Prize. Donnell received the American Sociological Association's Race, Gender, and Class Section Graduate Student Paper Award for 2002 for "When Race Matters: Racial Variation in College Enrollment Revisited." He is also the recipient of Princeton's Marvin Bressler Graduate Student Teaching Award for 2002 and was the Williamson Medallist for 1995 upon graduation from Franklin and Marshall College.*

DISCOVERIES

by CHARLES GUERRERO

"Of all the discoveries which men need to make,
the most important, at the present moment,
is that of the self-forming power treasured up in themselves."
—*WILLIAM ELLERY CHANNING, 1838*

Constellations

IT IS NOT THE SKY OF THE ANCIENT GREEKS that I now stand under, nor are they the same stars, their radiance during the Age of Mythology just now reaching the Earth. The configurations are the same, but more venerable since the shapes were given names: Ursa the bear, Gemini the twins, Cassiopeia the vain queen. I gaze up this night at the only one I've ever been able to recognize: Orion the hunter, his belt clear and bright, even in the skies over the Bronx. I have never understood how, back then, in a night sky ablaze with stars, a few were singled out and their celestial dots connected, their identities inscribed. I couldn't get past their individual points, their luminescent antiquity blinking infinitely in the dark. I have always looked at my life in that way; each event, whether major or minor, a solitary point, glowing in isolation in the firmament of my own personal history. It has taken me years to understand the interconnectedness of these events, and how, when joined, they delineate who I have become. One point stands out as the focus of this matrix, a beginning (though not a strictly temporal one) of sorts.

1982/1988

SPRING MELTED INTO SUMMER, and my hopes for a vacation full of fun and relaxation melted into the realization that I had forgone the hedonistic pleasures of the Big Park in the Bronxdale housing project for the classrooms of the Trinity School and more immediately Bus A, which now was wending its way through Harlem. I was one of the first students on the bus each morning and one of the last dropped off in the afternoon, which in some ways should have been an advantage. The reading I didn't do the night before could easily have been completed in the time it took to get from Story Avenue to 91st Street. I sat in the back (*all* the cool kids sat in the back), staring fixedly at an imaginary point outside the bus window. My stomach churned in synchronization with the wheels of the bus, and try as I might, I could not help attempting to determine the exact rpms; this succeeded only in making me more nauseous.

My sickness was no doubt fortified by the realization that nowhere to be found in my outsize backpack was my latest research assignment (eaten metaphorically, once again, by my trusty psychological canine, always to be counted on when I needed a rationalization as to why I didn't complete my work. I couldn't, at this juncture, admit that I was overwhelmed), and the knowledge that *The Light in the Forest* remained pristinely unread. I shifted my gaze to my reflection in the scarred bus window. I was unrecognizable, green about the gills, and disappointed in myself.

We made good time that morning, despite a brief stop in the middle of the 96th Street transverse for me to get rid of the plastic bag I had vomited in. I was hoping it would make me feel better, but it didn't; my next hope was that my bus counselor would make a sufficiently disgusted report to Bruce Ravage,[1] the appropriate calls would be made and I would be on my way back home. We pulled up to

[1]Bruce Ravage was dean of students for many years, responsible for bus transportation, disciplinary matters and recreation, among other things.

Trinity, and several other buses were just crawling off, empty yellow carapaces that had discharged their young. Streams of Prep students seeped into the building in rivulets. I walked more slowly, hanging back, assuming my most debilitated expression, my chest suffocated by the feeling of impending doom. When I entered the lobby, I was prepared to be appropriately pathetic for Mr. Ravage's benefit. Instead, I was greeted by my advisor, Frankie Cruz.[2] He was frustratingly optimistic in our meetings, full of the milk of human kindness. I did not know what I had done to deserve such unflagging devotion, so I chalked it up to the fact that he was just very good at his job. Today was no exception, unfortunately, and as he began to talk to me, ask me about my night, my ride to school and my work, my heart began to sink. He talked about our scheduled meeting later that day, and he also mentioned the fact that he was going to excuse himself from recreation to help me with my homework and organizational skills. I was moderately angry, because I knew then that he had me. I straightened up a bit, and when questioned by Mr. Ravage, I told him I was fine, just a little car sick. I wouldn't be going home early today; Frankie and I had an appointment . . .

It was years later that I got to stand at the front of the bus, like a sergeant inspecting the troops, my little battle-ready charges like recruits off to their first encounter (Frankie was fond of calling the Preparatory Component a "14-month academic boot camp"). I was always amazed by the almost unholy resolve, the dogged determination (at this point, unrecognized in myself). Some read, some slept, some joked and laughed, others stared blankly out the bus windows, watching the heat rise off the pavement, the way I used to do. It was my first tour of duty as a member of the Summer Advisory System, a job I took mostly because I felt a strong indebtedness to Frankie Cruz. I vaguely wanted to "work with children" (a phrase, I would come to realize, that comes automatically to the mouths of many who are often unsure as to what that really means), but I wanted to show Frankie that his investment in me had paid off. I was a good student now, one of the high

[2] Until enough Prep students had reached their senior year of high school, advisors were non-Prep students, often college students, recommended by the independent schools they had attended. During the summer of 1982, a few Prep for Prep high school students began to be added to the mix. Beginning in 1985, the Summer Advisory System became an all-Prep corps.

achievers, a completely different person from the mess of a boy who sat with him, eyes welling with tears as we searched through the detritus of my bookbag for assignments that were MIA, presumed dead.[3]

As the summer progressed, I became attached to each of my students, especially the tough cases. I took on each one as a personal crusade—they would make it through. One student in particular made me lose sleep at night. He was a second-summer student whose name appeared on the board every day, and he was always *this close* to being dropped. My meetings with him vacillated between imploring, cajoling, cheerleading and menacing. I was his friend, his coach, his own personal bogeyman, as the situation required. Exasperated with his seeming nonchalance during one of our meetings, I said to him, "Don't be surprised if I don't see you at Commencement. I guess it won't matter to you anyway." As it turns out, I was the one who was surprised—I saw him every day after that. The day of Commencement, I went up to him and said simply, "Glad to see you here."

"Wouldn't have missed it for anything" was his reply.

1996

THE GENTLE ROCKING of my little coracle-like sea kayak almost lulled me to sleep. I was lying down then, arms folded, happy to be buffeted about by the whims of the waves. In that position I felt like a water lily, buoyant, and buoyed. I must have looked like a Viking funeral, minus my horn and helmet, ready to be set aflame and set adrift. Through half-closed eyes, I could see the out-of-focus profile of the Campanile; I was facing approximately northeast. A little while ago, I had been able to see Alcatraz, so I had been spun almost one hundred and eighty degrees.

I had long lost sight of my friends, who were all intent on going *somewhere,* even though we weren't allowed to leave the boats. They had skittered across the surface of the bay like tiny water boatmen, obsessed, yet oblivious to the danger of fish below. None of that mattered,

---

[3] Charles had entered the program a full year younger than the typical fifth-grader admitted to Prep. Much of the difficulty he experienced that first summer was due to a lack of organizational skills, which was attributable largely to his age.

though. I was enjoying the salt smell of the water (really an estuary, not a bay, but in style-conscious San Francisco we *always* went with what sounded best) and the dappling of light on everything.

This urbanely bucolic scene made me, not surprisingly, reflective. I was not really thinking about anything particular, my mind being content to travel round and round but never taking off, like a pen tracing a Möbius strip, its tip never leaving the paper. Then I heard it. A gurgle at first, it quickly developed into an onomatopoeic *splash splash splashing.* I cocked my head warily, icthyophobia preventing me from taking too great of a peek. Its pinnipedal profile undulated on the surface, a perfect complement to the tender waves, curved, and curving.

There were several of the shapes on the water, some a mere arm's length away, if I cared to reach out my arms past the protective border of the boat. The barking began, deep in their throats (where in a sea lion does the throat begin and end?), guttural, squeaky like an old bicycle horn. I was in the midst of a pod of them, playing, wanting me to play. The wonder of that moment, that slow dawning of joy in my chest, burst forth over the bay, spilled over the edge of my little boat, dancing over the water like sunbeams toward the Golden Gate. Then it hit me; where there were sea lions, there were most assuredly sharks. Fear clamped down on my chest, stuffing my previous oneness-with-nature back down my gullet. I found myself looking into the now infinitely deep water, just seconds ago so bright, now so impenetrably dark.

1994

I COULD SEE MY REFLECTION IN ITS DEPTHS. It was misshapen, like a fun house mirror image. I peered over the edge, and I could recognize the pieces of it in the bowl; neat quadrants reared up out of the garnet liquid (a sauce finished with port, I remember), and I wondered how many of them were from the same place. To my initial dismay, the tiny lobes of brain looked just like they were supposed to. I had wanted them to be sliced and chopped neatly, obliterating any semblance of their cranial origin. Here they were, little replicas of the models you might see in a hospital or a science lab, the curious wrinkles folded over, the proverbial gray matter made crimson by the thick bloodlike sauce.

I had begun to fancy myself as some sort of gourmand; I spent a good deal of time eating out at some of San Francisco's finest restaurants. What kind of *mange-tout* was I, who now quailed at the prospect of taking my first bite of calf brain? I could hear, with knifelike clarity, Lady Macbeth's voice, exhorting me to "screw my courage to the sticking place" and put the fork in my mouth. And so, I did. The first thing you notice about a mouthful of brain soaked in a port wine reduction is the texture. Firm, yet yielding. Spongy, yet surprisingly concrete, like an esoteric philosophical idea. The taste was almost an afterthought. I couldn't discern a taste ascribable to brain per se; the taste was all sauce. Unlike the other bits of offal that floated in my stew (kidneys, sweetbreads, heart, all of which I had previously eaten, and all of which I loved), the brain was almost chimerical in its flavor, elusive, hiding behind anything else that would get in the way.

As I rolled the soft bits of bovine intellect in my mouth, savoring its shallow wit and my exuberant victory over squeamishness, I was transported back to a younger, simpler time. I immediately thought of my great-grandmother's tongue sandwiches, which my cousin DaRon and I used to obliviously devour at her kitchen table in the Bronx. I remembered going shopping with her at our local PathMark, pushing the cart down each aisle at a reckless speed, hurtling by boxes of prepackaged delights, until she stopped abruptly by the meat section. She picked up a curious-looking package and placed it in the fenced-in baby seat area of the cart. It looked almost obscene, gray and pimply, huge and vulgar in its insouciance. A disembodied taunt, the tongue strained against the binding plastic wrap.

"What's that?" I nervously asked.

"Tongue for your sandwiches" was the offhand, agonizing reply.

I instantly thought of all of the tongue sandwiches of yesteryear, and my mouth went dry and mealy. I had a sickening image of past tongues, which I had happily munched and enjoyed the taste of, tasting me back. I began to feel sick, unable to control my nausea, unable to voice my distaste with anything other than an involuntary "Moo."

That was the last cogent thought I had as I sat enjoying my triumphal meal of brain. I had a mind of spring; as I sat, mouthful after mouthful, my thoughts became filled with something like victory, and visions of bright sunny pastures and tender green shoots of clover.

1986

THE FIELDS WERE FULL OF CLOVER THAT DAY, perfect for honey. The sun was also beaming happily, as if drawn there by a kindergarten child, smiley face and all. I was sweating in my suit (part paper, part plastic) and my hat, with its cage of netting falling down my face like chain mail, or a bridal veil. I pulled on gloves of leather, checking the seal between cuff and sleeve, and smoke pot in hand, ventured toward the clamorous monolith sitting a few yards ahead.

The large screened-in hat and stiff Tyvek suit made me feel like an astronaut as I made my way across the field, which felt alien every time I walked across it because it was always subtly different and there was always the slight murmur of menace caught in the air. The field was full of bees, hanging in the air like stars in the night sky, or like motes of dust gently settling in the dusk. It was almost dusk then; it had taken us longer than usual to travel up to the apiary. Traffic on the Sprain Brook was bad—filled with workers jammed together, humming inexorably toward their homes, much like the tiny workforce that buzzed its way toward the monolith-like hive after an honest day's toil that I now had to tend to.

This hive, a bit shorter than I was at the time, wasn't their normal home. Rather, it was a newly constructed observation hive that I had spent weeks building (with the help of my local friendly apiarist, of course) in preparation for carting the greater part of my collection of *Apis mellifera carnica* to a Boy Scouts exhibition in the city later that month. This hive was slender, tall and clear (part wood, for the frames, and part Plexiglas), perfect for viewing the ceaseless activity within. It was very different from the short, private wooden square that served as their usual home. It was more like a busy skyscraper—nothing like the angry squat box that I believed the bees preferred to inhabit.

This day, all I had to do was check on the general health of the hive. Bees are notable for their total hierarchical interdependence. When you look at a hive as clearly as I could at that moment, you have the strong feeling that you are actually looking at a being incorporate, with a single mind and purpose, changeable moods and a swift, biting temper. The buzzing grew louder in my ears as I approached, my suit turning from a matte white to a dappled black and brown and mustard yellow as I became covered in honeybees. While I waved the smoke pot absently in front of me, the thin trail of smoke caused a few of the bees crawling across my face to fly away. I gently scooped the remaining few off the screen of my hat with a gloved hand. They darted off in livid protest.

I knelt down in front of the hive and began to scan the constantly moving interior for the queen. The apiarist who helped me build the hive had given me the queen at the start of the project. He had daubed a circle of Wite-Out on her back to make her easier to spot. Of course, her tremendous size and the fact that she was always the center of attention didn't hurt, either. There she was, dead center, surrounded by nurses who were frantically, constantly feeding her. As she ate, the thrum of the hive was one of contentment, and I could see the purpling sky reflected in the face of the hive as the sun began to set.

It took the hive a few hours to settle down after we loaded it on a truck and drove it from Westchester to Columbus Circle. The buzzing was near deafening with anger as we carried the hive, entrance now sealed, through the exhibition hall, the gasps of terror from the horrified onlookers drowned out in the din. The judges were suitably intimidated enough to award the colony third place. I was the only Boy Scout from the Bronx to get my Beekeeping merit badge. We celebrated that day by eating a square of honeycomb cut directly from the hive. I had gone out earlier and removed the frame myself. We removed the cappings and cut the large square into several smaller ones. They sat on individual plates, their geography the most perfect of geometries, oozing honey. We sat down, and with the first spoonful of honey I felt a deep pride and satisfaction buzzing in my chest, as the now less perfect square dripped its liquid gold onto the plate like a sunrise at the edge of the world.

1995

NOBODY WOULD ACTUALLY SAY THE WORDS "like a sunrise at the edge of the world," I decided. It was late; dialogue was never my strong suit and it became excruciating at two A.M. The *tap tap tap* of the backspace key was positively cheerful as it devoured the sentence. My wood was considerably less jovial, since the *As Du Volant* would still be left with nothing to say for the time being. I tried unsuccessfully to suppress a yawn, and at that point decided it was best to stop writing for a while.

I looked over Elijah's plans for the set: they were intricate, brilliant—a far cry from the first set I ever designed. At age eight, I had built a whole theater out of the serendipitous arrival of a large refrigerator box that I was allowed to keep. The simple system by which the "curtain" was raised and lowered seemed so advanced to me at the time. A cord running through the top of the box to a flap out front operated the screen with a simple pull. A ring attached to the end slipped around a hook, securing the whole mechanism in the open position. I could raise the curtain and operate one puppet with my free hand. I began to design more complex puppets and set pieces that fit the limitations of my theater—multiple puppets on runners that could be controlled with one hand, spooled drawings that could march across the stage with just the twist of a dowel. All were designed to make my captive audience forget they were essentially looking at me, in a very big box.

I was the type of child who enjoyed constructing things. Erector sets, Lego, Lincoln Logs, activity books filled my afternoons. My theater was the perfect outlet for my nascent desire to be a technical virtuoso. The plays themselves—the stories—in those early attempts were secondary to the spectacle. They tended to meander, unfocused, rushing headlong to the next carefully constructed scene change. Not much, it seemed, had changed in the intervening years. Sure, I had developed a particular love for the written word, carefully linked together, meanings so full of recombinant possibility like a lexicographic helix of DNA, but this enjoyment came as a spectator, not a practitioner. I loved the *idea* of being a writer, but I was always too impatient to develop any foresight about my writing. I had never even voluntarily written an outline for any paper I ever had to write (and when compelled to produce one, I usually wrote it *after* the paper was complete) until my sophomore year at Harvard. Each time I sat down to write, I produced a mental travelogue, a history of my mind's wanderings. It was never a carefully plotted scenario.

I stood up from the computer and stretched. I pushed PLAY on the tape deck that contained the score that Matt had written. I had to rework the lyrics to several of the songs. I have always found songwriting to be easier—it allows for a more relaxed, off-the-cuff approach. I never mastered the mathematics of music, but constructing the demure scansion of lines of song was a different thing altogether. It was right up my alley. I lay back and began to concentrate on the soft strains of the piano, reforming stanzas in my mind. I was asleep before the song ended.

The day the play opened, I stood in the middle of the Red Rocket Theater like a surveyor. Last-minute details waited breathlessly like suitors for me to tend to them. I hadn't slept that night; the projects that needed finishing were too numerous. We had spent a good deal of time making steering wheels; in a musical about an auto race in France, they were an important part of the mise-en-scène. Each one had to be made individually, each had to reflect the personality of the driver. It was the perfect overnight activity, providing a necessary distraction from the persistent vole of anxiety that had taken up residence deep in the pit of my stomach.

How had I gotten here? I narrowly avoided kicking over the still-hot glue gun as I waded through a pile of material. I had wrestled with the script for weeks, fighting for every line of dialogue. The musical was a now-bloated (by my standards) hour and a half, partly because it contained almost 50 minutes of music. I had made the decision to represent the loftier (and, truth be told, more cumbersome) sentiments in song instead of spoken dialogue. So even though the sunrise at the edge of the world was no longer present, some of its equally picturesque brethren were.

I sat in the still and quiet of the little theater, itself an altered box, but instead of holding a single refrigerator, it had once contained dozens of pairs of shoes. It would be several hours before anyone would tell me how much they enjoyed the show, but I already knew how much it meant to me. The amount of toil, sacrifice and love that Andrea, Elijah, Katie, Lecie and Matt had poured into the project was all the feedback I needed. I was reminded of my favorite poem by Elizabeth Bishop, and all around me the tiny theater with all the planks of wood and bits of material and everything was rainbow, rainbow, rainbow! And I let my anxiety go.

2002: A Postscript

"YOU'VE GOT TO LET THAT ANXIETY GO," I told my student, who squirmed like a landed fish in the chair next to my desk. "The college application process should be, well, *fun*." I could tell by the look of utter disbelief on her face that she didn't believe a word of it. I wondered if it was too late to convince her I was not the madman she thought I was, because we needed to have a pretty close working relationship for the next nine months. I had to regroup.

"Let me put it to you this way—unless you go crazy, fail some classes or get thrown out of school, you'll get into a college. And with your record, it will be a good one. Okay?" This remark was met with a tiny seed of acceptance. That was all I needed; that seed would grow over the course of the year; it was my fervent hope, of course, that it would blossom into acceptances at a few of the top colleges and universities in the country. As she left the office, I could see a tiny swagger in her step and a bit of a gleam in her eyes.

She deserved to swagger a little; as I read through her folder, even I was impressed with all that she had done. Since I had returned to Prep as the director of college guidance, I never ceased to be amazed at the students with whom I worked. There was such a vibrancy, a palpable energy that surrounded them. It was similar to the way an electroplaque works in eels; it was impossible not to get caught up in their field of electricity once you got to know them. There was such a fearlessness in their approach to everything. Sure, they were nervous when applying to college, but they didn't even think twice when it came to things like running organizations, questioning political figures or helping others in need. Could you find a distillate for that drive, that energy? Casting off Cap'n

Hook's temerity, I wanted to know what made the insides of Prep students tick.

The answer, predictably enough, started with a self-examination. As I sat trying to write a recommendation for a student who was applying for an internship in Senator Clinton's office, I began to think more about my own Prep experience. It hadn't necessarily led me to any place I had expected to go, or to do anything that anyone thought I would do. I looked for that common denominator, the through line that linked all my experiences at each locus like some metaphysical connect-the-dots. I had always felt the restless need, like a Magellan of the Bronx, to chart those places in my own personal geography that were as yet unknown. The resulting cartography was less a delineated map than it was the broad outlines of discovery.

History, as far as it goes, is important to us, but Prep students love to create themselves in their own images. There is a certain delight in doing that which no one else has thought to do. It is a testament to ourselves, a celebration (slightly Unitarian at a basic level) of the ability to create, and most of all to discover. The boundaries of our life-maps are pushed ever outward, and I always look forward to when I can return to those always changing shores and rediscover the most important mystery out there: myself.

It was then I began to see just how those bright and shining moments connected. The personal boundaries that were expanded during the Preparatory Component laid the foundation for all that was to follow. Certainly, those attributes existed prior to my involvement with Prep, but they lay dormant. That sense of adventure, of self-confidence, of determination—those were characteristics that began to grow and propagate in the intense laboratory that was the Preparatory Component, a short, intense 14 months that informed every choice and decision I have made since. It is not easy to isolate what Prep has meant to me because, quite simply, it *is* me. I can now lie back and see the constellation of my life. Prep has been an integral part of that, the central, and brightest, star.

CHARLES GUERRERO *is a member of Contingent V. Born and raised in the Bronx, he graduated from The Fieldston School in 1989 and received a B.A. in English and American literature and language from Harvard University in 1993. Following graduation, Charles moved to San Francisco, where he cofounded and served as artistic director of The Red Rocket Theater (1994–99) and was director of operations, marketing and production for Inspiration Stones, Inc. Returning to New York City, he became director of college guidance at Prep for Prep, a position he has held since 1999. An advisor during his high school years, he served as assistant head of the Summer Advisory System in 1990 and 1991 and as head of the Summer Advisory System in 1992 and 1993.*

STAKING MY CLAIM

by FRANCINE CHEW

THE FIRST TIME THAT SCHOOL BECAME DIFFICULT was during my sophomore year at Yale. Prior to that, academics had been challenging and stimulating, but not overwhelming. Fourteen months of PREP 9 classes, four years of Exeter's dormitory life and six-day class weeks, and freshman year at Yale had not daunted my academic expectations. The summer after my first year in college, however, I had surgery to repair a torn ligament in my knee, and I began a year-long struggle with depression. During that time, I questioned many of the motivations that had led me to Yale, and I wondered whether or not I had been charting my own destiny or carrying out the plans others had determined for me.

When I arrived in the United States, I was almost 12 years old. I had left Jamaica after completing the first form, the equivalent of seventh grade here, and I had always done extremely well in school. Within days of our arrival, my mother was hard at work finding the best schools for me and my siblings. By the end of our first month in New York, she had already enrolled each of us in competitive public school programs. I was placed in a junior high school that was 30 minutes from our apartment, even though there was one only two blocks down the street. My mother felt strongly that although it was less convenient, the Thelma J. Hamilton Junior High School was my best option because it had a "Gifted and Talented" program. A year later, when my guidance counselor recommended that I apply to PREP 9, my mother again jumped at the chance to improve my educational prospects.

I was admitted to PREP 9, and I loved it immediately. I had no deep connection to my junior high school or to my classmates there, but PREP 9 quickly became a community in which I forged close friendships and thrived in the classroom atmosphere. My mother never had to convince me that the program was good for me and never had to plead with me to do homework. I simply wasn't tempted by outside activities, and I threw myself into the social life that emerged from my interactions with other PREP 9 students. The friends I called when I came home from school, the friends with whom I went to the movies, were all from PREP 9. Even homework became a social event. I compared grades with close friends, read essay drafts over the phone and took pride in how long I spent completing weekly assignments. I enjoyed the PREP 9 classes so much that being on the honor roll seemed a natural result of all the fun I was having, instead of a goal that I had labored intensely to achieve. My mother's highest hopes for my performance in the program were realized without her ever having to articulate them. In fact, one of her few complaints was that on Friday nights, before the program's Saturday classes, my friends frequently called after midnight, still wanting to discuss assignments.

Exeter was not much different, and my four years in New Hampshire were an exciting time for me. I juggled much more than I had before, and reveled in the novelty of each new activity. I realized that I was capable of becoming a great athlete, and I rowed on Exeter's winning varsity crews for three years. I had a campus job, headed various groups and was a proctor in the dorm. As had been the case during the Preparatory Component of PREP 9, I was motivated by the sheer enjoyment and fulfillment I experienced while participating in my various endeavors. At the same time, I inadvertently did what my mother wanted and fell in line with PREP 9's goal to nurture my leadership potential.

Everyone was thrilled when I was accepted early to Yale. My mother not only celebrated my achievement, but also felt that my admission to an Ivy League university proved that she had made the right decision to move her family to the United States. Prep for Prep was pleased because its administration considered Yale a school that would provide enriching leadership experiences and further encourage me to set ambitious goals for my future. I had my own reasons for celebrating. I was happy because Yale was located in New Haven, where I would have the opportunity to work and interact with a large minority population, because it was possible for me to be a top rower on its crew and because it offered a challenging academic environment where I could continue to feed my excitement for learning. Although I knew there were high expectations about what I should achieve at Yale, I was not intimidated. What I had wanted for myself had always coincided with what others expected of me, and I had no reason to think that anything would be different.

I was well prepared for the challenges of college. I was used to lots of homework and living away from my family, so I could concentrate on classes, work and rowing. I did well academically, earned enough money to cover my daily expenses and, despite a knee injury, was voted Novice of the Year in crew. Ending my freshman year in high spirits, I planned to spend the summer at Yale. I needed to repair and rehabilitate the torn ligament in my knee. Having secured a part-time job as a research assistant, I could pay for my room and board while I focused on physical therapy.

The surgery was successful, but rehab was slow and painful. At a crucial point in the healing process, soon after I had stopped using crutches, I fell and reinjured my knee. This called for additional months of therapy, which was an upsetting setback.

After my fall, everything became a struggle. For my job, I was assigned independent projects that I was supposed to do from home. However, I felt so disheartened by my physical condition that I began to put off fulfilling those responsibilities. For two weeks in a row, I promised myself I would do my projects "later," and twice I failed to make good on those commitments. Both times I found myself with more than 30 hours of reading and analysis to do and less than 24 hours in which to complete it all. The quality of my work suffered, and the professor who hired me eventually called me into his office to communicate his disappointment in me. I was embarrassed by my performance and began to hate my job; unfortunately, I had to keep at it in order to pay rent and other living expenses. My physical condition was slow to improve, further dampening my spirits. The daily routine of getting up to go to the gym and then do my work became tedious. I had never before felt trapped doing an activity I detested, and I remember wishing that I could fast-forward through the rest of the summer. I wanted to move on to the fall semester, which I expected would be no less successful and enjoyable than my freshman year.

Fall term did arrive, but there was no emotional reprieve. Everything was difficult. My knee hurt all the time, and I often had to take the campus shuttle bus to get from one class to another. While I waited for the bus, I would watch other students rush to their various appointments and become increasingly frustrated that I also couldn't rely on my own two legs.

When the orthopedist told me I wouldn't be able to row until after the fall season, I decided I would take the semester or the year off. My physical limitations squelched my spirit, and my dour mood leached into every aspect of my life. It was still pretty early in the semester, and already I was unmotivated to go to class, to work or to the gym. I researched Yale's tuition reimbursement policy (depending on how much of the semester has passed, Yale reimburses different percentages of the tuition) and decided to call my mom to tell her I wanted to come home.

I knew she would not immediately agree with my proposal, so I carefully planned what I would say to convince her. My mom already knew that my days were a struggle and was concerned because I'd had no experience with that type of situation. I planned to remind her that I was unable to function effectively in New Haven. Then I would point out that I could recover almost all of my tuition if I left immediately.

The conversation never progressed to tuition reimbursement. My mom adamantly refused even to discuss a break from school. She pointed out that my sister had taken time off from Wesleyan and still hadn't returned two years later. She also let me know that my father had planned to attend Howard University as a young man, took time off and was still working toward his bachelor's degree at 50 years of age. She said that although I had been exposed to privilege, I should not forget that I was an immigrant who would have to create my own advantages through consistent hard work, even during periods of adversity. She pointed out that many people, from my family here and in Jamaica to everyone at PREP 9, had an investment in my achievements. I don't think she meant to be harsh. She was responding out of fear that a semester or year away from school would mean I wouldn't complete my education.

I tried to convince myself that I was tough enough to overcome the first real setback I had ever faced. Unfortunately, despite my best efforts to be more positive and enthusiastic, I still was not happy to be at Yale. I repeatedly caught myself in public places, audibly arguing point and counterpoint the reasons I was in New Haven. I marked the dates of the various tuition reimbursement deadlines on my calendar and watched the days go by until money was no longer recoverable. I trudged to the few classes I attended each week. Friends started to ask if I was okay, and I began to sleep more than 12 hours a day. Eventually I dropped one course because I was hopelessly behind.

What I couldn't grapple with was the sudden realization that my individual agenda might be secondary to my group obligations. For the first time, I was aware that others claimed some ownership of my actions, both positive and negative. Perhaps it's a bit unbelievable, but the conversation with my mom was what first led me to consider my various identities—as an individual, as a representative of my family and PREP 9, and as a potential minority leader. As a result, I began to nourish a powerful resentment. I felt that my identity and affiliations unfairly shackled me to a high level of performance that no one should have to consistently achieve. I felt burdened by other people's expectations.

Of course, I had always understood that I was being groomed for great accomplishments. Years as my mother's daughter and as a member of PREP 9 had made that goal obvious. However, my prior successes had delayed my own realization of what it meant to truly commit to the program and to the achievement of my mother's goals for me. That semester, I realized that the program's mission, to nurture the leadership potential of able young people from minority groups, had introduced me to lifestyles that were beyond my own social perimeter. Although success implied an overall improvement in my own life's prospects and, by extension, an improvement in the prospects of all people of color, maintaining a commitment to my mother's vision and the program's goal required a lot of perseverance. While I was fortunate to have experienced easy successes over the years, I had never been forced to consider whether I actually wanted to commit to the program or to my mother's vision.

With those unanswered questions still troubling me, I finished the fall semester and began the spring term. By this time I had rehabbed enough to return to crew, but I was still unenthusiastic about being at Yale. My academic performance in the fall had been dismal, and I was soon on track to do even more poorly. Still depressed, I could rarely muster the energy to attend classes, so I petitioned to reduce my workload to three courses. On most days, I only got out of bed to go to practice and to my job. Again, I watched as the deadlines to withdraw came and went, and wondered how long I would feel lethargic and indifferent. The more I talked myself into finishing another day in New Haven, the more I asked myself if I was strong enough to finish out the year.

I can't say that I effectively wrestled with or consciously articulated these issues while I was depressed. That might explain why, when deciding my summer employment, I sought out a fellowship that required me to work with members of the New Haven community. I chose to apply that fellowship to the Ulysses S. Grant Program (U.S. Grant), an educational organization for academically gifted New Haven students. At the time, I was not at all conflicted about working for a program that so closely mirrored PREP 9's goals. In fact, I don't think I was conscious of the irony of my choice.

That summer was a turning point. It was a welcome change to work with U.S. Grant, as it was the first activity in a long time that

I had voluntarily undertaken. Even though I still fought against a constant feeling of indifference, I started to become exasperated by my continued lethargy, which in turn made me determined to follow through on my commitment.

There was much that helped me achieve that goal. I had a busy schedule teaching classes, preparing lesson plans, and interacting with my students and their parents. In addition, all the U.S. Grant staff lived on the same floor of a graduate school dormitory, so it was impossible to withdraw to my room at night or miss a day of classes. Luckily, the bustle and activity at night and in the morning normalized the hours that I slept and kept me keyed into the program's activities. Also, my students frequently called at night, so I stayed up to answer their homework questions.

Whereas I had been apathetic about my own recent academic achievements, I was intensely concerned about my students' performance. Their questions and responses challenged me, and as the summer progressed, so did my desire to be a good teacher. Also, the more involved I became in my job, the more I noticed the activity in the city. New Haven comes alive in the summer months, with its International Festival of the Arts, Jazz on the Green concert series and weekly street fairs. As my emotional pall slowly lifted, I bought tickets to see some of the shows. My focus had gradually shifted from myself to the activity around me.

One day that summer, after I had written homework on the board, my students complained about the length of the assignment —they said it would prevent them from hanging out with their friends. I replied that if they wanted to succeed and make their parents proud, they needed to focus on their education. In the process of articulating that answer, I settled my own reservations about PREP 9's mission. I realized that my students were in the same position that I had been in only a few years ago. In a subsequent meeting, I told them a little about myself, and I think we were all motivated by the similarity of our backgrounds. I certainly felt less isolated.

I found myself thinking a lot about what it means to be a part of PREP 9. I realized that what is difficult is not the program's rigorous

Preparatory Component or the demanding education at wonderful schools like Exeter. Instead, a student's biggest challenge is the essence of Prep for Prep's mission—to transform what is learned into real leadership skills and to make the commitment to put those skills to good use. The brilliance of the program's goal is that it molds leaders who are not only comfortable in their own communities, but also able to transform their identities into assets, particularly when they assume leadership positions in the larger society.

Even though I had to stumble before I could truly understand the importance of Prep for Prep's work, I learned that the goals and expectations that others had for me were, in fact, the goals and expectations I had for myself. During my personal crisis, I questioned everything that for so long I had accepted as gospel, only to discover ultimately that I was a true believer.

Teaching at U.S. Grant had enabled me to rediscover my spirit and enthusiasm about life, about learning and about the possibility of making a difference. During the fall of my junior year, I tackled every activity with relish. My personal achievement went beyond simply conquering my depression or rediscovering my old ambition and familiar self. *I was conscious.* I was able to embrace my mother's and PREP 9's expectations of me because I had articulated them as my own desires.

I continued to work for U.S. Grant, this time as its academic director. No longer conflicted about my relationship with PREP 9, I used the program as a model for U.S. Grant, introducing new responsibilities to my role. For example, because some parents wanted their children to attend private schools, I arranged SSAT preparatory classes for those interested. I also organized a Secondary School Fair that was attended by representatives from New England boarding schools and New Haven magnet schools. I was convinced that despite all the probable adjustments the students would have to make, attending good schools would be advantageous to them in the long run. Therefore, I unequivocally encouraged U.S. Grant's parents and students to pursue private school opportunities. Best of all, in stark contrast to my state of mind the previous fall, none of my pursuits seemed burdensome.

I added additional classes to my academic schedule, this time petitioning to take more than the permissible number of courses. Despite a six-course load, I did well academically. The clarity of my insight also paid dividends in my athletic endeavors. Whereas I had struggled to make the varsity boat the previous spring, I quickly established my place on the crew. I was delighted once more to have fun in classes, in sports and in my job. Additionally, the awareness that I was working toward my own goals substantially increased the satisfaction and appreciation I derived from activities that I had merely enjoyed in the past. Through adversity, I had found myself.

FRANCINE CHEW *is a member of PREP 9's Contingent V. Born in Jamaica, she immigrated to the United States when she was 12 years old and settled in Brooklyn. A National Merit Scholar, she graduated from Phillips Exeter Academy in 1996 and received a B.A. in economics from Yale in 2000. She was awarded the Yale Presidential Fellowship in recognition of her commitment to community service. Since graduation, Francine has worked at Morgan Stanley & Co. in New York. For two years, she served as a financial analyst in the investment banking division, Corporate Finance Chemicals Group. Currently she works for the division's Investment Banking Management Group, managing the Worldwide Financial Analyst Program.*

VI.
NAVIGATING THE IDENTITY RAPIDS

QUESTIONS OF IDENTITY COME in all shapes and sizes. Some youngsters raise the question for themselves; others have the question thrust upon them by society.

The stories in this section explore a number of quandaries faced by many of our students and alumni. Some approach the issue of identity from the perspective of living in two very different worlds; another raises the possible implications for family relationships when, by virtue of success, an individual's life experience makes her "different." The final story, particularly relevant given the fact that which face of Islam triumphs is now a matter of grave concern to the world, suggests the potentially overwhelming complexity of identity issues. All five of the stories provide us with hope that there are ways to navigate these difficult waters and end up feeling whole and happy with oneself.

One of the cruelest legacies of racism in our society is the pressure on young people *not* to do well in school. For many, academic success is equated with selling out, and professional ambition and advancement are denigrated as "acting white." Prep has urged its students to be prepared to resist the demands to be politically or socially correct, to think and act and be what others expect, particularly at the college level. We urge our students to resist the pressures to marginalize themselves and to create their own glass ceilings. From Prep's perspective, students who succumb to the pressure to define the world of ambition and professional success as "the white world" have fallen victim to the worst ravages that racism has wreaked on our collective psyche.

Prep for Prep, I believe, is an affirmation of the human spirit struggling to realize itself—seeking to grow, to create, to dream, to deny the forces of poverty and ignorance and prejudice that conspire to put out the flame. Prep is an affirmation that academic excellence is not the province of any one group; rather, it is a standard, a level of achievement, to which students can aspire regardless of race, ethnicity or social class. It is a common ground, and therein lies its power.

CHASING THE DREAM

by JAMAAL LESANE

WE GOT ON THE DOWNTOWN NO. 1 TRAIN at 79th Street. We were six 10th-graders, all wearing jackets and ties, all incredibly loud. To most of the other passengers, we were privileged, obnoxious upper-class kids. To the group of 10 older boys at the end of the car, we were victims. We had all heard the story about the kid whose skull was cracked open by a hammer on the subway; we all had friends who had been brutalized on the subway. Though we tried to lower our voices and blend in with the rest of the passengers, it was too late. We had already been spotted, and we were next.

By the time the train pulled into the 72nd Street station, the boys had surrounded us. We could try to run out of the car, but like hostages trying to flee their captors, that would just further anger them. As the doors opened and closed, we realized that our last hope—a police officer getting on the train—had not materialized. The best we could hope for, at this point, was that they were out for our money, not our blood.

When I was in the first grade, I got 99 percent on a spelling test and the teacher told me my score was the highest in the class. I remember the feeling of pride and accomplishment that I had that day, the feeling that I had been the best at what I did. It was a great feeling . . . but one that I would run away from for the next 10 years.

Growing up an outsider in the projects of Brooklyn is different from being an outsider elsewhere. Normally, outsiders are worried about the social alienation that they feel. In Brooklyn, outsiders had to worry about their safety on a daily basis. I was an outsider at P.S. 307, where academic excellence was frowned upon. Kids who did well were called nerds; kids who didn't were viewed as cool. Fortunately, I was beat up only once, thanks to the fact that my dad came to the schoolyard the next day and scared the bullies away. Unlike his son, he was still from the projects and knew how to handle this kind of situation

When my family moved, I was determined to fit in with the kids in my new neighborhood. They were a few years older and light-years cooler than I was, and I knew I had to conform to their ways in order to gain their respect. When they told stories about cutting class, getting into fights in school and the like, I chimed in with similar stories. When they chugged wine coolers that they had stolen from the corner store, I grabbed one, too, but poured it out when no one was looking. I was living a lie, but for once I was accepted. I also felt a sense of protection. The neighborhood bullies knew who I was, and more importantly, they knew who my friends were, so they always left me alone. I was still plagued by that secret desire to get the highest score in my class, but that was something nobody knew. I did well at 307, but I made sure I didn't do *too* well; I didn't do any homework, I occasionally acted up in class and I never studied for exams.

For two summers when I was going to Prep for Prep classes and got off the yellow school bus in front of all the neighborhood kids, I let them think I was a summer camp counselor. I really couldn't explain to myself why I was willingly going to school during the summers, and on Wednesdays and Saturdays throughout my sixth-grade school year. I certainly couldn't explain it to them. When I got home, I would try to study, but I would hear them outside playing; afraid that I was missing something, I would put my work aside and go out to join them.

At the end of my first summer, Ms. Boyd, the guidance counselor for the Preparatory Component, called me into her office to discuss my grades. I knew I was in jeopardy of being kicked out of Prep, but conveying that information wasn't the purpose of our meeting. Rather, Ms. Boyd wanted to tell me that she expected much better grades *from me.* I asked around, and nobody else had been given that same speech. I felt honored. Prep was composed of some of the smartest kids in the city, and yet, for some reason, she expected more out of me! I felt the same way I had felt that day in the first grade, and I vowed to myself that I would really pursue that feeling because I wanted to experience it on a daily basis. But each day, when I got home, I heard the voices outside and thought back to the days when I hadn't been accepted by my peers. And so I put the pursuit of that special feeling on the back burner.

My first fall at Collegiate, I would shiver all the way to the train station. Every morning, my mother sent me out of the house with a blazer on; she would beam with pride when I walked out looking so distinguished. But I couldn't wear a blazer on the subway. I would lose my props, not to mention that I would become a target. Most mornings, I rode with one of my friends from the neighborhood. At this point, they were all in high school. I couldn't possibly tell them that I attended an almost all-white private school. So I told them that I attended Satellite West, the same public junior high school that several of them had attended. On some mornings, I would be given love notes to take to girls they knew at Satellite West. On other mornings, I would get off the C train at the High Street train station in Brooklyn, adjacent to where Satellite West was located. I would walk toward the stairs, watch the train pull out of the station, and then wait for the next C train to resume my commute to the Upper West Side.

I was living a lie in Brooklyn, but I was sure that I would fit in at Collegiate and be free to pursue the feeling that I had been secretly craving for years. Though I had never before been around white people (other than teachers), I was determined to look past the fact that mine was one of only a few black faces. Unfortunately, the differences were more than just differences of race. I went to school every day with boys from the wealthiest families in New York City. They invited me to their Park Avenue homes, where they had maids and doormen. Yet the one time I invited some of them to my house, they were chased by kids from my neighborhood while doing nothing more objectionable than walking down the street. They spent their summers in country homes and expensive sleepaway camps, while I spent mine playing football in the street on St. James Place. No matter how hard I tried, I felt like I would never understand them, and they would never understand me.

One day I borrowed a VCR tape from a friend at Collegiate, and that night my house was burglarized; the robbers took our TV, our VCR, our appliances and my friend's tape. The only thing that felt worse than my family's having been robbed was the fact that my friend did not believe me. He thought I had *stolen* his tape. In his world, burglaries did not happen, and he couldn't understand the world that I lived in. Once again, I was an outsider. Thinking that I would never fit in, I lived for the joy of street football games with my neighborhood friends. I was not doing well academically at Collegiate, but who cared? They would never accept me anyway.

AS THE OLDER BOYS APPROACHED US, we clustered close to each other, preparing ourselves for the worst. Just as they got within striking distance, I heard "Oh, shit! Whassup, Jamaal?" I looked up, and it was one of the attackers. Rather, it was my friend Sha, who lived one block away from me. His block and my block were friendly football rivals. We exchanged pleasantries, and then Sha called off his friends; they got off at the next stop . . . peacefully.

One of them did manage to steal a hat from one of my classmates, the same boy whose tape had been stolen from my house. Realizing that he knew I was friends with one of the boys who had just threatened us, I apologized to him. He smiled and thanked me, as did the rest of my classmates.

What struck me most about the incident on the No. 1 train was the look of confusion on everybody's face. Sha's friends were confused; they couldn't understand why or how he knew the nerd in the jacket and tie. My classmates were just as confused; they couldn't understand why or how I knew the mugger on the subway. The two groups lived in two separate worlds, parallel universes that represented the segregation and polarization that plague our country. They were all confused at how I lived in a world where I could wear a jacket and tie during the day and yet hang out on the block at night; how I could live in a world with no segregation and no racial barriers that couldn't be overcome. It was the first time that I felt accepted by my Collegiate classmates. It was the first time that I wasn't embarrassed about playing football in the summers instead of going to a country home. It was also the first time that I truly realized what a special opportunity I had before me.

My grades at Collegiate skyrocketed in the 11th grade. I was also voted vice president of my class and the next year, captain of the varsity basketball and track teams. All the while, I maintained the neighborhood friendships that I had worked so hard to cultivate. I finally understood that a world had been created for me in which I could feel free to chase that feeling of doing my best academically, while still being respected and accepted by my neighborhood peers. Ironically, I realized, it was the only world in which I could have felt truly comfortable, ever since I had gotten that 99 percent on my spelling test.

Unfortunately, the world I live in is only a dream world for Sha and for the rest of my friends in Brooklyn. No one has created it for them, yet. There is no doubt in my mind that had Prep not intervened in my life, I would have continued my quest to follow in their footsteps. Instead, Prep created a world for me in which I could be myself; it gave me the opportunity to find myself, not the person I wanted to be but the person I really was. It allowed me to appreciate my four years at Yale so much that I cried on the day I left. It allowed me to feel comfortable at a law firm where I am the only African-American associate.

I still live in the same neighborhood in which I grew up; I still have the same group of friends. Many of them attended community colleges but have yet to graduate. It often strikes me as unfair that an opportunity I was presented with when I was 10 years old is all that separates us. Yet, whenever they beam with pride when I tell them what I'm doing, the same way my mother did years ago, I realize that Prep allowed me, and everybody in my life, to be the dream.

JAMAAL LESANE *is a member of Contingent X. Born and raised in Brooklyn, Jamaal graduated from Collegiate School in 1994 and received a B.A. in sociology from Yale University in 1998. Subsequently he earned a J.D. from Harvard Law School in 2001. Currently, he is a second-year associate in corporate law at the New York office of Covington & Burling.*

THE LUCKIEST GUY ON THE LOWER EAST SIDE

by PANG LEE

i.

THE YELLOW TAXICAB PULLED ONTO the Exeter campus slightly after dawn. My uncle, a recent immigrant from China and the proud new owner of a taxi license, had insisted on driving my family up to New Hampshire. It would probably have been easier to take the charter bus that Exeter had provided for its New York City students, but I didn't mind the company. The only request my uncle had made was that we start our trip from Chinatown at midnight just in case we got lost on the unfamiliar roads of New England and needed an extra few hours.

I stayed awake during the entire six-hour ride partly because I was in charge of reading the English road signs, but mainly because I was reflecting on my decision to leave home. Michael Chung, my post-placement counselor from Prep during my years at Allen-Stevenson,[1] had encouraged me to apply to Exeter because the

[1] The Allen-Stevenson School is a kindergarten–ninth-grade school. About 10 of the NYC independent schools at which Prep students matriculate are K–8 or K–9 schools. Prep has on staff an out-placement coordinator who works closely with students who are graduating from these schools and must therefore go through the admissions process to secure a high school place either at another independent day school or at a boarding school. The coordinator's work supplements the efforts of the placement officers at the K–8 and K–9 schools.

school would offer me a better education and provide connections for the future. Truth be told, I was really more excited about the prospect of finally having my own room and taking a real shower. During my campus visit, a student guide had shown me a typical dorm room furnished with a bed, a desk and two lamps. Until that time, I had lived all my life in a railroad-style tenement apartment on the Lower East Side, where the bathtub was inconveniently located in the kitchen and I had to share a bunk bed in the living room with my sister, brother and grandmother. After deciding on Exeter, I spent all my time fantasizing about how I would decorate my room and how I would be able to do my assignments on a real desk instead of a greasy kitchen table. And I could only try to imagine how it would feel to take a long, hot shower in a real bathroom. During the cab ride, I could hardly contain my excitement, knowing that the next time I fell asleep, it would be in my very own room.

I was ready for boarding school. Unlike some of the other scholarship students, I was not a stranger to the world of private school education. I had spent three years at Allen-Stevenson, an all-boys school located on the Upper East Side, and I had already been exposed to students whose parents were executives and lawyers and doctors, *not* waiters or garment workers. It was certainly tough being so different at such an impressionable age, but I had discovered that nevertheless I could excel in school and be an integral part of the school community. Of course, there were times when I was teased for always wearing the same school tie or sporting a pair of fake-leather shoes instead of the more fashionable Sperry Top-Siders or not owning a fancy shirt with the Polo insignia. I never completely got used to the sting of these comments, but I drew strength from belonging to a larger Prep community that valued me for who I was instead of what I wore. The beautiful thing about being part of Prep was that you always knew you had an advocate, a guardian angel.

Despite my excitement about going to boarding school, I felt a deep sense of guilt about leaving my family. I worried for my mother, who was a garment worker in a sweatshop and needed me to look after my younger brother and sister when she worked late in the factory. What would she do now when her boss demanded that she stay until midnight to finish her work? My father, who had been disabled in a truck accident, needed me to translate whenever he had to meet our caseworker at the welfare office. Every three months, I would skip a day of school and accompany him to the Waverly Job Center on 14th Street to explain why we still needed welfare, food stamps and Medicaid. The appointments were always scheduled for early in the morning, but strangely our caseworker was never available to meet until after the noon lunch break. I dreaded sitting in the waiting room with all the other frustrated and angry people, many of whom were trying to call their caseworkers to come downstairs on the one greasy black phone that connected to their offices. The situation invariably got worse once we *did* meet the caseworker. He was Chinese and thought it was a disgrace that a Chinese family was on welfare. He often tried to shame us into discontinuing our case by muttering how lazy my father was. I knew better, of course. Lazy men don't risk their lives swimming out of China to Hong Kong (as my mother had also done) and eventually making their way to America so that they could collect a lousy welfare check. I was disappointed that my father was unable to find work after his accident, but I was not ashamed of him. I often wondered what the caseworker would have done if he had been run over by a truck and didn't speak enough English to find a job outside of Chinatown. Despite my guilt, I knew that I would be honoring my parents' dream of seeking a better life in America by going to Exeter.

As the yellow taxicab made its way onto the Exeter campus, I had a sense of purpose and resolve to make sure the tremendous opportunity that I had before me did not go to waste. Thanks to Prep, I was prepared to tackle the academic challenge and interact with people who had assumptions about their place in society that were so drastically different from my day-to-day reality. Ironically, however, I was soon to discover that the Exeter community had an ethos similar to the egalitarian community that was celebrated at Prep. Neither at Prep nor at Exeter was self-pity tolerated.

ii.

I WOKE UP IN THE TRAUMA UNIT at Bellevue Hospital, surprised to see Frankie Cruz quietly talking to my parents. Despite the pain medication, I could feel a throbbing from the two hammer blows to the back of my head, and my body was sore from the nine stab wounds that marked my arms, back and legs. I had a hard time breathing because one of my lungs had been punctured by an ice pick. Frankie, then director of Leadership Development at Prep, was one of the first people to visit me in the hospital. I had known Frankie since my Preparatory Component days, when he was still a Princeton undergraduate but returned to Prep each summer as head of the Summer Advisory System. I wasn't sure what Frankie was asking my parents, but he probably wouldn't have believed the story.

It was the spring break of my senior year at Exeter, and I had returned to New York to share great news with my family. Three years of hard work had paid off: I had been admitted to MIT, my first-choice college; I had just been announced as a semifinalist in the Westinghouse competition; and I had just come off of a 17-2 regular season as a varsity wrestler. Little did I know, however, that getting nearly killed by a Chinatown street gang would be the highlight of my senior year.

The police reported that my attackers had mistaken me for a rival gang member because of the red varsity letterman jacket I was wearing. But I knew better than the police what had really happened. I knew why I had been attacked while my two friends had gotten away unscathed. Instead of looking down at the pavement as my friends urged me to do, I had instead made eye contact and acknowledged a gang member who was standing across the street. When he and his seven fellow gangsters approached us, my friends took off, but I naively stayed. It would have been hard to run anyway, since I was sporting a pair of real Sperry Top-Siders instead of sneakers.

My years at Exeter had taught me to greet strangers when you met them on the paths. I certainly don't blame Exeter for teaching me to appreciate the goodness in people. I should have known better. Back in the old neighborhood, making eye contact with a stranger, especially a gang member, was an open invitation for confrontation. Gang violence was not a rap song playing on MTV or some news feature on CNN; it was a reality for all the neighborhood youngsters. Negotiating with gangsters was a part of growing up in Chinatown. The first time I had gotten mugged was when I was only 10 years old. I was playing softball with friends in Seward Park, a local spot of greenery notorious for drugs and prostitution, when three 15-year-old gang members took our bats and threatened to beat us if we didn't give them our wallets and watches. Muggings soon became a part of life, and I quickly learned how to navigate the streets to minimize unwanted encounters.

Seven years older but not much wiser, I had inadvertently let my guard down and forgotten momentarily where I was and with whom I was dealing. Getting stabbed was an unpleasant reminder that in my haste to make it out of the inner city, I had best hold on to some of the street smarts that had gotten me out in the first place.

I remember how upset Frankie was when he saw me in the hospital. In fact, I remember how upset and shocked everyone at Prep and Exeter was about the attack. But for some reason I, myself, never got very upset or angry with the people who had nearly killed me. Even though I was clearly the victim of a violent assault, I felt more sorry for my attackers than I did for myself. Many gangsters were FOBs (fresh off the boat) who spoke English in a heavy Chinese accent and had a hard time assimilating into the mainstream. Some had dropped out of school and spent their time hustling on the streets. These gangsters, with their outrageous spiky hairdos and baggy black pants, would have looked odd and much less threatening anywhere else outside of Chinatown. Their parents were probably like mine, having come to America to seek a better life. Unfortunately, however, these young men had succumbed to street violence as a way to seek self-esteem and personal worth. Perhaps things would have turned out differently for them if they had been afforded even a fraction of the many opportunities that I had had as a youngster.

The attack only fortified my resolve to make the most of those opportunities and of the future opportunities I was now in a position to create for myself. These days, the scars from my stab wounds serve as a reminder of how lucky I am to be alive and how quickly my life could change due to circumstances that are sometimes beyond my control.

iii.

I NEVER FELT THAT I WAS DISADVANTAGED by my social or economic background. Maybe it was because I grew up in a strong, loving family that valued education and had high expectations of me. Maybe it was because Prep and my family taught me that my self-esteem was not derived from the clothes that I wore or how popular I was at school. Sure, it was tough to see my private school classmates drive off with their parents in their Mercedes to their ski vacations. But I doubt they will ever experience the sheer exhilaration you get from outrunning a mugger chasing you with a jagged broom handle down Canal Street. That rush is better than any trail you could ever ski at Killington or even Tahoe.

I continue to straddle the world of the privileged and the poor. As a third-year student at the University of Pennsylvania Law School, I work as an advocate at the Guild Food Stamp Clinic, helping my clients deal with the state welfare bureaucracy. After graduation, I plan to work in a large law firm in New York but will return to live in Chinatown so that I can save money to purchase a house for my family. I already know that when I begin to practice law, working pro bono will always be part of my job. There is always a relative or friend in Chinatown who needs help with some legal matter.

I fully accept the challenges of my dual membership in two very different communities. As I have learned from my long association with Prep, I can be a member of both without having to compromise my identity in either world.

PANG LEE *is a member of Contingent IX. Born in Hong Kong, he arrived in the United States at the age of four and a half and was raised on Manhattan's Lower East Side. Pang graduated from The Allen-Stevenson School in 1990 and from Phillips Exeter Academy in 1993, and received a B.S. in molecular biology from Massachusetts Institute of Technology in 1997. At MIT, he was chairman of the Senior Class Gift Committee, which raised the largest senior class gift in the school's history. After working two years as an analyst for Andersen Consulting, followed by a year as coordinator of Prep's Annual Alumni Giving Campaign, Pang resolved to pursue a legal career. In May 2003 he received a J.D. from the University of Pennsylvania Law School. At Penn, he was president of the Asian Pacific American Law Students Association as well as president of the Guild Food Stamp Clinic. Pang has accepted an offer from the New York City law firm Kaye Scholer, LLP, where he will be an associate next fall.*

REFLECTIONS ON THE LIFE OF A YOUNG AMBASSADOR

by KEVIN L. STROMAN

THE DAY WAS MARKED BY EAGER ANTICIPATION of what I hoped would be the first of many interviews with an adoring press. *Business Week,* having identified me as a young African-American "Future Business Leader," had decided to interview me for an article about the increasing importance of recruitment and retention of minority talent in corporate America. Not bad, I thought, for a college senior. Donning my power shirt, with my tie crisply pressed and my corporate glasses polished to perfection, I felt confident, empowered and ready. I came armed with a strong GPA and the growing belief (soon to be confirmed) that I was poised to become the first African-American ever to be elected president of the senior class at Bates.

"Firstly, Kevin, I just want to thank you for agreeing to speak with us today. You're a very impressive young man."

Thus the interview began. I humbly thanked the reporter for his compliment and spoke briefly about how important I believed the article to be. For a few more minutes we exchanged pleasantries but finally got to the first questions that constituted official business, questions about my background. This happened to be a topic with which I was always comfortable, because I had grown accustomed to being able to evoke a certain type of predictable response from most individuals.

"If you wouldn't mind, for the record, could you restate your major?"

"I have just about completed a double major in economics and Chinese language," I responded.

"Wow, that's a pretty ambitious undertaking—economics and Chinese. So you speak a bit of Chinese, then?"

"Yes, I speak it fairly fluently. Actually, I spent some time sophomore year going to school in Nanjing."

"Really? That's so . . . interesting."

So far, it was going exactly as I had expected. I had grown accustomed to the manner in which people would proclaim "interesting" or "fascinating" and then, like clockwork, the punch line would follow:

"Please don't take this the wrong way, but what in the world, of all things, made *you* choose China?"

And there it was. I was always forced to grin like the proud scientist satisfied that his carefully chosen stimuli had served their intended purpose. Whether the source of the query was pale-skinned or darkly hued, friend or foe, family or foreigner, the question implicit within that question was always "Why have you, *black man,* decided to learn to speak Chinese?"

Now, those who know me personally know that there are really two answers to that question. What the interviewer heard that day was the following mass-consumption-ready response:

"It's evident that the future of our nation, in terms of its potential for continued economic growth and political stability, is unequivocally linked to the development of a sustainable synergetic relationship with China," I proclaimed. "Moving forward, therefore, I believe it is imperative for the leadership of tomorrow to develop a fluency in the language and culture of our important global partner. Currently, there is a void. Given my capacity for language, as well as my interest in and sensitivity to this nation that is at a crucial point in its transition, I believe I can begin to fill this void."

Another, more immediate reason, known only to my closest friends, had been the actual impetus for my foray into Chinese language and culture. In high school, having been an avid kung fu movie fan and fanatic, I had grown weary of trying to read the bouncing English subtitles at the bottom of the bootleg copies on which I found myself spending my meager allowance. Needless to say, however, I chose to go with the first explanation, which was also absolutely true. As a result, the interviewer was impressed with my knowledge of the world and the maturity of my perspective, and the remainder of the interview was carried on in a very positive manner. In the end, I was directly quoted in the article in a way that made me seem exceptionally smart.

While the specifics of this interview are not important, I recall the anecdote because of the questions I was prompted to ask myself afterwards. Whence have I derived the courage to be different? Where and when did I begin to take a special interest in the road less traveled? How and why did I develop a passion, and even a sense of morbid responsibility, for thrusting myself into situations of probable discomfort? Why did I feel such a strong attraction toward undertaking a certain kind of ambassadorship?

It was, after all, this sense of ambassadorship that had given me comfort in the midst of environments that represented huge departures from my place of humble origin. Oftentimes I chided myself, humored by my self-appointed title of Ambassador Stroman. Yet the title and the role have served me well during my educational tour of duty through foreign lands both within and outside the United States. At times it definitely seemed that being an African-American New Yorker attending a relatively small New England liberal arts institution shared certain similarities with being an African-American in China. In both situations, I was clearly identified as the authority on all issues pertinent to "my people," and I found myself often in discussion of what it meant to be an African-American. I remember explaining to large numbers of people in certain towns in China that there was actually a sizable population of individuals like me who lived in America. And I remember also describing the process by which my ancestors were brought to the New World.

It was a pride in the responsibility of my station as an ambassador that had given me the resolve to press forward in the face of adversity and had reminded me on more than one occasion of my mandate to succeed in life despite external factors. My ambassadorship was a source from which I was able to draw strength and maintain focus during my last two years of college with a parent lingering on the precipice of death; I was driven by the understanding that my accomplishment was not mine alone, but rather something my loved ones and Prep for Prep could share in and be proud.

From an early age, I was imbued with a sense of personal responsibility to proudly represent my family, my community and Prep. With each small victory, I became endowed with a bit more courage and confidence in my ability to reconcile dreams that often differed markedly from the reality I experienced on my journey. I became quite comfortable with a life of constant scrutiny in environments in which culturally and socioeconomically I was not the norm. This experience has allowed me to draw strength from my own individuality. With this emotional training that I received during my high school years, it is no wonder that I have felt compelled to seek places where my voice and the voices of those like me are infrequently heard.

One of the most important lessons I have learned is that there is power implicit in the notion that who we are and what we do is ultimately a reflection on the institutions in which we are reared. In my case, the primary institutions have been my family and Prep. Through our daily interactions we have the potential to be instruments of social change. We are challenged to walk through the doors of opportunity opened by those who have gone before us while opening new doors for those who will come after us. We are encouraged to know and be known by the world in places where our voices too often go unrecognized.

Ambassadorship of the type of which I speak is the realization of one's significance in history outside of oneself. It is this principle that has guided my footsteps on the path of personal and professional advancement. It has been a source of great strength and a gift from Prep for Prep for which I am most grateful.

KEVIN STROMAN *is a member of Contingent XII. Born and raised in Manhattan, he graduated from The Allen-Stevenson School in 1993 and from Collegiate School in 1996 and received a B.A. in economics and Chinese language, cum laude, from Bates College in 2000. Kevin spent the fall of 1997 at NanJing DaXue (Nan King University), enrolled in its Chinese Language Immersion and Market Study Program, and the 1998-99 school year at the London School of Economics and Political Science. At Bates, he served as president of the Class of 2000 and was the recipient of the Benjamin E. Mays Scholar Award for Academic Excellence and the Charles A. Dana Award for Leadership and Academic Excellence. He was also named the Andersen Consulting Intern of the Year in 1999. Upon graduation, Kevin joined the Strategy and Business Architecture Group at Accenture, where he served initially as a government strategy business analyst (in New York City and Washington, D.C.) and currently is a lead strategy analyst in Accenture's Global Government Operating Growth Strategy Group.*

THE PARTY

by Karen Young

"I DON'T WANT A PARTY," I stated clearly.

"Yes, you do," my mother declared. "Graduating from law school and having a job waiting in September is a big deal for this family."

"Please, no party. I haven't taken the bar exams yet. I need all the luck I can get, and you're going to jinx me."

"No arguments. Pick a Saturday, because we're going to celebrate."

It was settled. I picked a Saturday in June, and my Aunt Marilyn volunteered her backyard. I invited a few close friends. I knew my mother's sisters would come, and a few friends of the family.

I was back in New York to stay. For seven years I had been away at school, first college in Rhode Island, then law school in Virginia. I had missed a lot in those seven years, and frankly I wasn't even sure that anyone in my family besides my mother and sister would want to celebrate my return. I wondered whether any of the seven cousins I grew up with would come. We were all close in age, and they had been the center of my world when I was very young. Then, when I entered Prep, my world very quickly grew much larger.

School became the center of my life. Other activities and other people became my priority.

For the past decade, my cousins and I had seen each other about twice a year, usually on Thanksgiving and Christmas. We were always friendly and polite, but there was not much real conversation. Even when I was in New York for summer and winter breaks, I was working or hanging out with friends from Prep or Brearley or Brown. Would they come to this party when the focus was on the very thing that made us different? Would they come to celebrate my success? Did they even consider earning a J.D. success?

As the facts stood, I was the one who had left the group. I couldn't hang out with them in junior high. There was always homework to do or someplace to go; there were slumber parties, visits to the theater, museum trips, choral practice, watching my friends take dance class. There was another world out there, and I wanted to be a part of it.

In high school, there was even more to do: rehearsing for school drama productions, writing editorials for the school's underground newspaper, writing letters to protest apartheid or other social ills, working at a series of after-school jobs, exploring Manhattan with my Brearley friends and, of course, lots and lots of homework. My life seemed very full. There was no time to linger.

While my cousins had a short bus ride or walk to school, my commute was an hour long. I spent most of my commute crammed into a No. 6 train. Seventeen subway stops separated 177th Street in the Bronx and 86th Street in Manhattan, and the subway became a place where I did some of my homework. In hindsight, my commute was priceless. I became acquainted with writers, some of whom became the most significant literary influences I have experienced. Langston Hughes, William Shakespeare, William Faulkner, Charles Dickens, Jean-Paul Sartre and Toni Morrison were just a few of the authors I came to know and love on the No. 6 train.

I could not share these experiences with my cousins. We had shared childhood secrets, toys and candy, but I could not share how I adored Shakespeare's sonnets, Mozart's music, Broadway musicals and the Metropolitan Museum of Art . . . how *Huis-Clos* and *Les Jeux Sont Faits* blew my mind . . . how it felt to be voted junior class president, when only a few years before I had felt out of place at school . . . how it felt to spend the summer in Paris when I was 17 . . . how it felt to go back to Paris three years later and fall in love with the city all over again . . .

I could not share how it felt to go to Brown and not be intimidated by the academic expectations, or how it felt to be called on in three classes during my first week of law school. Nor could I share how it felt to have three guys, one from Harvard, the second from Yale and the third from Princeton, come up to me during that same first week and ask me to be in their study group because they were impressed by my answers in class.

At holiday dinners over the years, my mother and aunts often spoke about how well I was doing. "Karen did this. Karen did that." But no one ever spoke about the challenges I faced. Never a word was uttered about my hatred and fear of math. Geometry, pre-calculus, calculus—how hard I worked on those horrid subjects. When I was thinking about removing pre-calculus from my schedule in 11th grade, Miss Conant, the chair of the math department, sat down with me and told me not to be afraid. She told me that *she* had no doubts about my ability. That short conversation made all the difference. I gritted my teeth and faced pre-calculus and then calculus.

None of this was talked about at family gatherings.

No one talked about my struggles at Brown. Juggling classes, a campus job and numerous activities while always worrying about financial aid and the ever-increasing loans: these were not fit subjects for family discussion. Seeing Ku Klux Klan membership flyers all around campus and not feeling safe because I was the only black woman in my dorm: this was not something to be shared with family members except for my mother and sister. I stayed across campus for a few days with a friend from Prep (three of us had gone to Brown together my freshman year) after returning to my dorm one night to find that the flyers I removed had been replaced with even more KKK flyers and racial epithets. There had been no family discussion about my having turned my fear into action by holding a dorm meeting and working to make the dorm a comfortable environment for everyone, or about how I had sat down and explained to a hulking football player in my dorm, known for physical confrontations, why his frequent use of the word "nigger" was offensive.

There was no talk about the challenges of law school or how I constantly worried about my grades, my mother's health and those ever-increasing school loans. I kept to myself how incredibly afraid I was of failing the New York and New Jersey bar exams, and how the specter of John F. Kennedy Jr.'s multiple bar failures haunted me. A Kennedy could afford to fail. I could not.

My cousins knew none of this. All they'd ever heard about were my "successes," and why would they want to endure more of the same at a party in my honor? If the tables had been turned, I don't think I would even show up. I would probably send a card. Best regards. Congratulations.

Yet I really wanted to call them and say "Hi" and ask them how they were doing. Maybe I would even summon up the courage to ask them if they were coming to the party. I really wanted to see these childhood friends. We had sprawled out on the floor and colored in our coloring books; they had often teased me for coloring outside the lines. We had played Uno and Trouble. We had shared Now-and-Laters and M&Ms. We had danced and jumped rope. All of a sudden, I realized I *needed* to see them. I had broadened my horizons, but now I needed to come home. Although I had learned many lessons over the years, I still believed that family is one of the most important things in life. I needed to connect with my cousins to prove to myself that I had not lost touch with my family. I needed to know that my decision through the years to pursue other interests had not irrevocably severed my ties with my familial peers.

June 17, 1995. Party day. Beautiful weather. Scrumptious food. Jamming music. Friends and family. I decided to enjoy the day even though I was still uneasy about celebrating prematurely. While many friends were in attendance, by midafternoon none of my seven cousins had yet arrived. Though disappointed, I figured that they, like me, knew we had grown apart and there was no real reason to come. To my surprise, however, as the afternoon progressed, most of those cousins did show up. They ate, talked and laughed, but mostly they just hung out with each other. There was no real conversation with me, only polite hellos and hugs, not much more.

As the party started to wind down, my mother presented me with a gold watch and a plaque from the family. I joked about getting plaques and watches when you retire, not when you first embark on your career.

The plaque read in part:

You Exemplify an Eagerness to Succeed and a Strong Sense of Identity and Commitment.
Your Family and Friends Honor Your Principles and Achievements.
We Wish You Good Luck, Good Health and Much Happiness.

A week later, I watched in shock as my cousins spoke to me on tape. My mother had hired a videographer to memorialize the party, and I had watched him goad my friends into telling wretched stories about me in front of the camera. Without my knowing it, he had also approached my cousins and asked each of them to say something. One after the other, they told me they were proud of me and wished me well. I had inspired one of them to apply to college. I had shown another that anything was possible. Two of them told me they were working hard to follow in my footsteps.

As I watched the tape, I looked for signs of inebriation, insincerity, jealousy or sarcasm. I found none. I looked for signs of nudging from my aunts and uncles. There were none. All I could see and hear was genuine pride and sincere good wishes.

It's a good thing I watched the tape alone, because I began to cry. Maybe it was the stress from studying for the bar exams. Maybe it was the relief that there was no ill will between my cousins and me. I had taken a different road, but I was still one of them. Maybe, after all, all the craziness of adolescence and early adulthood doesn't obliterate the secret handshakes and pacts of childhood.

The party, plaque and videotape gave me renewed energy and confidence to take and pass the New York and New Jersey bar exams. Since then, I have seen my cousins more often, though still not often enough. We have real conversations. We joke around. We share parts of our lives. Although there are still many parts of myself that I haven't shared with them, that doesn't matter as much anymore. What matters is that I am not a stranger in my family. My place in the family did not vanish over the years; it simply evolved.

For better or for worse, my cousins and I are moving forward in our own distinct ways. Nevertheless, my cousins know who I really am. No matter what I do or where I go, to them I will always be the girl who colors outside the lines.

KAREN YOUNG *is a member of Contingent IV. Born in Brooklyn and raised in the Bronx, Karen graduated from The Brearley School in 1988 and received a B.A. in political science (with honors) from Brown University in 1992. Subsequently, she earned a J.D. from the University of Virginia School of Law in 1995. From 1995 to 2000, Karen was a commercial litigation associate in the New York office of Thelen Reid & Priest, LLP. Currently, she is a staff attorney at IBM, providing legal support in the financial services and and life sciences industries. At Prep for Prep, Karen was head of the Summer Advisory System in 1990 and 1991 and has been an active member of the Annual Alumni Giving Campaign Committee since its inception, serving for several years as a vice chair. She has been chair of the 7th and 8th Annual Alumni Giving Campaigns.*

THE INNER WORK OF CARVING A SELF

by SARAH SAYEED

"Out of the night that covers me
Black as the pit from pole to pole
I thank whatever gods may be
For my unconquerable soul."
—FROM "INVICTUS" BY WILLIAM ERNEST HENLEY

HERE I AM: TRANSPORTED FROM the Asian continent to America, raised in the Bronx, a graduate of Prep, Chapin, Princeton and the University of Pennsylvania's Annenberg School for Communication, standing before students in a third college. The Baruch student body is considered among the most diverse in the nation. Many in the School of Public Affairs are from lower- or middle-class families, and most are full-time workers coming to school at night. These are real people with real-life concerns, balancing and juggling work, studies, marriage, parenthood and community obligations. They are much like me. Yet, somehow, I feel different.

What is it that sets me apart? On the first day of the course, my students see a woman with a long skirt and long-sleeved shirt, topped by a *hijab*, a scarf that observant Muslim women wear. So I come into the classroom distinct in appearance from most professors in whose company these students have sat. Yet, somehow, the differences between us feel deeper than appearances. They are defined by our life struggles and the meanings we ascribe to them. And it is the concept of differences that excites me to teach about using communication to broaden thinking, deepen understanding and create stable bridges between individuals and groups.

Through my struggles, I have learned that differences among individuals and groups, and even internal polarities, are valuable for personal and community growth. My travels from India to Baruch have been awash with encounters in which I have been pulled in multiple, even opposing, directions. I continue to examine facets of my identity and face the same question from new vantage points: who do I want to be as a Muslim American female of Indian and lower-middle-class origins?

I formulated my identity question at an early age. I was compelled to do so by virtue of the differences between the South Asian Muslim culture I was born into and the American culture in which I was raised. No matter whether the choices were simple or difficult, their implications felt and feel weighty. In 1976, as a new third-grader in America, I faced peers who performed a Native American war chant when they first saw me, because they confused being an Indian from India with being an American Indian. I ignored their teasing. In fifth grade, I decided I no longer wanted to wear my hair in two braids every day. Even this choice entailed a decision about which model of femininity I wished to adopt: the girl who is Indian Muslim or a new all-American. By the end of seventh grade, my parents had decided they wanted me enrolled in an all-female academic environment, and through Prep for Prep, I landed at Chapin.

But the gender homogeneity at Chapin did not hide other heterogeneities and other disparities. In five years of commuting from the Bronx to the Upper East Side, I daily crossed from my own blocks marred by arson, drug abuse and urban poverty into a neighborhood of buildings with doormen and homes with Persian carpets and expensive paintings. I continued to be aware of myself as racially and religiously different from my peers, but I was lucky to have teachers who valued my unique perspectives.

When I left home for college, I traveled from the same dilapidated blocks to Princeton's Gothic arches. I left the spiritual comfort of home, parents and Chapin and entered a class in which the ratio of men to women was three to one. I had to figure out how to deal with the other half of the human race, and honestly, I thought we were from different planets. That was years before I ran across John Gray's book *Women Are from Venus and Men Are from Mars.*

At Princeton, I declared my major as sociology and my minor as Near East studies. In my junior year, I went to the Netherlands, West Germany, Yugoslavia and England as part of the Antioch Women's Studies Program. During this semester abroad, I met social service providers who assisted immigrant families, and I relived my own struggle in the acculturation of women much like me—newly transported from the East into a Western cultural context. I returned home more pro-women than ever. I insisted that I would reconcile my feminism and my religious identity, despite the common refrain that feminism and Islam are incompatible.

As my social consciousness blossomed, I decided I wanted to have a career that would help me "make a difference." I reconnected with Prep, where I worked for some time before I felt the urge to return to graduate school. At Prep, "making a difference" meant helping students and alumni to make the most of Prep-sponsored opportunities that promoted their personal development. "Making a difference" now means teaching communication and doing research in a public service–oriented institution.

Between graduate school and Baruch, however, other layers of my identity came to the fore: I married and became a mother. Working and having a decent family life became part of the equation that had to be balanced. I also became far more immersed in my faith identity than I had been until that time, and began to wear my spirituality comfortably. I adopted the *hijab* as an expression of my commitment to live out the beauty of my faith and to be a good role model for my son. As I learned more about Islam, I came to see myself first and foremost simply as a *person,* and thus the identity questions with which I had for so long grappled became more muted. But just when I thought I was settling into life and my humanity, I entered into September 11, 2001.

I am still unable to grasp the events and meanings of that day, but like everyone else, I am shaken. For several months I felt intellectually paralyzed, unable to focus on my research about adolescents and drug prevention. I started to think that my research and writing in health communication was a moot point, not at all "making a difference." All of a sudden, I wondered: for whom in the world do I want to make a difference? It relates to a basic tenet I teach my students: know your audience, and use your knowledge to shape your message.

In my life choices are messages about my abilities and my values. My audience is the group of people whom I want to serve with my work, as well as those who will hear and observe my legacy. To which group did I belong? To humanity? America? Muslims? Women? Minorities? The poor? What did I want to communicate, and to whom? As I faced again the same inner questions about the interplay of faith, gender, nationality, race and class, I realized that I had assumed too quickly that my life answers had been figured out. It has been strange to find many of my lived internal tensions thrust now into public discourse in the paradigm of a clash of civilizations. I have had to quietly remove myself from the jarring frame of a clash, to fall back on the hope of a dialogue that creates wholeness from fragments.

I have also decided to do something unorthodox for someone on a tenure track. Into my third year of the tenure clock, with only two years left to go, I added a focus on media coverage of the current detentions of Middle Easterners and Muslims into my research program. Perhaps a cost of this change will be that I proceed more slowly on health research, and that I publish less. But as I told a colleague, I have only one life to live. I need to be engaged in research that I find substantive and meaningful.

What carries me through the oppositional pulling is a quest to live one word: *integrity.* The Random House College Dictionary defines integrity as "the adherence to moral and ethical principles; soundness of moral character; and honesty." What is more meaningful to me about the noun *integrity* is that it has the same Latin root as the verb *integrate*: "to bring together or incorporate parts into a whole." The meaning of *integrate* is precisely how I define my life goals. My quest has been for wholeness.

The completeness for which I strive requires intellectual commitment and fearless self-examination. I cannot allow the pain that sometimes accompanies growth to encumber me, and I must strip down experiences to their bare essential meanings. I must consciously strive to retain a sense of simplicity, despite the complexity inherent in my life questions and experiences. All of us have to live through the struggles of life. All of us give meaning to them, and we move forward. I believe I, too, can do this work of finding out just who I want to be. An actively pursued education has repeatedly exposed me to new people, new ideas and new ways of being. But more importantly, in the skills imparted by my teachers and their firm faith in my potential are the hammer and the anvil that I need to make sense of these new encounters in ways that promote the unique expression of my selfhood.

Prep has remained as a reference point in my life journey. My choice of profession is a reflection of my passionate commitment to the principle that is at the heart of Prep for Prep: *Education can transform lives.* Prep has certainly provided me with access to elite educational institutions and nurtured in me a strong faith in my own intellect. Its most significant contribution, however, is that it has planted in me the desire and courage to seize the opportunities in each new environment I have entered. It has given me the confidence that I can chart my own life.

SARAH SAYEED *is a member of Contingent III. Born in India, Sarah immigrated to the United States when she was eight years old and was raised in the Bronx. She graduated from The Chapin School in 1986 and received a B.A. in sociology and Near East studies, cum laude, from Princeton University in 1990. Sarah subsequently earned a Ph.D. in communications from the University of Pennsylvania's Annenberg School for Communications in 1998. At Penn, she served as both a teaching assistant and a research assistant and was awarded a Dissertation Fellowship. Following completion of her doctoral work, Sarah remained at the Annenberg School as a postdoctoral fellow in Health Communication (1998–2000). In September 2000, she assumed her current position as an assistant professor of public affairs at Baruch College in New York City. She is the author and coauthor of numerous government reports and monographs, two UNICEF reports, and chapters on the development of effective antidrug media campaigns in two books.*

VII.
PREP FOR LIFE

FOR ME, THE HIGHLIGHTS OF A YEAR AT PREP are the often unscheduled, unanticipated moments. A senior at Yale calls to talk excitedly about plans to go abroad next year and teach in West Africa. A junior at Williams stops by my office and proceeds to lecture me on the imperative of studying Japanese. A newly minted graduate of Georgetown arrives with a plaque from his mother and the news that he has been awarded a Jack Cooke Kent Fellowship that will fund his entire law school career. A young woman who is moving up the management ladder of a major consumer products company stops by with two of her children when she is "home" to visit her mother for the weekend.

I think back to Prep's own admission folders over which I agonized, to the first tentative steps each of these alumni took toward becoming a real student, to the risks, the obstacles, the stereotypes they were determined to challenge. And I remember that each of them worked as a Prep advisor and was by turns both stern and compassionate with other youngsters who were trying desperately to be like them. And I know that each of them holds to a profound belief that people have the capacity to help others change the direction of their lives.

If this book were being compiled 10 years from now, some of the stories would be about the intervention by the Undergraduate Affairs Unit at critical moments in the lives of some ultimately very successful individuals. But such specific "Prep to the Rescue" stories would be far less compelling, I believe, than the stories included in this section. In different ways, they each suggest the ongoing influence of Prep on the lives of its undergraduates and college graduates in terms of their values, their sense of purpose, their peer network and the strength many derive from a shared sense of history and of having played a role in the making of that history.

Three summers ago, one of the advisory units chose the phrase "Prep for Life" to emblazon on the backs of their T-shirts. If we said the right things to them when they were young, and if we said those things with enough conviction, the echoes of conversations long past will bear fruit for years to come. I believe the T-shirts were an acknowledgment of this.

"GET ON THE BUS WITH A DOG ON ITS SIDE"

by PRISCILLA AQUINO

i. angels

Striking Forward

In young faces lie places of doubt
As body becomes new and curiosity brings new pleasures
So you battle street wars, you grow on uncharted land
No one quite knows like you—working from dark section
of room to lit centers of stage
Finding hope in baseball uniforms and talent show spotlights

If I could explain how much I see in your big bright eyes
dipped in past struggles of parents
It has taken second and third generations—counting scars on hands,
face, feet
If you could know that all that was created in this classroom would try
to give faith that life's plan goes beyond the high school acceptances
and stares from downtown passers-by

Keep head turned up searching, wishing, praying, wanting—fighting
Sun shining for you to find your chosen path
Growing towards a mañana so bright you will need a shade in tall trees
Enjoy the walk and always look for the tomorrow you never imagined

JUNE 2002

AND AT THAT MOMENT THEY CLAPPED FOR ME. Twenty-eight eighth-graders, South Bronx raised, they had just found out that I had graduated from Harvard only months before becoming their teacher. Deafening to my ears was the ripping open of the box marked "Do Not Open Until . . ." I had completed a process of taking all that I had experienced, all that I had learned, all that I had earned and all that I had been given, and turning it into something for someone else. Nothing could quite compare to opening eyes and hearts to the knowledge, the lessons in life, that others had shared years before. At the end of that school year, their message was clear—thank you for believing in us. I hoped they truly understood the message was mutual—thank you for believing in me.

That hot, muggy June day in 2002, my students glowed with an unmistakable pride. In them I saw all the dreams I had ever had for myself; in their faces, in their walk, I saw that fearless spirit exuded on days when everything seems right. Looking out into a packed auditorium, with tears making trails down my face, I knew I'd had something to do with the spirit of the students sitting before me. When they cried in my arms as we posed in front of cameras, I thanked them for letting me into their lives. I'd had no idea when I sat in my bare classroom 10 months earlier, surrounded by no more than seven mismatched tables and a handful of chairs, that so much would happen when my students came through that door. I had planned to teach for as long as I could remember, and yet at that moment I asked myself for the first time, "What do you think you are going to do?" The human spirit is divine and is able to derive so much from the spirit of others.

United States history, the subject I taught, included comments from the Latino and black students about how the National Guard never found its way to Crotona Park, and discussions about the Young Lords and Black Panthers making changes. Many of my students had never left the Bronx, so we traveled together through books, pictures and trips around the city. I wanted them to demand more for themselves and also more *from* themselves. I saw that "more" in the faces of the young people who graduated that day. After that year, I don't think I could ever look back and not be satisfied with the decisions that had brought me to this Bronx classroom. Standing before these students, I knew I had already begun to be that leader, that catalyst for change, that Prep's mission statement predicted.

I thought about the teachers who spoke through me as I led lectures and discussions and found an animated tongue, hoping to provoke thoughts, questions and most of all arguments. Children have an amazing way of reminding you of the "buts," and that is what will always make the clock tick and the tables turn.

ii. nuestro lugar

$128,000 later . . . this I learned

Draped in the sweat of father working in factory
We packed up yearbook, new college sale items from K-Mart,
promising to keep in touch with friends
Determined to not turn into TV character sipping on screwdrivers
while A grades turned into B grades
Promised to never change while trippin' into new music
Redefining friendship as friends became family that woke
you up in the morning and turned off your light
as you fell asleep pens open books unread
As family saw your tears because you came home
And when the day to day drowned you family never lost faith
never believed you less because you failed any test or could not get
out of bed too tired to fight battles that Tuesday
So while you grew and learned loss, your eyes kept family standing
When going home became harder your now extended family
understood and laughed tears away in late meals and babble
I see silhouettes of your faces crying, laughing, but mostly fighting
And as we dance across our stage—taller—we dance together
In the footsteps of Flaco, Pigón, y Lupe you can hear the drummin'
Y allí unimos past and present on one stage.

JUNE 2001

THE "NEVER COULD HAVE BEENS" ceased to exist the day I stood in the Tercentenary Theater and wore a black robe. Surrounded by the friends who had become my hermanas and hermanos, we led the graduating class out to our seats, by happenstance belonging to the house that led the line that year. I remember thinking, as I walked across the Mather Courtyard, that I had not seen a more sunny day in Cambridge. The sun gods had paid us a visit that made our parents' eyes sparkle and our smiles larger. It was a blessing to graduate by house, as my Prep and Harvard family could enjoy this day together. I never would have imagined that the beautiful events of college, all culminating in this ceremony, could be shared with my hermanas: Maria Cruz and Manuela Arciniegas, whom I had met when I was 10 and 14, respectively, and who had shared Prep memories as celebrants at Hotchkiss, as advisors, as roommates, but most of all as familia. Here, in the sun-dappled courtyard, our families recognized each other, and each complimented the others on their daughters' success. This long journey had been made with the comfort of familiar faces. It was only right that, on this day, these same faces were there to support and enjoy all that had come to be. My little sister, Sakai, one of "my kids" from my first year as an advisor, also came to celebrate this day. From all stages of my life came people to enjoy this day. I remember walking across the stage, looking for my father, mother and brother, and pointing the oversize crimson envelope in their direction. This belonged to them, too.

Mama and Papa had taken three days off and arrived on Class Day to hear my friend Amma Ghartey-Tagoe address our class and to hear our guest speaker, Bono from U2. They had invested in a digital camera to have a record of the event, thinking "regular" pictures could not capture the laughs and stories that we shared as our families sat and ate together.

That night we all gathered at Maria's home and brought our families so they could converse freely in Spanish as we barbecued in the yard. That night was shared with the closest members of my extended family, with Maria, Manuela, Kiara, Lizzie and Cielo. Maria's little sisters tried to play basketball with Kiara's little sisters, my mother discussed Costa Rica with Kiara's stepmom, Kiara's father and my father stood over the fire, and the powerful energy of conquest was radiant in our glow.

That moment is what Harvard was to me—a translated version of the Harvard that has been shown in movies and written about in books. I was not supposed to go there and live the same version that my classmates lived; I was supposed to live a new and equal version. When I looked out into the crowd, diploma in hand, I knew that I had done just that, and that, in doing so, we had changed Harvard forever. I remembered visiting the campus in the fall of 1996 and asking about the role that Latinos played at Harvard. An African-American student told me that Latinos did their own thing, and he was not really aware of what their role was on campus. Above all else, the impetus behind wanting to come to Harvard stemmed from my determination to make the Latino voice one of which the Harvard community was aware. In my loud four years, as a community, we had accomplished that.

iii. triumph of heart

battlefield

joined in the name of Mexican glory
they spend their days off in marked fields as dirty bodies
a world repainted with Adidas cleats while drinking a doble equis
con la carne asando they go home to a world where Aztlán
is not just a slogan
where their eyes hold the manuscript of post-invasion

allí over the sunset in the playground
where minimum wage is not what makes a starter
where the only thing tus carnales look at is the color of uniform and
the pass and the goals
donde la Raza can comfortably sit on the terrace of the manzana city

allí over the sunset where the veijitas cook as if back on stoves in casas
sweating over flames
with hands moving tan rapido to make your plate

allí over the sunset no one cares if you have no education
and clean floors for a living
where the inglish you speak goes unused
blows back in the trees, is swallowed like serpent to eagle
here lo que importa is your game.

SEPTEMBER 1991

"THE NIGHT BEFORE MY FIRST DAY at Nightingale, I had a long talk with Papá. 'There are going to be people with more than you, but you remember you have more in your heart than any gold or money that anyone on this earth has.'" I wrote this about my father for my college applications. He is the inspiration behind so much of my life that I can only think to write about him as I write about my life. Born in Cuatla Morelos, Mexico, Papá came to this country, as many immigrants have done, for a better life. He promised me that even as we made sacrifices to make ends meet, he would always continue to pay my tuition year after year. He had always wanted more for me. Papá realized that Prep had opened the possibilities, and he never looked back after that. During my six years at Nightingale, he came to soccer games, cultural nights, award ceremonies, always sitting along the side of the auditorium or the churches. I would always walk up to him, and I would always receive a warm hug. He taught me to want what nearly everyone else had decided was not within my reach. Papá insisted on normalizing the experience I was having by expecting big things from me and silently smiling as I came into my own.

SEPTEMBER 1997

THE DAY MY PARENTS DROPPED ME OFF at college, I entered unknown territory that changed our relationship. My friend Elbert had volunteered to drive me to school, since no one in my family knew how to drive. He tried to comfort my parents on the way to Cambridge, knowing that on the way back to New York he would have to continue to talk to them about the world I was about to enter. I knew that it would not stop my mother from sobbing or my father from worrying, and yet we all knew this was the way it should be. Stepping onto Harvard's campus, I became a member of the same university that had housed presidents, authors, politicians and so many others who had gone on to do great things. We were all somehow aware of this as we turned onto Mass Avenue. The red brick buildings seemed to say, "Come on in . . . we were expecting you."

After we had located my dormitory and carried my belongings to my room, we looked at each other in my new home, and I knew that we were all scared about what was about to be my life for four years. My father pulled me aside, saying, "This is one of the most important days of our lives. Here I know that you will grow and change. Know you will never be alone and that you deserve all that this place can give you." I handed him a letter that I had written for Papá, Mamá and Paolo. I knew that eloquence would escape me as I stood blubbering, and yet I knew that I would have so much to say. We kept our good-bye brief, but all of it was uttered as we cried into each other's arms, knowing we would simply miss each other. The irony of the day was illuminated when I later reached for the wallet that my parents had accidentally taken with them back to New York, leaving me with no ID card to enter buildings and eat in dining rooms. Once I got back into my room, I sat among my boxes, good-luck cards and so many pictures, and just released. I thought of the day that my father had arrived in this country with only one hundred dollars and the directions to get on the bus with a dog on its side. I had a different challenge, but I knew he had prepared me well to make Harvard mine. College had begun, and laughing as tears fell from my eyes only seemed right.

iv. lessons de mamá

The Woman Who Raised Me

I remember looking at my mother, mad. Why did she never do anything in her life.
She never finished school and although it has been 26 years since she came to the U.S. she still insists that she cannot speak English.
She stayed home with the nenes, a good wife.

Her reluctance to be 'American strong' used to make me feel like she had low hopes, I was choosing to look at her like a converted gringa
A feminist badge-wearing niñita who thought she knew everything about power and success.
I thought there was a clear distinction between the independent world I planned to enter and the submissive and weak woman I saw.
I guess I was looking the wrong way.

One of mis abuelas, the grandmother in México belongs to a large family.
A strong man leads them, but a stronger woman holds them together.
He was taught to order the cleaning and maintenance of the home.
She learned to comfort hungry cries and bitter hearts.
Along the way she lost her own cares, because family always comes first to a woman.
Between the cooking and the cleaning she created power and hope in children devoid of a dream.

Today she stares at a world so fast with its internet access to people that do not matter to her; in a modern world too far to mean anything.
Instead she takes care of a home remembering years in fields, years in kitchens, years in poverty.
She learned that poverty cares very little about how good you are to your children or how well you can cook.

These women have so many parts to their day as the wife that inspires
As the mother that gives herself to her children as they criticize her un-American ways
As the woman that maintains pride at all times and always demands respect.
She knows what it is to be twice un-human.
Her strength as a bronzed mujer survived is what I want.
There is no formula guaranteed, maybe that means that we all have a chance to find that power.
Yet I know I have seen the power at its best in the woman who raised me.

1991–1997

SHE WANTED ME TO GO TO BED ON MOST NIGHTS that I insisted on staying up to finish work. I used to think she wanted me to fail. I had not learned to love her way of trying to take care of me. It took going to a school full of women and living with a new set of women to understand my Mamá. She was the rock of my family, and no one wanted to acknowledge that because she stayed home and did not have a job to go to daily. No one ever stopped to think about the magical things that were right around the house; clean rooms, filled fridge and warm meals. This was not enough because we had decided that the work regulated by a time clock is more valuable than the work that never ends. As I became more aware of the various roles that women have had in society, I came to appreciate the role that my mother played in my life. The point was for me to evolve as I focused on me at an all-girls school and as I treaded a new path in college.

Learning Mamá was learning what could be as we praise all that is good and all that makes someone else's day a better one. It fell into place with the help of the women who surrounded me at school, and it became even clearer when I heard some of the most impressive professors at Harvard discuss what it meant to create a family. Time away from home has been time to understand the power of women as the force that connects members of a family and holds the pages from the past. Mamá led me to a place of freedom from rigid formulas, and there I find the me that blends the past, the present, and the future that I will create for myself.

v. at nightingale

Whispers

And in walked this Jewish man
in what was most unlike the salsa on my walkman
or the graffiti writing on concrete Spanglish walls
pero allí we found each other as I fought new language
you translated in your tired eyes and belligerent mouth

wanting the earth and sky to have a different tint—a tint you did not see Shanghai underneath your feet
there you helped me shine with the distinct glow of endless lust for más
lost twelve-year-old y un hombre cansado we found peace
now unable to see the end of the horizon as light hits the ground
and the serenade of children fills my head with a familiar rhythm
in that delirious state between lying and rising you gave me the spirit to move
when ears did not want to listen
when I did not know how to stand center stage
when no one could get angry
when I could not stop being angry
and there you stood at the corner of the stage when they called my name
scholarship and praise—you made them consider me
pouring soul into forty-five minute sessions that transported age-old understanding of what can happen if you keep eyes wide open
there in the distant mist I see my dreams.

1993–1997

AT NIGHTINGALE, ONE TEACHER made it his particular goal to help me reach my full potential. Mr. Feig refused to let me want anything but *more* for myself. He told me once that students like me were the reason he continued to teach. A Holocaust survivor, who refused to allow us to be stenographers, he loved history and teaching about the events that have shaped our world. He taught us to think. It was a simple task, really, but one that gave trouble to many students who were just as happy giving him what they thought he wanted to hear. He changed what "education" meant to me. Sitting in his class, I saw the power of an educator who bothers to challenge students and who demands that students challenge themselves.

Mr. Feig and I would sit in the cafeteria and talk about life after Nightingale. He believed that I could go where I wanted and never stopped talking to me about many things that were so foreign to me. I hear his words now, years after he passed, and I know that his spirit brings my classroom an energy that makes history come alive. I hear his words through my voice, as I try to elevate the desire to learn and the hope that education not only brings you more but allows you to *be* more.

vi. holding hands

Stage Fright

curled around each other
rainbow of opportunity in unknown faces
shiny bright eyes that could only hear half the words from speeches
itching to get to pizza and cake
playing with stem of rose
letting petals drop when getting rid of thorns
high-pitched voices lifting heads from books
busing around the city
new streets
parando cada vez a new name was read
pausing as taller led
learning about century-old traditions as they happen
names engraved onto mahogany plaques
etching into a part of history once denied
hand to hand we make history our own.

AUGUST 1995

THE SECOND TIME I SAT ON THE STAGE in the Chapel, the main auditorium of Trinity School, I had flashbacks to a day that seemed like a blur four years later. I heard my name walking me onto that stage filled with the same pride that had filled my frizzy head in 1991. Before Prep, I had never been a part of solemn assemblies, during which students actually listened as speeches were given. There I sat, eyes glued to Mr. Simons, who promised me everything I could imagine if I kept the faith, if I believed in myself, if I continued to take from and give back to this community, a small part of which, merely one contingent of students and their summer advisors, sat before him. Those same eyes still believed the words that promised forward motion. As an advisor, I had the privilege of having those whom I always called "my kids" ask me why they needed to attend classes during those long summer days, why they had to endure the long bus rides to and from their homes. The only response I could give them was one that would be with me for years, as I came to answer the question for myself. Vehemently I assured these younger beauties that it all had a greater meaning, so great that the rays of the sun could only explain how big it could all be.

Moving-Up Day[1] was an event that all Prep students must remember. Mr. Simons called each student's name, perhaps the first time most of the children had ever heard their name amplified by a microphone. Leading each unit onto the stage were two advisors, who followed a path that years earlier they had experienced for the first time. As the students were called, each one received a rose that represented the beauty of each individual child. While advisors and students sat onstage in six rows, Mr. Simons began to discuss a half-empty and half-full coffeepot. This pot would ask us to think about how to look at life. There as we thought about looking at life in different ways, it meant thinking about Prep as a helper in the pathways left uncovered. Young eyes looked on as "I can't" began to leave our language. There we heard that it was up to us to use the tools being placed in our hands to figure out where we wanted to take ourselves. As we recited "Invictus" line by line, we were saying that we knew that we were to take this world into our own hands, conquer this world and make dreams into realities. We said those lines together as a new community, and there we accepted this new responsibility to want more and to work together to achieve more. There as each individual stood and helped the next individual stand, we symbolized that community, that link that we would learn to depend on years later. The unbroken chain of administrators, advisors and students proceeded down the aisle of the Chapel. The silence was unique, almost cathartic. At the end, we stood in a circle holding hands

[1] Moving-Up Day celebrates a contingent's successful completion of its first Summer Session.

in the Trinity dining room. There we raised hands and said the one word that reminded us that the journey would be shared. We said "Together."

Sitting on that stage at the end of each Summer Session, during the five summers I served as an advisor, I heard the Moving-Up Day speech, understanding it all more each time, as I became the keeper of this world that had been all talk before I was able to see the development, contingent after contingent, of "my kids," year after year.

Knowing that only Prep students had sat and shared this ceremony on this stage, that we were participating in the early years of a tradition that would be remembered years later, made us a part of our own history. We were creating the family that Prep would always be for us. For many of the Prep students whom I know, there is that one friend, colleague, classmate, wife, husband, soul mate and kindred spirit who always understood. There is that one person who remembers the T-shirt slogans, talent shows, speeches, performances, marriages and children. The tie became solidified on that stage when I was 11 years old and each person, having stood up, reached to help the next person stand, and we held hands eternally connected in memory and desire. That linking of hands finds us chasing after each other's children, crying at each other's weddings, and saying good-bye as maybes become plane rides. The family has always understood that we must leave each other so that we can each do our own growing. Every summer session has come to an end with the same bittersweet tension in the air as students cry into each other's arms and as advisors look on with a certain nostalgia, knowing that these moments will become all too familiar. Those two summers and school year of classes, of bonding, of struggle, had exalted the possibilities, and so much that could not be measured in final exams or faculty comments had emerged for each of us. The very last summer I worked with the Summer Advisory System, I wrote in my journal, *"We always cry—five years, and it actually hurts more with each year. I guess it is because they are not a job, they are us. We are working with ourselves."* We are always helping each other stand up and holding hands as we discover the world together.

vii. growing pains

Pa'lante

Draped in effigies of santos y virgenes
Bronzed defiance peaks from my shoulders
Holding someone else's babies as some held me
Allí shine in my gaze I believe in the mañanas that seep out
from misty days in the laugh of children that can only
make you believe that rainbows lead to the pathway of
faith and that young hands can only create freshly molded
statues standing closer to the rays that beat on trees outside
of classrooms
Believing the only determinant is ganas—the all-mighty right
of want
Y allí en el amanecer que toca cada día
Allí I can raise head from pillow and know that it lies in them
and what I can teach them to desire
Caminemos—we have much left to uncover.

SUMMER 1991

LITERATURE WAS FIRST PERIOD. I didn't know why they called it that, but it sounded like the most important class I would have that summer. English was my second language, but I could not wait to understand the literature that no public school had bothered to integrate into its Macmillan series of Language Arts books. Sitting there in the warm rooms of Trinity School, it was solidified in my mind that this was a preferred way to learn. That first summer took its toll on my energy as I struggled to keep up with the work, and as I learned what it would take to get more out of every day. The memory of those two summers are glazed in the days that I spent finishing essays while the heat drained the energy away from my body. At home, water and strawberries placed by my side for fuel, little did I understand that from afar my mother looked on confused as I refused to leave the table until it all looked the way I wanted it to look. The next day in class, I fought to keep up and wondered if I would make it that first summer, if I would be invited to continue with Wednesday and Saturday classes in the fall. And yet there is this interestingly painful memory of "singing" at the Talent Show that preceded the ceremony on Moving-Up Day, the type of singing only an 11-year-old can do, filled with joy and no musical ability. The school year and second summer of classes would almost fly by without my being able to slow down to see them pass.

Cesar Chavez once said, "Once social change begins, it cannot be reversed. You cannot uneducate the person who has learned to read. You cannot humiliate the person who has pride. And you cannot oppress the people who are not afraid anymore." His words, when I read them years later, rang true, for I had known when I was 11, that I could never be the same person again.

Yet I remember the room I had at Hotchkiss, where my contingent had come for four days to celebrate our successful completion of the Preparatory Component. I sat in my dormitory room, knowing that this was the sort of place I would find myself in more and more. I knew that much, but I was not one hundred percent sure of what it meant. It was all so new. Full of anxiety, I thought about the future, dreaming under a starry night that was so uncommon in Washington Heights. Looking into the glass of the doors that lead to the Hotchkiss dining room that last night of the trip, I saw a vision of older people who were going to be in important places. I caught my reflection for a moment and thought about the world I had seen for six years before coming to Prep. I knew that I would continue to be a part of an educational system that would decide for many other children the difference between the two paths I could have taken. There in that glass pane, I saw myself teaching students just like me. In this image of me teaching, I was standing in front of students of color and using the lessons and materials that my teachers at Prep had used with me. It was to become a recurring dream, one that stayed with me long after trips to Hotchkiss had become only fond memories.

Translations of Spanish Words and Phrases

a doble equis—a type of beer
allí—there
caminemos—let's walk
casas—homes
con la carne asando—with the meat grilling
donde la Raza—the race (referring specifically to the Mexican community)
familia—family
ganas—will
gringa—a white American woman
hermanas—sisters
hermanos—brothers
lo que importa—what matters
mañana—tomorrow
manzana—apple
más—more
mis abuelas—my grandmothers
mujer—woman
nenes—kids, children
niñita—little girl
nuestro lugar—our home, our place
Pa'lante—Forward!
parando cada vez—stopping every time
pero allí—but there
santos y virgenes—saints and virgins
tan rapido—so fast
tus carnales—your peers
veijitas—old ladies
y allí en el amanecer que toca cada dia—and then in the dawn that touches each day
y allí unimos—and there we unite
y un hombre cansado—and a tired man

PRISCILLA SAMADY ZAMORA AQUINO *is a member of Contingent XIII. Born and raised in Washington Heights, she graduated from The Nightingale-Bamford School in 1997 and received a B.A. in sociology, cum laude, from Harvard University in 2001. In addition, she earned a Latin-American Studies Certificate and completed the Teacher Certification Program offered to undergraduates by the Harvard Graduate School of Education. She was the recipient of a grant that funded her senior thesis research assessing the education system in Cuba. During her last three years at Harvard, Priscilla served as an undergraduate minority recruiting coordinator for the Admissions Office. Upon graduation, she spent the summer as a research intern at the After-School Corporation and then began her teaching career at I.S. 129 in the Bronx, where she taught social studies to seventh- and eighth-graders (two of her six sections were bilingual classes). She is currently teaching U.S. history to eighth-graders at a Title 1 school in the Austin Independent School District in Texas. At Prep for Prep, in addition to her years as an advisor, Priscilla served as head of the School-Year Advisory Corps during 1996-97 and as assistant head of the Summer Advisory System in 1998.*

TELLING THE TRUTH

by STACEY IRIZARRY

I LIED TO EVERYONE ABOUT MY FATHER'S DEATH. I said he died of lung cancer. Accepting AIDS as the cause of my father's death was difficult; telling others the truth was unthinkable.

The repeated lies occupied my mind, preventing me from dealing with my grief, drawing me downward in an emotional spiral. Usually a motivated and ambitious student, I became reclusive and directionless. I spent my days sitting through lectures with a lump in my throat and my nights alone, walking aimlessly around the Princeton campus or sitting quietly in the library trying to force myself to read. My grades dropped dramatically, and the resident advisor asked me to consider taking a leave of absence.

One afternoon, after having received an especially poor grade on an organic chemistry exam and feeling like I'd reached bottom in my academic and personal life, I opened my mailbox and found a copy of Prep for Prep's Annual Report. There, alongside words of praise for Prep students and alumni in Mr. Simons' traditional opening letter, was a black-and-white picture of me in a lab coat conducting an experiment. The previous summer, Prep had set up an internship opportunity for me with Dr. Anthony Cerami at Rockefeller University in New York City and had sent a photographer to capture a few moments of me at work in the laboratory. It was one of those images that had been chosen to represent the typical Prep student whom Mr. Simons describes in his letters. I wondered how someone who felt as sad and lost as I did at that moment could be someone whom Prep for Prep viewed as a high-achieving member of the Prep community. Looking back at me from that glossy page was a person who was strong, smart and dedicated. Would I ever be that person again?

While reading Mr. Simons' letter, I was reminded that courage and integrity were two of the core values that Prep instilled in each of us. I knew I had to have the courage to redirect my life. I also realized that my emotional response to my father's death could be no longer an obstacle, but my inspiration. During the course of his illness, my father had succumbed to profound mental deterioration. In his final days, he could barely speak and he didn't recognize me. As an aspiring scientist, I wanted to know why this was happening and how it could be stopped or prevented. As a Prep student, I had always felt an obligation to give back to the community. It became clear that my way of giving back would be through dedicating my efforts to scientific inquiry. I decided to major in chemistry, and throughout college I took on challenging course loads. The sense that the Prep community believed in me inspired me to believe in myself, which motivated me during many late nights of studying in the chemistry library. I spent my summers doing research in labs, bringing me closer to my goal of going to graduate school. Studying basic science-related aspects of neurodegeneration and neurological disorders would become my passion and, ultimately, my career.

During my final years of college, I became an outspoken advocate for AIDS education, counseling and research. I told people about the impact my father had had on me—both in his life and in his death—with the hope of inspiring them to be true to themselves. Maintaining my integrity meant not ever feeling shame about who I am, where I came from or what I had experienced in life. That afternoon in the mailroom, as the lessons I learned at Prep once more helped me change my life, I knew that I would never lie about my father's death again.

STACEY IRIZARRY *is a member of Contingent VII. Born in Manhattan, she grew up in Brooklyn. A National Merit Scholar, Stacey graduated from Poly Prep Country Day School in Brooklyn in 1991 and received a B.A. in chemistry from Princeton University in 1995. She subsequently earned a Ph.D. in pharmacology from Yale University in 2001. In 1991, Stacey was awarded a Summer Undergraduate Research Fellowship at Rockefeller University. During her undergraduate years, she served as coordinator of the English as a Second Language (ESL) Program at Princeton and spent a summer as a White House intern. As a graduate student at Yale, she served as a member of the Graduate and Professional Student Senate, co-organizer of the Pharmacology Colloquium, Department of Pharmacology Admissions Committee member, and communications chair of the Graduate Student Research Symposium. Her dissertation research focused on the properties of anti-epileptic drugs and their neuronal targets. Currently, Stacey is a postdoctoral fellow at Yale University, where her research focuses on cellular proteins important in both neuronal and cardiac functions.*

A MORAL COMPASS

by DIAHANN BILLINGS-BURFORD

i.

DO YOU THINK THIS LAWYER knows what he's doing?"

"It looks like it, for all I know. He doesn't have very much to work with, given all that Denyse said at the grand jury hearing. But what does it matter, Mommy? Denyse cannot afford to pay for her own attorney, so we just better pray the public defender is a good one, right?"

My mother and I both knew the question I was really asking her: *Surely you are not thinking of wasting your money on an attorney for Denyse?* Though I was a "grown woman" when I asked my mother this veiled question in the summer of 2000, I still knew that I had to speak to her in a certain tone of voice. Besides, we'd had this conversation in various forms on countless occasions in the past. The particular words changed, the setting varied, but the core of the conversation was always the same.

This time my mother and I were sitting in one of my least favorite places, Brooklyn's State Criminal Courthouse. There was nothing I liked about the courthouse, not the decor, not the odor, not its purpose. I hated waiting in the line that wraps around the building in the morning with a crowd of primarily brown and black faces. I hated to see the children there for family members who acted as though this was a natural place for them to recreate. I hated seeing how young many of the detainees being arraigned were, how their body language and verbal responses revealed how commonplace a trip to jail was for them. The only thing that bothered me more than coming to the courthouse was the thought of my mother going by herself. So on this day I had skipped my morning classes and hoped I would make my afternoon seminar, which I really could not afford to miss.

"Well, once I found out that Denyse was arrested, I called a few friends. Henry suggested a lawyer that really knows the ins and outs." My mother was a smart woman. I had no doubt that the lawyer she considered calling could do a good job.

"Why, Mommy? Why do you think this would be a good thing? Will the lawyer stop her drug problem? Will it help to have Denyse on the streets again?"

My mother's exasperation was obvious as we got up and walked out of the courtroom to meet the public defender who had just represented my sister on the losing side of a bail hearing. "I am not stupid, Diahann. I do not think the streets are the best thing for Denyse, but I do not think that jail is, either. Do not forget that prior to this relapse, she was clean for over a year and watched your son."

My only answer was silence. I had not forgotten that my sister was clean for a while. I had not forgotten how helpful and how much a part of the family she had become once again. I also could not forget how many times we had been down this road. I could not seem to face the situation with the hope and determination that my mother did. Instead, I faced the situation with little hope for change and anger at both of them. I was angry at my mother for feeling any sense of responsibility for my sister's addiction, and I was angry at my sister for making what I viewed as decisions that were obviously wrong and totally avoidable. Sitting in the hallway, half listening to the public defender explain attorney-client privilege and my sister's situation "based on what I can tell you," I contemplated whether this fight was worth it and wondered for what seemed like the hundredth time why my sister kept making the same bad decisions and why my mother felt time and time again that she should try to soften the blow, the consequences of those decisions.

A little later, walking down the street, my mother and I ended our argument by agreeing to disagree. I did not tell her that she had done more for Denyse than most children get in a lifetime from their parents. I did not tell her that a 57-year-old woman, who was a great mother, should not be paying for *anything* for her able-bodied 37-year-old daughter. I just wondered, as I entered the train station with tears of frustration and sadness in my eyes to make my afternoon class at Columbia Law School, how my mother felt any responsibility for my sister's situation, given the two very different lives that her daughters were living. Why couldn't she see that she had been a constant, not a variable that could account for our differences?

ii.

IT IS DIFFICULT TO WRITE THIS PIECE without potentially offending those whom I love. Perhaps the positive impact the truth can have is more important than sparing feelings.

I cannot say that I have ever known true poverty. I have never missed a meal. I have never been homeless. I am fortunate to have been born to a woman who understood the value of education and loved me. My mother was the one who discovered Prep for Prep and insisted that I take the test. On the other hand, my family life has been far from idyllic. My parents' marriage was at best dysfunctional, and I did not come to appreciate my father on any level until I reached my twenties. I have one sister who is incarcerated and has had a serious drug problem for many years. My other sister is my best friend, but she, too, could have become a statistic; she had been a single mother in her early twenties with no college degree. While growing up, I did not consider myself poor, but there were many times when my mother could not pay all the bills when they came due. My experience at private schools also taught me that comfort is subjective. Observing the lifestyles of some of my peers, I became incredibly aware that there was plenty materially that I did not and could not have on my mother's income and my father's contributions.

I know that I have leadership qualities. I know that I am an intelligent person. I also know that there are others like me who were never exposed to another way of life and thus continue cycles of an existence that is below them and their potential. At that courthouse, I could literally see a possible lifestyle for me if I had not become a member of Prep for Prep. For sure, I do not think it would have been a wholly negative one, but I sincerely believe that my aspirations and most importantly self-expectations would have been entirely different. My family and my faith have done much for me, but I know that without Prep for Prep I would be leading a much different, less fulfilling and less "successful" life. If I were to think of my life or myself as a tree, I could not determine if Prep was the soil that supported my roots, the water that has been necessary to facilitate my growth, the sun that I strain to reach and which provides sustenance, or the roots and the branches of the tree itself, because this program is simply a part of me. My dreams, ambitions and goals have all been formed in part by the program and the roles that I have played in it. As a student in the Preparatory Component, I became cognizant of my determination, work ethic and commitment. As a college student and later as an employee of Prep, I redeveloped a sense of purpose, an understanding of my God-given abilities and the necessity to use those abilities to make my community better.

I have particularly keen memories of two moments during my time in the Preparatory Component. The first is of sitting with my advisor, Allison, in the carpeted section of the hallway on the third floor of the Lower School building of Trinity School. Allison was "discussing" a writing assignment I had submitted during the first week of my first summer at Prep.

"Diahann, Mr. Reardon assigned you an essay. You cannot possibly think this is an essay. It's only two paragraphs long."

In fact, I had no idea what exactly an essay was. At that moment I realized there were fundamental skills that I was lacking. I also realized that this program was going to require that I truly work. Surviving the Preparatory Component was going to mean learning at a pace faster than I was accustomed to and that I take the initiative to learn what I did not know. There would be no finishing homework while the teacher was assigning it or before I left school for the day. There would be no short cuts.

Later that summer, as I sought to complete yet another essay assignment, I experienced a meltdown. I can remember that night, or rather early morning, as if it were yesterday. I remember sitting in tears at the desk in my mother's room. I can almost feel the chair and see the revisions of the essay all around the final document that I just could not seem to properly conclude. I also remember making another huge decision, and that was *not* to give up. I'm sure that making that decision at such a young age to give my everything, to lose sleep, to push myself as hard as I possibly could, has been the key determinant in my "success." I believe that once one makes a decision to accomplish goals at all reasonable costs, this approach stays with the individual for life.

Many years later, in May 2002, I completed law school. During my three years at Columbia Law, I maintained a marriage, raised a son who is deaf, gave birth to a daughter and endured the death of my best friend and confidante, my mother. The first question people often ask me about my law school career is "How did you manage to do so well with all these things going on in your personal life?" In fact, one of my friends called me "la machine" a while ago, and I thought his label was totally hilarious.

Upon reflection, I know the answer to that question was formed in a Trinity hallway when I was 11 years old, listening to my advisor talk about my "essay," and at the desk in my mother's room when I finished my crying jag. Like the Preparatory Component, life demands that we work, that we meet challenges head on, that we be committed to completing any endeavor as best we can. Deciding to meet those demands determines success, and Prep was not only where but also *why* I made my decision.

iii.

WHEN I BEGAN WORKING AT PREP as a full-time employee in the fall of 1995, I was a bit weary. After graduating from Yale, I had spent a wonderful year teaching at an independent school in Connecticut. Coming home to New York, while comforting, also occasioned some moments of worry. And working at Prep was another type of "coming home." My main concern was failing: failing one of my mentors, Gary Simons; failing my "Prep kids"; failing my reputation in the Prep community. I had already been an advisor and a teacher during the summers. In addition, I had represented Prep on two television shows. The question loomed, "Would I be a good college counselor and Aspects of Leadership[1] facilitator?" I fully understood the importance of college counseling to the Prep for Prep program, and I was acutely aware of the consequences for my Prep kids if I did a poor job. I was unaware, however, of the exact importance of my responsibilities as an Aspects facilitator, as the project did not yet exist when I was a student in the Leadership Development Component of the program.

During my first few Aspects retreats, I learned how invaluable this position was in creating and maintaining the relationships I would need in order to talk candidly with my seniors. During the next set of retreats, I came to respect the intricacies of the curriculum and decided to master teaching as many of the modules as I could. (Later I discovered that such a goal was not such a good thing, as I became serviceable on almost any retreat.)

During my second year facilitating Attributes & Tasks of Leaders I and II, I began to realize the profound effect the curriculum was having on my life. My view of the program, my role in it and my own larger purpose all evolved as I continued to explore issues of ethics and effectiveness with my students. As I pushed them to take their free time to think, I, too, began to question more and focus more. It was during this time that I first came to see Prep as a great experiment, perhaps one that would really correct

---

[1] See page 367 for a description of the course called Aspects of Leadership, consisting of 11 modules (each three or four days long). Prep's high school students are required to complete at least seven of the modules.

some of our society's ills, rather than merely a program to help gifted people of color reach their potential. There is a value to the latter, but the former is by far more important and requires more of me and my peers. I began to see my role as one of helping my kids and their parents to navigate the complicated processes of college admissions and financial aid, but also as a pivotal step in the aforementioned experiment.

On the first day of the Presidents Day Weekend Retreat in 1997, one of my students questioned the necessity of Aspects for all Prep students. In effect, she was implying that not all Prep people were like me, that not all of us were meant to be leaders and do great things. My immediate response was the usual, as her core question was raised by someone on almost every retreat I had taught. The class and I explored the meaning and the different faces of leadership. We also discussed the role of an active and conscientious followership. For the rest of the retreat, however, I privately mulled over her comments about me. Somewhere along the way, I had stopped seeing myself as a leader. Besides being incredibly flattered, I remembered that I had seen myself in just such a light in years past. Somewhere I had lost the purposefulness that I had led numerous discussions about in Aspects.

iv.

OVER TIME, I REALIZED when the transition had occurred. It happened during my first year at Yale, when I had had the unfortunate opportunity to experience racism and our society's inability to deal with it firsthand.[2] One Friday evening, when I was hanging out with a group of my friends, we were put out of a pizzeria on campus that was very much a part of the Yale tradition. After returning to one of the residential colleges, my friends and I were stopped by the proprietor of the restaurant and the New Haven police. What followed was as close to pandemonium as I have ever been. The owner of the pizzeria yelled racial slurs while the police officers demanded that my friends and I stay put so they could "figure this whole thing

[2] The incident dealt with in this section of Diahann's story is also reported in Orlando Bishop's story, pages 86–87.

out." No arrests were made, even though by the end of the evening there were six police cars at the college gate.

Before the end of my first semester, I had to appear before the college's Disciplinary Committee. According to the police report, I called the restaurant owner and the police officers profane names, threw pizza on an officer and even shoved one. Aside from the fact that I had a serious situation on my hands, I found the report amusing; as an African-American, it was entertaining to think that one person did all of this to at least six police officers and was not arrested or even restrained. There was also discriminatory treatment on the part of students and the administration. One article that appeared in a student publication accused me of not understanding the teachings and legacy of Martin Luther King, Jr. This, too, was amusing, since the writer had never even bothered to interview me and referred to me as "he" throughout the entire article. Many student forums dealt with the incident, but I only attended one. It was clear that outside the black student community, there was great angst at the suggestion that a Yale tradition might not be perfect and that racism did, in fact, still exist in our microcosm. I did not believe, however, that the institution's overall unwillingness and inability to deal with racism was my load to bear.

In the end, my friends and I attended a mediation session with the owner of the restaurant, during which he stated, "I did not know that you guys were Yale students." It was obvious to me that any discussion of race was lost on this man. He did not see that his conduct should have been the same whether I was a black person from New Haven or a Yale student who happened to be black. I believe my friends and I signed some paper stating that the mediation was successful; in reality, the mediation was at a remote location, none of us had cars and we just wanted to leave.

I was the only student brought before the Disciplinary Committee. The dean of students explained that the meeting was only happening after an extensive period of fact-finding but then had no response when I pointed out that neither I nor any of the other seven black college students had been consulted about the facts. The committee placed me on social probation for a semester because I had violated the rule requiring students to present their identification to a school official when asked. The campus police had in fact asked for my identification, and I had in fact refused to show it.

I have no illusions about why I was not "disciplined" more severely. After I called home the Friday evening following the incident, my mother spent the weekend planning her attack. By Friday of the next week, there were letters and calls to Yale from the types of people she knew mattered in these situations. In addition, it was clear that the one African-American professor on the Disciplinary Committee thought it was ridiculous that while we, a group of students, had been harassed, here I was being "disciplined."

For sure, I had experienced racism before, but never as an adult, when the stakes become higher and one's emotional well-being becomes less important than politics and real-life concerns. As much as is possible at an institution such as Yale, I began voluntarily to segregate myself. I lived off campus with a friend, who was also African-American, and most of our other African-American friends lived within a three-block radius. I never stopped seeking out or accepting leadership positions, nor did I ever stop participating in worthwhile endeavors. But sometimes consciously, and most times unconsciously, I limited my scope. I remember the master of my residential college approaching me in my junior year and asking me to apply to be a freshman counselor. I never turned in an application and was honest enough to tell him that I had no intention of doing so. At that time the position held no appeal to me, but it was a position the old Diahann would have loved.

In fact, were it not for an experience that sought me out rather than one I would have had to seek (I was "tapped" by one of Yale's famous senior societies), I could have graduated without any emotionally involved relationships with non-African-Americans. The contrast and change were obvious, since in high school I had served as student body president, captain of three varsity sports, co-founder of the black student organization and the Anti-Bias Coalition, and was awarded the Poly Cup for having made a major contribution to the life of the school. When I graduated from Yale, I had been the president of my sorority, historically an African-American organization, as well as a coordinator for the Afro-American Cultural Center and the curriculum developer for the Brother and Sisterhood Mentorship Program.

In retrospect, the only thing that kept me from becoming consumed by the bitterness that discrimination engenders was the fact that I had spent a considerable amount of time with people of many races. I knew that this one set of white people and their actions did not represent an entire "race." As simple as it may seem, experience had taught me that all people could discriminate, hate, be ignorant and lack morals. Fortunately, and more importantly, I had firsthand knowledge of people of all races who did not hate or discriminate. In short, the actions of the non-African-Americans whom I loved and respected overshadowed the ignorance of others.

v.

AT 25 YEARS OF AGE, Prep had once again forced me to make a life-changing decision. That is not to say that I now have a mission or a life plan all mapped out. I am, however, more aware of my leadership abilities, and I work toward setting goals with a larger purpose in mind. I am more aware that as my life gets more comfortable, I have an obligation not to become complacent about the injustices that exist. I am more aware that there exists a need for leadership on all levels, and I have to recognize when the situation requires that I perform the tasks and exhibit the attributes of a leader.

As conscious as I was of my struggle with the issue of race and discrimination, I was unconscious of some of the effects that my encounter with racism had had on me. My student's comment and the Aspects curriculum pushed me to go back, reevaluate some of my life choices since freshman year at Yale and regain my greater purpose, my belief that I was given the gifts I have to make a difference on the largest scale possible. Grappling with racism is not easy for any of us, whatever our color. There are no pat answers. Our society is plagued by it, and our society renounces it at the same time. This paradox makes for difficult situations.

In the Ethics of Leadership I module of Aspects, we introduce the idea of a *moral compass.* Perhaps my earlier analogy of my life or self as a tree was all wrong. I think Prep has been throughout my life a moral compass that is always with me, but that I only inspect closely from time to time. It guides me to my destiny. It does not provide my end point, but it reminds me that I have much to do, and it reminds me also that *how* I do it matters as much as *how much* I do.

DIAHANN BILLINGS-BURFORD *is a member of Contingent VI. Born and raised in Brooklyn, Diahann graduated from Grace Church School in 1986 and from Poly Prep Country Day School in 1990. She received a B.A. in psychology as well as Teachers Preparation Certification from Yale University in 1994 and earned a J.D. from Columbia University School of Law in 2002. At Yale, she received the Nguza Saba Award for Political and Social Leadership. After teaching history for a year at the Kingswood Oxford Middle School in West Hartford, Connecticut, Diahann worked full-time at Prep for Prep as a college counselor, director of College Guidance and director of the Network for Undergraduate Affairs and Professional Advancement, an executive staff level position. She has also been an advisor and subsequently a teacher in the Preparatory Component and has served for several years as a vice chair of Prep's Annual Alumni Giving Campaign. At Columbia Law School, Diahann served as a student senator, a moot court student judge, chair of the Alumni Committee of the Black Law Students Association, and a teaching assistant for Professor Theodore Shaw's course, Race and Poverty Law. She was named a Public Service Fellow and a Lumbard Fellow and was a summer intern in the Criminal Division at the U.S. Attorney's Office for the Southern District of New York. Diahann is currently an associate in the litigation department at Simpson Thacher & Bartlett in New York City.*

VIII.
JOURNEYS

THE APPLICANTS COME, more and more bright youngsters each year. They come because, in what has always been quintessentially a City of Immigrants, a proud gateway to a Nation of Immigrants, Prep for Prep beckons as one of those places where determination that grows into ambition is a ticket to a brighter future.

From South Jamaica and the South Bronx, East Harlem and East New York, these boys and girls come armed with a love of learning and a willingness to work hard; they still believe the American dream can be theirs. As they take the first tentative steps toward fulfilling that dream, Prep commits itself to a sustained effort to strengthen their resolve and embolden their aspirations. Fourteen months of classes at Prep and six years at independent school (or four years at boarding school) challenge them continually to reaffirm their faith in themselves and in the fundamental principles that in America should determine who succeeds and how.

Time and again I am swept up by the wonder and drama of the journeys on which our young people embark. For many of the boys and girls I've come to know and admire, the odyssey that begins in Crown Heights or Bedford-Stuyvesant or the Lower East Side is not unlike an American pioneer's decision to set out by covered wagon to cross a continent. The routes and the obstacles are different, but ultimately the success of each such journey depends on individual will and the desire of an individual to be all that he or she can be. Each such decision represents an unwillingness to make do, to resign oneself to mediocrity, to give up one's dream. There is a power and nobility in the human spirit, and I see it every day with each step a student takes on the way to a better tomorrow.

MAKING PILGRIMAGE TO MYSELF

by LORELEI SEPTEMBER WILLIAMS

" . . . and i dance my
creation and my grandmothers gathering
from my bones like great wooden birds
spread their wings
while their long/legged/laughter
stretches the night.
and i taste the
seasons of my birth. mangoes. papayas.
drink my woman/coconut/milks
stalk the ancient grandfathers
sipping on proud afternoons
walk with a song around my waist
tremble like a new/born/child troubled
with new breaths
and my singing
becomes only the sound of a
blue/black/magical/woman. walking.
womb ripe. walking. loud with mornings. walking.
making pilgrimage to herself . . ."
—SONIA SANCHEZ, "PRESENT," IN *SHAKE LOOSE MY SKIN*

THE SILVER GLARE OF THE SUN cast a magical light on the huts whizzing by on my left. High in the vivid blue expanse of sky, in the company of wispy, iridescent clouds, this almost arrogant sun made me feel how small I was, and I loved it. It is easiest to feel God when you put yourself in the context of the sun and the ocean and when you are surrounded by endless green fields and the huts of people who have lived the same way for centuries. I shifted my weight in the seat, the numbing pain of metal bars through the thin cushion bringing me out of my reverie momentarily. We were on the road to Durban via the Eastern Transkei, making an eight-hour trip in a little school bus that was ill equipped for the journey.

It was my third month in South Africa as an exchange student. Since my arrival, I had developed the habit of listing myself, of trying to put the pieces of my selves together to make a verbal mirror. The practice had become habitual because the pieces were changing and coming into focus in a way they had not done before. I wanted to keep track. Away from my world of family, friends, New York, New Haven and Yale, there was nothing to distract me from myself. Stretching my legs across the length of the tattered plastic seat, I reached for my journal and pen and shifted toward the light. I began the third version of my list: tourist, American, Black, woman, young, poor, independent, poet, people-person, activist, faithful, survivor, daughter, sister, aunt, beloved, loving, adventurous, child of God . . ." I wrote until the sun set as the bus chugged along the dusty road and the scenery changed from Coca-Cola ads and ANC signposts to meandering cows and moonfaced women bearing baskets on their heads and babies on their backs, walking miles along the highway.

That was almost five years ago.[1] Now, at 26, some of the items on that list have fallen away and others have come into sharper focus. In the span of time between today and that trip, I have lost a father and an aunt, seen my mother through her bout with cancer, fallen in and out of love, started and quit a consulting job, graduated from Yale and the Kennedy School of Government at Harvard, and

[1] The story was written in late October of 2002.

traveled to Cuba, Haiti and Brazil for the first time. One week from today, I will return to Brazil on a yearlong Fulbright fellowship. In many ways now, the list seems almost inane. Life and the identity it creates for us defies words, labels and logic. But if I did try to make sense of my selves so far, the activist, the artistic and the spiritual dimensions of my life have been the most salient. And everything has been marked by the fact that I entered this world Black and female and spent the majority of my youth in poverty.

WHEN I WAS YOUNG, my mother made a desk for me by laying an old wooden board from her sewing machine across an open dresser drawer. I was 12 at the time, and we lived in a studio apartment with my sister and father. My mother wanted to make sure, no matter what the circumstances, that I had a place to study. Education, in her eyes, was my escape route to a better life. She was right. However, escape was not my only dream.

The sharp socioeconomic contrasts I encountered growing up in that Harlem studio (and later in the Charles B. Rangel projects) while attending a private school on the Upper East Side of Manhattan politicized me at an early age. At home, battling poverty, family drug addictions and incarcerations, and domestic violence, I learned first-hand about the dynamics of power and inequality. At school, I was one of two African-American students in my grade. On my daily morning ride downtown on the Madison Avenue bus, I watched the scenery change from torn-down and abandoned buildings, liquor stores and glass-littered parks to clean streets, doormanned buildings, boutiques and beautiful Central Park. As I walked from the bus stop to the school, classmates would arrive in their families' chauffeured limousines and Lincoln Town Cars. On visits to classmates' homes, I found bathrooms that were larger than my whole apartment. My friends spent the equivalent of my family's whole budget for a week's worth of dinners on one lunch that would be half eaten. Negotiating the realities of my world—a world of penthouses and country homes, the projects and eviction, a world in which my brown skin was at once a rarity and at other times a banality—race and class took on a razor-sharp saliency in my life.

Surviving those early years compelled me to help other young people struggling with similar challenges. Throughout my life, I have always felt particularly invested in the struggles of youth trapped in the web of racism and poverty throughout Africa and its Diaspora. Knowing both their challenges and their potential called me to action.

Most of my life has been spent trying to make sure that fewer children know the childhood I knew. Or if they know it, that they can find the good in it, the wisdom and the power that is born in survival. If there is any work I feel called to do in my life, this is probably the most important to me. It comes partly from a natural love of young people and from helping to raise my niece and nephew. It comes largely from the fact that I attribute so much of my success to people and programs that helped me when I was young. When I look at many of the young people I work with, I see my own face 10 or 15 years ago. I am filled with excitement when I think of what is possible for them. And I am also filled with a sense of urgency when I think about what they're up against.

Over the past 10 years, I've worked in various capacities to empower young people in New York City, New Haven, Cambridge, South Africa and Brazil. Since my first trip to Kenya in the 10th grade, I have been fascinated by the idea of Diaspora. I have traveled to Cuba, Haiti, Zimbabwe, France, the U.K., Jamaica and the Dominican Republic in search of the ties that bind and do not bind Black people globally. Family ties in Jamaica and the U.K. also heightened this interest. In my travels (and also in my studies), I began asking the "brutal questions." Why was it that in every multiracial country I went to, most of the poor and homeless were Black? Why were so many Caribbean and African countries dependent on Europe and America for their economic welfare and their public policies? And why did they seem to constantly be losing control of their natural resources and self-determination? Why did Harlem, Soweto, Kingston, Liberdade and Port-au-Prince all look so similar to me? Why did the young people I met there tell so many of the same stories, over and over again?

Clearly, Black people's lives are not identical globally. But what I have found both intriguing and disturbing is the extent to which the oppressions we bear are so similar. Black populations throughout the United States, Latin America and Europe, who suffer disproportionately from poverty, unemployment and poor education, health and housing, continue to find themselves at the bottom of the socioeconomic and political ladders of their societies. The position of Africa and the Caribbean relative to the rest of the world mirrors those same patterns of marginalization. Many of the commonalities for Black people worldwide are created by the intersections of race and class in the global capitalist economy. In addition to the common problems are many of the cultural commonalities that we share in terms of food, music, religion and sometimes just the rhythms in our walk and talk. And so, when I look at the faces of my students in the Langa township (South Africa) or in Alagados (Brazil), I still see my own face years ago. I still see all the potential and all of the challenges. And I see them playing a big part in generating solutions to those challenges if they are given the resources, support and opportunity to do so. I believe, like one of my heroines, the late Lisa Sullivan, that

> [urban] youth must be organized to formulate their own questions, to define their own problems, to find their own solutions, and create their own institutions. . . . [The] undeveloped social capital and untapped leadership potential of the hip-hop nation can re-energize the post-modern freedom movement.[2]

My own vision is more internationally focused than Lisa's, but it runs along those same lines. Eventually, I plan to launch my own nonprofit, DAYLIGHT (Diaspora Alliance of Young Leaders Initiating Growth, Hope and Transformation), which will develop a new cadre of leadership in Africa and nations of the African Diaspora. An avid student of racial politics, international development and leadership development, I believe that solutions to many of the problems facing developing countries can be found through effective leadership and governance. As John F. Kennedy once said: "The future promise of any nation can be directly measured by the

---

[2] Larry Bellinger, "Late to Bed, Early to Rise, Keep the Faith and ORGANIZE!: Lisa Sullivan Has Set Her Heart on Politicizing the Hip-Hop Nation," *Sojourners Magazine,* June 11, 2001.

present prospects of its youth." Helping youth improve their own prospects is a major part of my life mission.

DAYLIGHT will train the next generation of young leaders throughout Africa and its Diaspora for careers as public servants and social entrepreneurs and create a network of young Black leaders who will work in coalition to address common problems plaguing their communities and countries. Through DAYLIGHT, I hope to combine my beliefs about the need for linkages between grassroots and institutional strategies, connections between theory and practice, my obsession with the idea of Diaspora and my passion about young people—to try to create an organization that saturates Black communities and countries with more effective public decision-making skills, greater civic participation and a more informed participation in the global political economy.

THE JOURNEY TO DAYLIGHT began early on in life. Growing up poor, Black and female, I often felt like I was living in the stratosphere of society far away from anything "normal." That feeling was intensified during my first years in private school. My life seemed to contrast in every way possible with the lives of most of my peers. As I got older, however, I realized I was living not in society's stratosphere, but right in the intersection of a momentous societal traffic jam. So many of society's most contentious issues seemed to be embedded in my daily realities. The war on drugs, the criminal justice system, welfare, unequal education, public housing, violence, the "inner-city crisis," affirmative action—I knew about it all from a first-person perspective. I didn't need the nightly news or any elaborate policy studies to explain what was going on. Most times they got it wrong anyway. Because of that vantage point, I began to feel that I had a right and a duty to say and do something about these things. I began to feel that all people who were living simultaneously at the margins of society and also in the middle of that dangerous intersection had a right to share the insights, creativity and answers that their lives had given them.

This consciousness led me to commit to various community service projects during high school and to advocate for attention to race and diversity in my high school. In the ninth grade, I became one of the founding members of the Women of Proud Heritage group (a support group for the Black students in my school). During my four years in high school, I launched a campaign to get the school to buy more books by African and African-American authors for our school library and to get an area studies course that focused on Asia, Africa and Latin America. I also initiated an Upper School Diversity Night and took part in my headmistress's Committee on Diversity.

It was when I joined the Prep-sponsored group Students Advocating for Young Children (SAYC) that my activism began to engage with the larger world. SAYC is a high school child advocacy group that often works with the Children's Defense Fund. During my two years with SAYC, I helped organize an antiviolence Youth Conference, a child immunization campaign in Harlem and a "child watch" program to heighten awareness of children's rights at various institutions in New York City. When I attended a Children's Defense Fund conference in Atlanta with SAYC delegates, my activism took on a national context. And after attending a meeting of the Black Student Leadership Network (BSLN), run by the fiery young Lisa Sullivan, I began to realize it would always be a part of my life somehow. BSLN was a new organization, also affiliated with the Children's Defense Fund. At this meeting, Black college student activists from all across the country were gathered to craft strategic plans and policies to attack the poverty and hopelessness in their communities. As a 15-year-old, this was an awesome sight for me. Meeting Lisa and another woman, Deirdre Bailey, my sister and I were ushered into a new family of activists. For the first time, I felt that my preoccupation with race, inequality, poverty and young people could actually have some direction and centrality in my life—that it was worthwhile and something I could and should give myself to. I was in awe of Lisa and Deirdre; I looked up to them and felt something catch fire all the way down in my bones.

That fire traveled with me to Yale. All the work I had ever done and all the rage I had ever felt about racism, sexism and poverty was finally put into context when I stepped foot into my first-ever political science class, "Politics and the Black American," with Cathy

Cohen, my first-ever Black female professor (and incidentally only the second Black female teacher I had had since kindergarten). I had never had a teacher like her before. All of my classmates and I held her in the highest esteem, and each class session we didn't quite know what to expect. Truth be told, I think we were somewhat intimidated in those first days of class. Professor Cohen was strict, no-nonsense, and fierce in all the good ways a Black woman can be fierce. I came to class every week eager to see what she would teach us—this short, sharp, dreadlocked woman with dry wit, keen intellect and real heart.

Professor Cohen became my favorite professor at Yale, a mentor and one of my most trusted advisors. I would sit in the Cross Campus Library for hours reading every mandatory and suggested reading for that class, my mind wide open and in awe. Names like Manning Marable, Carol Swain, Lani Guinier, Audre Lorde, Cornel West and Michael Dawson became familiar to my tongue. New and strange terms like "marginalization," "intersectionality" and "reflected consciousness" became part of my vocabulary, and a deeper understanding of power, privilege, justice and democracy began to frame my understanding of my own past and my present. I was able to situate my experiences of public and private education, living in the projects, occasional periods on welfare, and encounters with the criminal justice system through my father and brother within a legal, socioeconomic and historical context. I understood how the little picture of my life fit into the big picture of America. I began to understand the trends that contributed to other children growing up as I did and other adults living the lives my parents lived.

But it wasn't enough for me to keep this understanding in the classroom. It has always been my pet peeve to be able to talk about a problem but not do something about it, so in addition to declaring a major in political science and African-American Studies, I became very active in Yale's Black community and in New Haven. I worked for and eventually headed a student-run tutoring and mentor program for New Haven youth. I also joined the Black Student Alliance at Yale (BSAY) and became one of its chairs (my twin sister was the other) during the second half of my sophomore year. With my sister and the BSAY board, I initiated and organized Yale's first Black Solidarity Conferences. We wanted to create a substantive space where Black college students could come together to explore and address issues of concern in our communities, beyond the typical one-day cultural celebration (Black Solidarity Day) that BSAY had carved out 10 years before our matriculation. We shied away from the typical elite focus of most similar conferences at Ivy League schools and invited students from a variety of public, private and community colleges. Deirdre Bailey, one of the women we met at the Children's Defense Fund conference in Atlanta, played an invaluable role advising us. She and Cathy Cohen and Lisa Sullivan were among the conference's speakers in its first two years, as were Angela Y. Davis and other activists, artists and politicians from across the country. The event was entirely student-led, and we negotiated with the college administration, faculty, city businesses and community members to achieve our goals. The conference brought together about 200 students from across the country in its first year and will celebrate its eighth anniversary this year.

WHILE I HAVE ALWAYS had a strong interest in working to effect change domestically, I was also drawn to the international sphere early in life. A high school community service trip to Kenya (offered through a partnership between Prep for Prep and the U.S. Experiment in International Living) had introduced me to the politics of the developing world and to the idea of "Diaspora." Up to that point, all I had really known of Africa was the Ethiopian famine of the 1980s and Tarzan. As I built huts with women of the Masai tribe, they taught me what it was like to live during the British colonial regime and the independence movement led by Jomo Kenyatta. I began to see the commonalities and differences between the Black American and Kenyan liberation movements and to think about broader socioeconomic struggles throughout the developing world.

When I went to South Africa during my junior year in college, the trend continued and my commitment to a Pan-African struggle for human and civil rights was intensified. In South Africa, I understood what Jim Crow must have felt like to my great-grandfather.

Many of the Black people there were still fearful. They looked like tourists when they left the townships and entered the cities, and they were quick to move out of the way of whites on the street. Others were not so timid. A friend, Andile, had taken part in the infamous Soweto uprising and told me what it was like when the police descended on his secondary school with tanks, tear gas and guns. He told me how they shot his brother's girlfriend in front of his eyes and carted his brother off to jail, where they ripped off his fingernails, pulled out several of his teeth, beat him and starved him almost to death. Andile told me how he took to the streets with the other children that June day, how he wanted freedom, equality and dignity and didn't care that he might die for it.

Again I drew the parallels to the African-American freedom struggle, and again I tried to involve myself in the momentous changes that were sweeping over the country. Teaching at a Langa township school and interning in the South African Parliament, I got a close-up look at the post-apartheid realities, from both the grassroots and the federal perspectives. One day, I was fortunate enough to sit in on a Parliamentary session when Ugandan president Museveni addressed the entire body. Looking down from my perch in the balcony, I realized I was in the same room with Nelson and Winnie Mandela, Mangosotho Buthelezi, F.W. de Klerk and countless others who had been active in the formation of the new South Africa. It generated such excitement deep within me; I knew I always wanted to be in the midst of change-makers such as these. While I did not agree with the types of change some of them advocated, they were the people who had the power to shape a society.

After graduating from Yale, I briefly moved away from the world of political activism and joined Andersen Consulting (now Accenture). Although I stayed for nearly two years, the corporate world was clearly not for me. I was happy to leave and pursue a master's degree at Harvard's Kennedy School of Government, where I gained a useful skill-set in political advocacy, analysis and management. This training also allowed me to go to Brazil between the two years of classes, and in Brazil I heartily dove back into the grassroots work I love.

Designing and teaching a course on leadership development for two Afro-Brazilian youth groups in the summer of 2001, I felt something akin to the alignment of an internal compass. The response I received from working with these groups felt like an amazing confirmation that this was the work I was supposed to be doing—and that following graduation from the Kennedy School I should try and begin the work of founding DAYLIGHT, the nonprofit I had dreamt about for three years.

In many ways, Brazil brought me full circle back to the roots of my activism. Working with the young people there and listening to their stories of survival reignited my fire. Many had been abused and were homeless; they were in poor health and had little access to education. But they were adamant about making something good of their lives and helping their communities in the process. They kept insisting on life in the midst of an environment of social, emotional and physical death. One conversation with a 16-year-old girl reminded me of a conversation I'd had earlier in the year with a young Haitian boy. Lucimara challenged me to really think about her daily reality—one in which her mother had to choose between medicine for her sick infant and bread for the family. "Sure, you had a hard life," she said, "but life for Black people here in Brazil is far worse than anything you'll ever know." In her country, the brownest children are most often the ones you see sleeping barefoot on cardboard in the drizzle, selling peanuts in the street, sniffing glue behind the Barra Lighthouse or picking discarded cans out of the muddy, filthy gutters. There are almost no Black faces on the TV and barely any Blacks governing the country, even though Afro-Brazilians make up arguably more than 40 percent of the country's population.

Her Haitian counterpart, a little tourist guide I met in the mountains of Milot, reacted to me the same way. Etienne was a precocious youngster, about 10 years old, very intelligent and outgoing. Winding up the mountain toward our destination, the 300-year-old Citadelle fortress, he schooled me on Haitian history and culture, even teaching me the Creole names of roots and plants along the path. His mood changed suddenly, though, when I asked him what he wanted to be when he grew up. "When I grow up? When I grow up? *If* I grow up. And job? There are no jobs for anyone here. Not for my mother or father and not for me—unless I can go to school or get out of Haiti." The outburst caught me off guard, but I was not completely surprised. This 10-year-old, in his tattered clothes and too-big sneakers, was already a politician. Like me, his life had given him plenty of ammunition. I liked the fire in him—his insistence on keeping it real and challenging me to think about his people's dire situation. I wondered what it would be like for him to dialogue and work with other young people from Soweto, Harlem, Kingston, Havana, and Liberdade in Brazil.

In the past two years, I have begun to build the framework for DAYLIGHT, the vehicle that will bring together the Lucimaras of Brazil, the Etiennes of Haiti and the Andiles of South Africa, along with their counterparts across the Diaspora. To honor this calling is a synthesis of all I have learned and struggled with living in the intersection of race, gender and class, working as an activist and as a student of political science and public policy. However, I will take a yearlong detour to pursue a different calling to work in Brazil beginning next week.

My Aunt Barbara once said to me: "If you want to see God laugh, make plans." Well, despite my passion and plans for DAYLIGHT, I have been blessed to receive a Fulbright that will enable me to return to Salvador, Bahia. There I plan to work with three NGOs[3] whose aim is to develop the professional, educational and leadership capacity of Afro-Brazilian youth in Salvador. These three programs specifically focus on the arts, environmental preservation and college preparation. I'll be doing a comparative study of these nonprofits' organizational structures and capacity, programs, pedagogy, and program evaluation processes. For the second half of my project, I'll be working with each organization in a consulting capacity to help them strengthen one aspect of their organization, for example introducing new fund-raising strategies, curriculum, or program evaluation methods. Basically, I want to understand what models of leadership development are being used in Salvador, how

[3] Nongovernmental organizations similar to what we would call not-for-profit organizations in the U.S.A.

effective they have been, how they might be improved those models might be useful in other countries.

Working to understand and strengthen youth leadership de- opment programs in Salvador will be a crucial step toward my goals for DAYLIGHT. While teaching my own leadership development workshops in Brazil this past summer was successful, I learned that it is also important to understand and learn from existing local models that have proven successful. Instead of bringing my own American ideals of what leadership looks like, it is crucial that I understand what works for the people I want to help in other countries. And I cannot find that in a textbook or in a Harvard classroom. I can find it in the people who are living it.

"To whom do I owe the power of my voice, what strength I have become? . . . To whom do I owe my survival? . . . To whom do I owe the woman I have become?"

—AUDRE LORDE, *ZAMI: A NEW SPELLING OF MY NAME*

PREPARING FOR THIS TRIP TO BRAZIL and recently celebrating another birthday has made me very aware that I am standing at a crossroads in my life. As the future stretches out before me, I am sometimes giddy imagining the tremendous possibilities it can hold. When you are bathed in the power of possibility, it's almost like a natural high; every cell jumps for joy. Sometimes I feel full enough to burst. I think of all the poems I want to write, the people I want to meet, the countries I want to see, of being married and having a family of my own, of seeing my own children grow up, seeing my organization develop, and helping to train and convene a new international generation of Black leaders. I have always been a dreamer and I always dream big. In every person and every event, I see an opportunity, an opening, a possibility.

In many ways, *possibility* is my favorite word. It is ironic sometimes, considering that so much in my early life pointed toward impossibility. Some days I wonder, like Mahalia Jackson, "how I got ovah." How did I make the move from paralysis to power? Mostly,

I have to say it was grace. I look at other really gifted kids I grew up with who were dealing with a lot of the same realities I was; now many are strung out or in jail, had kids really young, ended up on welfare quasi-permanently or ended up in oblivion somewhere. I know I'm no better than any of them—that really it was by the grace of God that I happened to survive and to thrive.

Family, mentors, a vibrant spirituality and strong faith, along with artistic expression, also played an important role during those years; they still do. And there is little doubt in my mind that I would not have had the same incredible opportunities, education and access without being part of Prep for Prep. It is to this constellation of support and guidance that I owe "the power of my voice" and "the woman I have become."

My mother's endurance and the way she stressed the importance of education in my life as a vehicle for mobility, always seeking out new programs and good schools, was a foundation—a solid rock in my world. She paid our tuition God knows how (we still had to pay some despite being on financial aid), while she supported all four of us (my twin sister and father included) on her meager salary. It was also my Aunt Barbara and my older sister Lisa who, with my mother, formed the trinity that kept my twin sister, Andrea, and me well loved and nurtured.[4] Another factor was the role models I sought out, mostly older Black women I encountered at my various internships or through various events. Most of the time, I didn't talk about what was happening at home, but I enjoyed learning from them and the vision of opportunity and possibility they gave me.

Finally, Andrea and I joke about the fact that we are also what kept each other sane. Knowing we were not alone in the crazy situations we found ourselves in made them easier to bear. We gave each other a much needed reality check, much love and much laughter. Also, through our competitiveness, we probably pushed each other to achieve more than we might have without each other. The thought was, if she can do it, so can I. So we did, constantly pushing each other's standards higher, constantly meeting and exceeding those standards.

4 While Lorelei attended The Convent of the Sacred Heart, Andrea attended The Spence school.

And through it all, there was Prep for Prep. It was definitely a godsend for me and for Andrea. In addition to all the academic and professional support it offered, it gave us a community of young people who shared an almost identical reality to ours that helped us navigate the very complex worlds around us. When we were younger, my mother always encouraged us to attend the various theater and movie outings, ski trips and other activities. Anything Prep offered, we were usually among the number there. We participated for several years in the Inspirational Choir with Jeree Wade, took part in Santina Goodman's acting class and went on several college visits. I had my first job, at 14, with Janice Peters, working on the first Prep for Prep art show. Undoubtedly, it was through Prep that I had many of the earliest and most pivotal experiences in my life—doing child advocacy with SAYC, traveling to Kenya, working at MTV through Prep's Summer Jobs Bank and obtaining a White House internship when I was an undergraduate.

As an 11-year-old, I remember looking up to my Prep advisors and other older Prep students and alumni like Cherell Carr, Orlando Bishop, Samona Joe and Monica Dennis, among others who advised and supported us. I met many other people at Prep events who would become important mentors in my life—women in politics and in the media and film industry. Together, these advisors and mentors gave me a vision of what was possible for my own life. I was able to see, very concretely, what life had to offer beyond the four walls of that studio apartment my family lived in when I first began the Prep program. The possibility that had been birthed and strengthened in me through my family, my faith and my own striving blossomed and was made manifest in the opportunities Prep gave me. At this point in my life, 15 years after I first walked through the doors of Trinity School to my first Prep classes, I can only hope, through my own life and through DAYLIGHT in particular, to be such a wide doorway, a vessel for someone else's blessing.

LORELEI WILLIAMS *is a member of Contingent X. Born in the South Bronx and raised there and in Harlem, she graduated from the Convent of the Sacred Heart in 1994 and received a B.A. in political science (American government) and African-American studies from Yale University in 1998. Subsequently, Lorelei earned a master's degree in public policy (international development and nonprofit management) from Harvard University's John F. Kennedy School of Government in 2002. While at Yale, Lorelei served as program director of the New Haven Youth Program (sponsored by the Urban Improvement Corps), chaired the Black Student Alliance, was a summer intern at the White House in the Office of Media Affairs and spent the spring of 1997 at the University of Cape Town (South Africa) as a participant in the Semester Exchange Program in Political Science. While in Cape Town, she served as an intern for the Parliamentary Women's Group in the Parliament of the Republic of South Africa and was a volunteer teacher at The Chris Hani School in the Langa Township. She was a recipient of the Yale University AACC Award for Outstanding Leadership, Scholarship and Community Service (1998), a Political Science Department Research Grant (1998) and the William Pickens Senior Thesis Prize (1998). While at Harvard, Lorelei received a John F. Kennedy School of Government Non-Profit Management and Leadership Opportunity Fellowship, a John F. Kennedy School of Government Community Service Award, Center for International Development Summer internship grant, and a David Rockefeller Center for Latin-American Studies research grant. In the two years between graduation from Yale and matriculation at the Kennedy School, Lorelei worked as an analyst for Accenture. She is the recipient of a Fulbright Fellowship that is enabling her to spend the 2002-03 academic year in Brazil working with several Afro-Brazilian youth organizations.*

A LONG WAY FROM ST. ANN'S BAY

by KEVIN JOHNSON

IT'S THANKSGIVING DAY, 2002, and I'm in my final year of med school, waiting to hear back from residency programs in radiology while hoping my research gets accepted for publication by a reputable journal. Those are my primary concerns at the moment. From a narrow, short-sighted perspective, I have a good deal to be stressed out about. But if I were to zoom out and view life from a big-picture perspective, I must admit that I have good reason to be thankful. Heck, things could certainly be a lot worse.

How did I get here from such humble beginnings? In some ways, I've benefited from a combination of hard work, divine intervention and being in the right place at the right time. My success, however, is rooted in Prep for Prep. Perhaps mine is the quintessential Prep story of each opened door leading to the next with an almost *Alice in Wonderland* feel to it. Prep's mantra, "Leaders don't just happen," has rung true in my life. I am *who* I am today because of my education, and my education is a direct result of my membership in Prep.

AS A FOURTH-GRADER at St. Ann's Priory Primary School on the north coast of Jamaica, I followed a familiar routine of waking up early to catch the usually crowded minibus. The trip entailed a 2-mile walk as well as a 20-minute drive along the scenic coast overlooking the Caribbean Sea. The khaki uniform, playing soccer with tattered tennis balls in the 90-degree sun and the occasional lashing for speaking when not spoken to all remain vivid memories of my youth. My primary education in Jamaica provided an important backdrop for my immersion into the New York City public school system. I was soon to discover that schoolchildren in New York were much more assertive than children in Jamaica. Perhaps the pervasiveness of corporal punishment and the widely held cultural belief that one must respect those in authority served to keep us in check. Jamaican students are taught to work hard in school from an early age. We were poor, and education was thought to be the key to upward mobility.

My family's search for upward mobility, however, took us to the United States. It began in 1985 when my mother was recruited to work at Kings County Hospital in Brooklyn. If there had not been such a tremendous nationwide shortage of nurses, our family would still be living in our house in St. Ann. A little over a year after my mother's departure, my dad, my brother and I took an American Airlines flight to New York City, where our new life was to begin. My dad, who was raised in the hills of rural St. Ann, thought of a plane trip as a formal occasion, so we all wore matching tailored three-piece suits for the trip.

We left behind a small two-story hillside farmhouse overlooking the sea, and several chickens and dogs, not to mention the mango, breadfruit and coconut trees. When Dad informed us that we were spending our last school vacation in Jamaica, my feelings were mixed. On the one hand, there was the sense of hope and wonderment for what the future would bring. America! The land of *Dallas* and the Cosby show! Didn't all black Americans live the Cosby lifestyle? A few days in my family's new apartment in East Flatbush taught me otherwise.

East Flatbush was a scary place. I was worried less by the childhood threats of ghosts and more about the real dangers of being harassed by older children on the way home from school. We lived in a building where the landlord's son was a tall, gaunt, unemployed addict who borrowed eggs and other grocery items on a weekly basis.

The police presence was minimal, the music was loud and the winters were cold. There were street gangs. The crack cocaine epidemic was at its height; for evidence of this, we had only to look outside our windows where the vials could be seen littering the streets like empty candy wrappers. Rap music, which was taking root as the music of the streets, was still a foreign language to me. I was a long way from St. Ann's Bay.

More than coming to the city of bright lights to start a new life, my trip to New York meant my reunification with my mother. Bruised knees, below-average grades and fears of the bogeyman outside my bedroom window were best handled when Mom was around. An almost religious sense of togetherness was an attribute shared by all members of our family. It was good for us to all be gathered under the same roof once more. Sure, we encountered a harsh new world in Brooklyn, and yes, Dad changed jobs at least four times during our first year in the United States. But we were the Johnson family. We had a work ethic and an unremitting faith in Providence that would rival the Puritans who had come centuries before us.

SPELL *PHOTOSYNTHESIS.* What is photosynthesis? These were the testing instruments used to assess my intelligence by the placement officer at P.S. 235. I failed miserably. Cultural bias? Maybe. The bottom line was that I was destined to spend fourth grade in a class for mediocre students rather than in 4 SOAR A, the class for gifted students.

My class was taught by a stern, jherry-curled teacher in his late thirties with a lot of pride and a very short fuse. His name was Mr. Purvis, and each morning he greeted the class with the deafening command "Silence!" His cold stares could instantaneously ice the hottest of classroom commotions. I wasn't sure if his mannerisms were just a façade to intimidate and earn the respect of rogue nine-year-olds or just his natural demeanor. It was only a matter of time before I realized that casual conversations and loud outbursts of laughter were possible only in his absence. As I adjusted to the American school system, I brought home mediocre grades that year.

While I didn't get spanked, the fear and dread instilled by my American teacher were as effective if not more so in keeping me from misbehaving.

The next year, it took a system of positive reinforcement to bring out my best. I was very fortunate to be assigned to the class of the most devoted, most caring teacher in Brooklyn. Mr. Bresnyak, or Mr. B as we affectionately called him, had a star incentive system that rewarded the class's best academic effort on a monthly basis. Homework assignments, quizzes and tests took on a whole new meaning because each star that was earned was tabulated to determine who would win that month's bowling outing or trip to a taping of the Cosby show. Not surprisingly, my interest in schoolwork reached a record high. Tamara Small and Kevin Johnson were the co-winners of the monthly prize for the majority of my fifth-grade year. Not long before the end of the semester, in fact, I was informed that I would be placed in 6 SOAR A, the most advanced sixth-grade class in my elementary school.

It was at J.H.S. 211 that I came to hear about Prep for Prep for the second time. As a fourth-grader, I had overheard conversations about a program that sent gifted minority students to the city's premier private high schools and had presented the idea to my parents, who quickly balked at the idea of my taking the train into Manhattan without an adult. Now I discovered that Prep had a separate component for junior high school students.[1] At age 12, I was more amenable to jumping on the subway for hour-long rides to the Upper West Side. Besides, I knew of two other students who were also candidates for the program. We could travel together.

AFTER A BATTERY OF TESTS AND INTERVIEWS, I was accepted into PREP 9. While Prep aims to enhance the mathematical, writing and analytical skills of its students, the most valuable lesson I learned relates to the passion for our communities that is instilled in Prep students. We were taught to believe that we are special and that each of us has a unique mission that entails ultimately uplifting the

[1] While Prep for Prep admits fifth- and sixth-graders for placement in New York City day independent schools, PREP 9 admits seventh-graders for placement as ninth-graders in boarding schools.

various communities whence we came on as large a scale as possible. All the Prep students whom I came to know have a design for using their careers to reshape their neighborhoods or for "giving back" to improve society at large. This sensibility came from speeches we heard in the program, leadership modules we studied on retreats, and the energy and idealism we felt from being around each other. We were a special group, chosen from a new generation, for whom a program had been created to save America from the failures of its past. Before we saved America, however, it was imperative that we obtain the appropriate academic credentials. So 14 months after my arrival at Prep, I was on my way to an independent school in rural Connecticut that I had never even heard of until I entered the program. The school was named Hotchkiss.

HOTCHKISS WAS A TIME OF EVOLUTION and maturation. It was a time of becoming, a time of trying my hand at photography, singing Broadway tunes from *Carousel* and *Shenandoah, and* acting in a variety of plays including *Antigone* and *A Raisin in the Sun.* Of course, there were the low points, too, such as getting tossed in the school lake by overzealous members of the varsity football team during an initiation rite and experiencing my first relationship, my first kiss and first breakup all in a matter of one week. It was a time of making friends from all walks of life, friends who were Muslim, Christian and Jewish, friends who were white, black, Asian and Hispanic. Going to Hotchkiss was like going to college at the age of 14. I welcomed the freedom from the overprotectiveness of my parents at home and slowly grew to appreciate and love the tranquillity and natural beauty of the campus nestled in the foothills of the Berkshires.

Hotchkiss was also a time of triumph. Since my days in junior high, I had always enjoyed being the halfback in pickup football games or stealing a base during an informal game of softball. On the blue six-lane track at Hotchkiss, I discovered my passion for sprinting. I had never imagined I could be *that* fast. Besides raw talent, excelling in athletics at the prep school level required a bit of dedication and a solid work ethic. The workouts and meets were equally exhausting. Able to excel in both the short- and middle-distance events, I participated in no less than four events in each meet, the most grueling of which was the mile relay. While my teammates rested on their recent victories, I was dutifully warming up for the race that often determined the outcome of the meet.

Track taught me the importance of dynamism and making my presence felt. Even more important than my personal success, however, was my impact as captain of the Hotchkiss track team during my senior year. I led our lads to a long-anticipated New England championship, a fondly remembered experience that also strengthened my team-building and leadership skills.

AFTER HOTCHKISS CAME HARVARD. If high school was a time for shaping character and fostering independence, college was my introduction to adulthood. I encountered all the expected scholarly trappings: outstanding faculty, brilliant students and unlimited resources. I also came to discover the adult vices of alcohol, sex and wild parties. I was no longer subject to curfews, study halls or limited visiting hours for members of the opposite sex. Needless to say, my introduction to college life, as it has been for many another naive freshman, was an eye-opening experience. While I continued certain traditions like going to church (when I wasn't hungover or too tired), running track (even when hungover) and working my tail off to get respectable grades (prior to going out and drinking, of course), I made time for certain extracurricular activities I never dreamed I would bring myself to indulge in during my boarding school days.

The end of my innocence came the semester I joined the Phoenix, one of Harvard's exclusive final clubs. The club was a mix of guys from all races and socioeconomic backgrounds who enjoyed each other's company and tried to straddle the fine line between work and play. It's a wonder I made it into a decent medical school. Perhaps my most important achievement at Harvard (besides setting a new school record in the indoor 400-meter dash) was simply learning how to have fun.

While I was learning to enjoy life, my undergraduate experience was abbreviated when I graduated a year earlier than my entering class. Harvard allowed its students to apply the credits earned from high school advanced-placement classes toward graduation requirements. At the time, it made perfect sense to put them to use and save some money in the process. In addition, I had already completed my premed requirements and been admitted to Yale's medical school. My reasoning seemed logical at the time, but in retrospect, graduating early was one of the worst decisions I've ever made. I will never be able to recapture that year of lost experiences at the country's oldest institution of higher learning.

SINCE I'VE BEEN AT MEDICAL SCHOOL, my focus has shifted. While I've had to intensify my academic efforts to survive Yale's science research labs, qualifying exams and taxing ward experiences, I have also been given opportunities to focus on the New Haven community. My most rewarding community service activity thus far has been running the Health Professions Recruitment and Exposure Program (HPREP). As the program's coordinator, I have recruited students from the local community and, with the help of fellow medical students, exposed them to topics in medicine and public health. Each year, at the end of the program, the most outstanding students are rewarded with scholarships payable upon their admission to a four-year college or university. My interest in sacrificing precious study time to involve myself in this activity is a direct result of the seed of community consciousness that was planted many years earlier by Prep for Prep.

Besides the attention given to community service, an important component of the medical school experience at Yale is the emphasis placed on scientific research. In 2001 I collaborated on a one-year immunobiology fellowship with professors George Tellides and Alfred Bothwell. This work culminated in my research thesis, "The Role of Adhesion Molecules in Pig to Human Xenotransplantation," and conference presentations in Hawaii, Texas and California. For someone who had no prior background in basic research, I wasn't doing too badly. This experience also laid the foundation for my future pursuits in academic medicine.

Most recently I completed my pediatrics rotation in Ghana through an international travel fellowship awarded by the Herzig Foundation. My experience in Ghana was nothing short of life-changing. While working alongside residents from the University of Ghana Medical School, I saw a staggering number of patients who suffered from preventable infectious diseases such as typhoid fever, cerebral malaria and dysentery-related dehydration. The depth of poverty I encountered there prompted me to help to raise financial support for development of the university hospital. I hope eventually to start a foundation that addresses the causes of widespread unnecessary illness.

THE TRUE MEASURE OF ONE'S LIFE is the degree to which one has positively affected the lives of others. It is difficult to acknowledge Prep's role in my life without sounding as if I'm shamelessly plugging the program, but the impact that Prep has had in making possible my achievements and fostering my outlook on life is extraordinary. I wouldn't even have heard of Hotchkiss had I not been enrolled in Prep. Would I have gotten into Harvard had I not gone to Hotchkiss? Very unlikely. This academic domino effect extended to medical school and my experiences with HPREP and in Ghana.

The bottom line is that my exposure to elite educational institutions all began with Prep for Prep. I have tried to make the most of each opportunity, and to this day my plans and ambitions have not diminished in size and scope. I have Prep's mission to accomplish.

KEVIN JOHNSON *is a member of PREP 9's Contingent IV. Born in Jamaica, Kevin immigrated to the United States when he was nine years old and grew up in Brooklyn. He graduated from The Hotchkiss School in 1995 and received a B.A., cum laude, in economics from Harvard University in 1998 while also completing all premed requirements. Kevin is currently enrolled at Yale University School of Medicine and expects to be awarded his M.D. degree in June 2003. He has been named a National Congressional Black Caucus Scholar (1997-98), a New England Society Scholar (1998-99) and an Association of Black Cardiologists Scholar (1999). In 2001, he was awarded the Farr Scholarship in recognition of superior performance as a medical student coupled with leadership, integrity and intellectual honesty in the pursuit of medical knowledge. In 2002, he was awarded a National Medical Fellowship grant, a Herzig International Fellowship Award and the Wilbert Jordan Research Award in recognition of his first-place standing at a student research forum. He has served as Student National Medical Association national treasurer (2001) and coordinator of the Health Professions Recruitment and Exposure Program at Yale (1999-2000). He has worked with Genetics Department chairman Rick Lifton and pediatric cardiologist Peter Bowers to isolate a candidate gene believed to be implicated in hypoplastic left heart syndrome and subsequently conducted research with cardiothoracic surgeon George Tellides.*

THE JOURNEY OF A THOUSAND MILES[1]

by JANICE CRUZ-ROWE

AS CHILDREN, MY THREE SISTERS and I were carefully protected because we were girls growing up in East Harlem and there were plenty of ways that trouble could find us despite the tremendous sense of community among our neighbors. For that reason, my father was our protector, not hesitating to defend us against young perpetrators who stole our hats in the winter or knocked us off our swings in the summer. My mother was our faithful escort who accompanied us when we ventured out of our apartment; we were almost never permitted to go out alone.

Despite my family's overwhelming desire to shelter me from any kind of harm, I was nevertheless fortunate to experience many things that broadened my world and enabled me to see possibilities beyond my immediate environment. Each summer, we packed our belongings into a covered shopping cart and ventured out in the early morning hours to Penn Station, where we boarded a train for a three-day journey to Kansas City, Missouri. The days prior to the trip were filled with excitement as we washed clothes, picked out our favorite toys and packed bags of chips, graham crackers and peanut

[1] The title is from Lao-tzu's Chinese proverb "The journey of a thousand miles begins with one step."

butter sandwiches. We crept out long before our neighbors awoke and were forbidden to tell anyone of our trip, lest our apartment be burglarized during the four weeks of our absence. Taking the train was our favorite part of the experience, with three days of landscapes rolling by, transforming skylines of buildings to wooded expanses, to rows of cornfields, tractors and cows, and finally to the small train station in Kansas City where our grandfather would be waiting for us. The weeks that we spent in Kansas City allowed us to experience a different existence, one in which there were houses with crisp green lawns, cool basements with stacks of canned vegetables and freezers filled with meat, and car rides to Dairy Queen as part of our daily adventures. When we returned to New York City, to East Harlem, to our small, dilapidated apartment with two bedrooms, we felt a shock to our senses and longed deeply for the open spaces and fresh air that we had left behind.

When my younger sister turned 10, she joined a dance company in Harlem whose members received free tickets for dance events all over the city. My mother reluctantly allowed her to attend the performances and I served as her escort, since by then I was familiar with the New York City bus system from my daily commute to Friends Seminary. On one particular night, we had tickets to go to Lincoln Center to see the Dance Theater of Harlem perform *Giselle.* We rode the Second Avenue bus, carefully clutching our wallets and transfer tickets, and watching for the street signs that would indicate when we needed to switch to the crosstown. Dressed in our best slacks with colorful matching sweaters, we walked into what seemed like a palace of light. Women swarmed around us in sequined gowns, and men walked by in black tuxedos. We were so amazed to see African-American ballerinas that after the performance we weaved through the crowd, working our way from our rear orchestra seats to the very front of the theater. We peered up at the cinnamon faces of the dancers, so graceful and lovely, and caught the eye of one who looked down kindly upon us. We left Lincoln Center beaming as we looked back to see the huge windows shimmering in the night and boarded the bus uptown to our apartment.

However, the most important vehicle that exposed me to new challenges and made me believe that anything was possible was Prep for Prep. Throughout my years in the New York City public school system, I had always been placed in the IGC track, the classes reserved for "Intellectually Gifted Children." But despite the system's effort to provide accelerated learning, I had never truly been challenged. I remember once being out sick from school for a week and having the week's homework sent home to me; I completed it all in about an hour. It was Prep for Prep that raised the bar for me and prepared me to strive for a standard of academic excellence I had not even known existed.

The day I received the letter inviting me to be tested for Prep, I walked into my apartment anxious to tell my mother the good news. My mother, however, was completely focused on the evening news and the flashing headline that President Ronald Reagan had been shot. As a 10-year-old, my most salient image of the president stemmed from a report that the year before, when he had driven through Harlem, he had condemned the new housing development, Tiano Towers, as being "unnecessary luxury housing" for the poor. My family's long-standing dream had been to move out of our tenement apartment, where we battled our landlord just to have running water and heat in the winter, to this new oasis, which had a 15-year waiting list for applicants.

Ten minutes after my arrival home, my father came in with more news: his friend Tomas, who suffered from depression because he was unemployed, had committed suicide, leaving behind his wife and children. Needless to say, that day my news of Prep for Prep remained an undisclosed prospect in the backdrop. But as I look back now, it is so clear that this was one of the most important days in my life. It marked the beginning of doors being opened and the removal of obstacles that were invisible to many.

What I learned about *myself* during those first 14 months at Prep has stayed with me ever since. It gave me the courage and confidence to keep raising the bar for myself, at Friends, at Brown, at Columbia Business School. Prep also redefined the benchmarks that my family set for me. My grandparents both had grade school educations, and my parents had finished schooling at the high school level. Although my family certainly valued education (in my family, we rarely missed a day of school), they did not understand the importance of higher education for success in this country. I remember my grandmother's delight in the fact that my sisters and I could read, as she would test us with various street and traffic signs. Her academic aspiration for us was really just the base expectation for surviving in this country.

Prep also provided me with a network of peers with similar academic goals. In my East Harlem community, most people I knew viewed school, to a large extent, as something to get over with. Seldom had I met peers who relished learning and sought out academic challenges. As a perpetual bookworm, I would pass the time during school breaks flipping through the dictionary, looking up new words. When I entered Prep, I finally found a set of friends who enjoyed the challenges of learning and were not embarrassed to admit this. I found teachers who were passionately committed to teaching and did not view the end of the school day as "quitting time." At Prep, I found an intellectual home.

Excelling at Friends Seminary opened the door to Brown University. The support I received from college counselors at Friends and at Prep was critical in my decision about where to attend college. I had never met anyone who had attended an Ivy League institution, and as a result I was unsure that Brown would be a good fit for me. Luckily, a persistent college counselor persuaded me to apply anyway and helped guide my decision to go there. Although some may argue that attending the "right" institutions is not important, I have seen firsthand the fact that many of the best companies only recruit from a very select group of colleges and universities. I had just graduated from Brown University when I entered the brand management program at Quaker Oats, reserved primarily for MBAs. I was one of only two undergraduates in the nation to be given an offer.

I have been fortunate to have had such experiences despite the harsh realities of poverty in which I spent my childhood years. I wonder, if I had not had these opportunities, would I have believed that growing up on public assistance meant that this type of existence was to be my own adult destiny, that living without basic necessities like heat and water was normal, that alcohol could fill my spirit if there were no dreams. Instead, I was allowed to believe that there was something better, and that it was only a matter of time, hard work and perhaps a little luck to realize my dream.

JANICE CRUZ-ROWE *is a member of Contingent IV. Born and raised in East Harlem, she graduated from Friends Seminary in 1988, received a B.A. in psychology from Brown University in 1992 and earned an M.B.A. from Columbia Business School in 1998. Following her graduation from Brown, Janice worked for three years in brand management at the Quaker Oats Company and for one year at Lever Brothers. She later joined McKinsey & Company, where she is currently a consultant serving as a project manager. She has served clients in the health care and consumer products industries.*

A LIFE WORTH LIVING

by KEVIN OTERO

ONE DOOR CLOSES, ANOTHER OPENS

AS A KID, I WOKE UP EARLY EVERY MORNING, before my parents, to my knowledge before anyone else in the building, and figured out things to do to pass the time before the rest of the world opened its eyes. What I often ended up doing was eating from a large bowl of cereal while staring outside the window of our 15th-floor apartment in the third building east of First Avenue on 122nd Street in East Harlem's Wagner Houses. What I thought about was a product of what the plans were for that day. Occasionally, however, I would think beyond that day, into the future, and wonder what my life had in store. I imagine most children feel that they are put on this earth for a reason; that they are special; that they are going to do something with their lives. At a young age, I had that feeling, but with no idea how my background and my parents' lack of wealth could affect my ultimate destination.

As I grew up, I realized that school was an avenue that led somewhere. That is what my mom impressed upon me, and I became a sponge in school. Early on in my education, my mom realized I had a knack for the academic setting. Teachers at my local public school encouraged me to apply to private school. On their advice, my mother contacted UNIS, the United Nations International School, and eventually I interviewed with the admissions staff there. I fell in love with the school, and UNIS, in turn, seemed to be interested in adding me to its incoming third-grade class.

My mother did everything she could to afford the family contribution that the financial aid package required, but she was unable to come up with the money. I remember the morning she came into the kitchen with tears in her eyes and told me I would not be going to UNIS. I had no real idea of the depth of her disappointment. What I saw as a missed opportunity for fun with children from all over the world, she saw as a missed opportunity to open the doors of the world to me.

After fourth grade, my mother learned about Prep for Prep and had me take the admission examinations. I clearly remember walking into Trinity School and seeing the mass of children with whom I was competing that day alone, knowing there were numerous testing days. My mother told me not to worry, to try and do my best, and if things didn't work out we could always move to another state where the public schools were better. Somehow I maintained my composure, sat down at the assigned table and took the exam with confidence. Several weeks later, after receiving word that I was selected for second-round testing, which consisted of an IQ test and interviews, I began to get excited about the real possibility of admittance into the program. All the while, my mother was preparing to move away from New York City, should luck not be on my side. After several rounds of testing, however, I became less confident of my chances of being accepted. And as I learned more about what Prep entailed, I was unsure if the program was what I wanted or whether I was what Prep was looking for.

On a Saturday morning during the spring of fifth grade, I woke up early as I always did and this time cooked some French toast, a dish that was usually reserved for special occasions. I sat happily, excited about the breakfast, the nice weather outside and the planned event of the day: a trip to the planetarium, one of my favorite places. My mom woke up that morning in a good mood, excited for the day as well. We gathered a bag together and entered the elevator, which unfortunately put a damper on the morning because it smelled of urine. As we exited the elevator, my mom laughed and said, "Thank

God! I couldn't hold my breath much longer." She then opened our mailbox, gathered up the mail and was about to look through the pile when she decided to leave it for that evening. I smiled, knowing that the day would be better due to that decision. Opening the mail often brought about more worries than joy.

We took the crosstown bus to the Hayden Planetarium, which seemed in so many ways worlds away from my neighborhood. At a very early age, I had developed an interest in space and other worlds. My mother, being more a person of faith, tolerated more than shared my interest. Nevertheless, she accompanied me on my romps around the museum's exhibits.

While I stood enthralled by a display of one of the Apollo missions, I saw my mother rummaging through the mail in her handbag. After observing her deadpan expression as she sifted through what I imagined must have been bills and junk mail, I saw her eyebrows rise and the lines on her forehead wrinkle into the threefold pattern I recognized from the times I either scared or surprised her. She opened an envelope, read a letter and began to cry. As I was about to ask her what was wrong, she looked at me and said, "Baby, it looks like we won't be moving. I'm so proud of you." While I was overjoyed, it is only today that I can begin to understand the happiness that my mother must have felt. For her, it was the opening of the heaviest but most important door in the world.

Pulling a Mussel from Its Shell

DURING THE FALL AND WINTER TRIMESTERS of the Preparatory Component, my mother and I were faced with a decision that we had waited for all my childhood. As one of the students who had been doing quite well, I was in the fortunate position of being able to apply to a number of the most competitive and academically challenging private schools in the city.

I had become enamored of a group of institutions called the Hilltop Schools,[1] located in what was known to the area residents as Riverdale but to my mother and me as the Bronx. My mother was

[1] Located in Riverdale, the most northwestern and affluent section of the Bronx, this group of schools comprises Fieldston, Horace Mann and Riverdale Country School.

kind enough to appease my interest, and after a visit to Horace Mann my own decision-making process was over. I clearly remember walking around the campus, marveling at the buildings, trees and fields, imagining what it would be like to go to school there, in what compared to my concrete-filled neighborhood seemed, to my eyes, like the Botanical Gardens and, to my mind, the Elysian Fields. My mother, always the more pragmatic one in our relationship, pointed out that the decision should not lie in my love for a campus. She promptly explained that much hinged on scholarship awards and that in any case I was not mature enough to handle a three-hour-a-day commute.

One day, after we had visited about six different independent schools, my mother and I met with Gary Simons to discuss the school choice.[2] During the meeting, Gary emphasized that part of the program was about teaching leadership skills, which included decision-making and accountability. To that end, choosing a school was in large part up to me. I explained my reasons for wanting to attend Horace Mann, while my mother countered with reasons why Horace Mann would be a serious mistake. One of her most memorable arguments centered on the neighborhood legend of a child who arrived home late from school and was kidnapped, taken to the roof of our building and killed. Gary Simons, while empathizing with my mother's concern, stood by his opinion that Horace Mann was among the most appropriate schools for me and that the decision should still be mine.

After that meeting, I went on a campaign to show my mother that I would be fine taking the train to Horace Mann. I insisted on traveling to and from school and Prep classes on my own. During the course of my efforts, I began to realize that the problem was not my being able to handle the commute. Sure, my neighborhood was not the safest, and sure, bad things did happen from time to time, but letting the neighborhood dictate my decisions would be

[2] As part of the placement process, each child and parent is expected to visit about six schools which at that point are considered viable options. These "preliminary visits" are arranged by Prep staff with each participating independent school. Following these visits, individual conferences are held with each child and his or her parent(s) at which it is decided to which two or three schools actual applications will be made.

counter to what my mom and I had been doing all of our lives. The problem was that my mother was scared to death of sending me off alone, out of her sight, beyond her protection. For a mother who until then had escorted her child to and from school all of his life, having me go off to Horace Mann was like pulling a mussel from its shell. There was no way she was going to let me go without putting up a fight. After vehement resistance, my mother and I, one Sunday, walked over to the M20 bus stop, boarded the bus together and traveled for approximately half an hour before arriving at 106th Street and Broadway. We then walked to 110th Street and Broadway to board the train that would take us to the last stop on 242nd Street and Broadway in the Bronx. During the trip, my mom gave me her little primer on street knowledge, tips to keep me from getting into trouble. While I appreciated the tips, she of course underestimated what I had already picked up on my own in my short lifetime.

That day was the last day my mother accompanied me on the commute to Horace Mann. However, for many of my years as a student at Horace Mann, I could count on seeing her looking out from our 15th-floor apartment, making sure I made it home safe. For the rest of my life, I will feel that wherever I am, my mom is watching for me from that window, wondering how I am. Nonetheless, I believe deep down inside, she knows I will be fine.

Experiential Learning: A Ticket to Anywhere

My first year at Horace Mann was filled with expected and unexpected challenges alike. In a way, I felt I was being parachuted into an experiment. How I fared, I thought, would be completely up to me, but in reality there was help along the way.

Toward the end of September, a classmate invited me to his house for the weekend. I was grateful for the ease with which this new friend was welcoming me into his life; I, for reasons of fear and immaturity, had not been as welcoming. At the end of classes on a Friday, we left together on the school bus headed to his home in New Jersey. On the bus ride, my friend asked me to forgive him because his house was a little small and under renovation. Thinking

I had connected with someone of a similar modest background, I told him not to worry, that I, too, lived in a small home.

Once we arrived at the doorstep of his home, I had my first taste of the old adage: all things are relative. What he considered small was an expansive, Mediterranean-style villa. That weekend was an awakening of sorts for me. I realized I was entering a different world, as my mom had predicted, and I knew that I would undergo a transformation. My experiential learning experiment would be filled with moments that would test my will and makeup. No matter how well I did academically or socially, the trajectory of my life, while seemingly on an upward curve, would no doubt encounter some dips along the way.

During my sophomore year, my parents were in the middle of a divorce so heated that I decided to move into a friend's house. I needed the time away from the distraction, to focus on school, to keep my eyes on the prize. During the months of my parents' divorce, there was extreme bitterness and sadness in me, but I knew that I needed to rise above the emotional stress while remaining aware of it. Between my friends and my ability to immerse myself in school, I was able to succeed academically, but whether I would succeed emotionally was a different story.

After rebounding from an emotionally turbulent summer, I returned to school, excited to be back. Some of my closest friends were in the same classes I was taking, and I was looking forward to a good year.

It was during that year, however, that I started to see life as an unsettled time frame in which to live, learn, feel and absorb. I remember one particular 24-hour period in November as if an artist had etched it in my mind. A friend and I were looking forward to having dinner together on a Friday night before attending the "sweet sixteen" party of a girl who at the time I thought was the most beautiful thing I had ever seen. Besides the excitement over the prospect of possibly consummating my crush on her, all of our friends were going to attend the party. To make things even better, the next day many of us planned to meet to buy sneakers, play basketball and then head to a comedy club with a group of girlfriends. For the high school student, this day would be hard to beat.

The party was a blast, and the following morning I declined an invitation from my friend Strasser to hang out for the day. I kept my other plans to shop and play ball, all the while anticipating an evening laughing at the comedy club. The day was a beautiful one, about 65 degrees, my favorite temperature, and the sun was shining in a way that seemed unique in terms of how the sun rays broke through the minimal cloud cover. After expending energy on shopping and playing, my friends and I needed to refuel so we went to our favorite Mexican place.

During dinner, I went to a pay phone to check in with a friend and find out when and where people were planning to meet. The moment he answered the phone, I picked up some crackling in his voice. I suspected girlfriend troubles, but then he asked me, "Where are you? Can you sit down?" and I knew that something was wrong. "There was a car accident," he managed to say. "Strasser is dead, and Andy is in the hospital."

In complete disbelief, I screamed at Eddie, "Stop fucking around! You can't be serious!" At that point, my body buckled, and I hung up the phone and began to cry. I felt as if the sky were falling down, as if my mind were fracturing to pieces, as if I would cry forever. I walked around the block several times, kicking garbage, yelling, trying to somehow gather myself and grasp what had happened. How could I have passed up seeing my friend for the last time? How could God let this happen? Why were such genuinely good people taken away?

With the heaviest weight on my chest, I went back to the restaurant to break the news to my friends. A night that was supposed to be one of laughing with friends became a night of crying with friends but, more importantly, a night of *loving* friends. That night was a turning point in my life. I knew I had to open my eyes a little more, take more of the world in and make even more of the opportunity, the privilege, to be alive, to take the good and bad of life, to make my friends and myself proud.

With this new attitude, I went about life in a different way, though sadly aware of what it had taken to remove the veil. I found solace in academics, athletics and community service, anything where I could give a part of myself. In short, I found comfort in living.

With a Little Help from My Friends

In the second half of my junior year, I had to prepare for the SAT and begin to think about where I would attend college. At Horace Mann, parents were invited to the first meeting regarding the college admissions process. After reviewing my record, the college advisor gave my mother and me an assessment of where he thought I should apply. We were pleased with some of the schools he mentioned, but then we proposed other schools in which I was interested. To my surprise, he was somewhat dismissive about my interest in certain schools and advised that I be more pragmatic about my approach. After feeling somewhat insulted that he did not see the merits in my experiences, background or scholastic record, I began to convince myself that he was not out of line, that he might just be looking out for my best interests and that I may have been too ambitious.

One day soon after that meeting, on the way to the Prep offices before a retreat, I ran into Frankie Cruz outside Trinity School. A Prep alum and member of Contingent I, Frankie was the director of the Leadership Development Component at Prep, which included responsibility for college counseling. Frankie and I had remained friends since my early years with the program, and while we were catching up, he asked me what colleges I was considering. I recounted my experience with the college advisor at Horace Mann, and he expressed a mixture of surprise, disappointment and even anger. When we met later on in his office, he told me he thought I had a chance of getting into Yale, which was the school I dreamed of attending.

My confidence soared. With the help of Frankie and the college placement staff at Prep, I worked endlessly on application materials. I remember trying to capture my essence in the college essays and realizing that the staff at Prep had a better idea of who I was and what I wanted to do. People in the program had seen me grow up, develop interests, acquire skills and find myself. It was and remains invaluable to have people who know you in such a unique way. Having such a genuinely interested support system allowed me to present myself to the admissions committee in the best way possible.

A year later, I was in a car on I-95 on the way to New Haven. Soon after receiving a letter of admission from Yale, I had also received a letter of apology from the Horace Mann college advisor.

So off I went to college, the event that my mom had so patiently awaited but at the same time dreaded. It was now time for me to get in the driver's seat and choose my own route in life's complex highway system. Where I would choose to go, my mom could certainly not predict. Her main goal had been to get me to the point where I could choose. With choices, she knew, I would "see the world and live a life worth living."

An Ethos Worth Living By

A MONTH AGO I SAT IN A HOTEL ROOM, being interviewed by a partner at one of New York's most prestigious law firms. After some conversation about my life to date, the attorney posed questions that evoked a much more emotional response than I had expected to give. "What are you good at?" he asked me. "What motivates you?" "What is your greatest weakness?"

I would describe my approach to life as governed by a "fear of mediocrity." Some people like to sleep late; I do not. Some people like to structure their lives around fun; I do not. Some adopt the approach of "eat, drink and be merry" or *"que será, será,"* but I do not. For some reason, I generally feel as if I need to work on something, to work *toward* something, to be something more than I already am. I want to interact with the world, learn from the world, truly live in this world.

In the film *Amadeus,* the composer Salieri recounts his envy of Mozart's genius, all the while illustrating the writhing pain and paralyzing effect that a fear of mediocrity can have on a man. For my part, I use this fear of mediocrity as fuel for the pursuits I choose to engage in. I am well aware of the pressure that such an approach puts on me, for I am rarely satisfied with my accomplishments. It is not that I am overly competitive with my peers; it is rather that I compete with myself, constantly trying to push the boundaries of what had been my limits. I am hard on myself because I feel I know myself well and am strikingly aware of my faults. I try to improve on these faults instead of working around them.

I like to think of my life as my art. Before me, I have time, my abilities, and everything in the world as tools with which I can carve out a truly unique expression of myself. It is by how I live my life, what I choose to do with it, the relationships I form and cherish, that people will understand a part of me. Life no doubt has a way of making us feel naive at various points, but nonetheless I truly believe that there is a basic underlying ethos that ties together the disparate parts of our time here. For me that theme is the avoidance of mediocrity. Some may ask, "Well, how do you avoid something so relative, so subjective?" My answer is simple: by thinking about it; by being aware of how precious life is. Is it not the duty of all who live to *truly* live, to reject the option of being passive, to contribute to the improvement of this world in our own small but unique way?

I have settled my mind on a path that satisfies me. My fear of the mediocre will always inform what I choose to do and the way I attempt to do it. This ethos is what gets me up in the morning, lets me sleep at night and makes me, quite simply, me.

KEVIN OTERO *is a member of Contingent XII. Born and raised in East Harlem, Kevin graduated from The Horace Mann School in 1996 and received a B.A. in sociology (Program II with political science), with distinction, from Yale University in 2000. At Yale, he served as managing editor of the* Journal of Sociology *and was named the Seward Henry Fields Scholar and a Schwartz Fellowship Recipient. During his summers, he was a legal intern in the Equal Employment Opportunity Division of the Washington Lawyers' Committee for Civil Rights and Urban Affairs and a White House intern for Vice President Gore's Reinventing Government Project. Kevin is currently a second-year student at Columbia Law School, where he is on the* Law Review *and is a recipient of the C. Bainbridge Smith Award (Dean's Scholarship). In 2002, he was one of only three first-year students to serve as a summer associate at Wachtell, Lipton, Rosen & Katz, where he rotated through the litigation, creditors' rights and corporate departments.*

IX.
MAKING A DIFFERENCE

FOR THOSE OF US WHO ARE STILL DEEPLY MOVED by the words "I lift my lamp beside the golden door"; for those of us for whom the image of Abe Lincoln, the backwoods lawyer rising to lead a troubled nation, still resonates; for those of us who still believe that America does have the capacity to be "the last best hope of mankind": for us, the students and alumni of Prep for Prep offer hope. We take from knowing them the hope that an America far more true to its own most cherished ideals is still an America that is possible.

It is almost impossible to go the route a Prep student has gone and not be at least aware of, and more likely pained by, the continued and in fact increasing inequality of opportunity that persists in our country. The stark differences in living conditions, in educational opportunities, in the ability to be heard and taken seriously by those in power are too evident to go unnoticed. Our youngest students can see the differences when they compare their new independent schools with their old public schools. As they grow older, they become ever more aware of options that are not available to neighborhood friends and often not even to siblings and other family members. I have watched them grow into exceptional young men and women who will not only achieve; they will also contribute, and in due time they will lead. "Making a difference" has always been a key theme at Prep. By virtue of their own experience, our students develop an understanding that people *can* make a dramatic difference in the lives of others.

I remember a meeting of our board of trustees at which three students who had been White House interns were invited to make a presentation about their experiences. When they left the boardroom, there was a visible reluctance to move on to the next agenda item. Here were three individuals who had started out with all sorts of strikes against them and yet were highly positive in their outlook. Each of them was quite different from the others, yet what they had in common was an eagerness to take on the world, to be players in a society desperately in need of their faith that America has a place for them. It was a moment to savor.

Scattered throughout this book are the stories of individuals who hope to rise to positions of influence in business, education, law or the media. Many of them could have been included in this final section. There is among Prep alumni an ongoing debate about how to be most effective in working for change. Some believe in working directly with the problems that clearly exist, attempting to do as much as one can to ameliorate the situation. Others believe it is more effective in the long run to build their careers and rise to positions in which hopefully the values they espouse can inform either public policy or private philanthropy on a larger scale.

JULIO AND I

by YAHONNES CLEARY

DURING THE SUMMER OF 1994, after my sophomore year in high school, I ran into an old friend. In elementary school and junior high, Julio[1] and I had been in the "gifted and talented" class together and got similar grades. We often bet on which one of us would make more money when we grew up. But in the two years that we had been out of touch, our lives had diverged significantly. Dressed in shirt and tie, I was doing a weeklong internship in the Family Court's Juvenile Delinquent Division as part of LDSI.[2] Julio, recognizable to me by his dark, curly hair, wide eyes and nonchalant swagger, was being arraigned for drug sales. The caseworker with whom I was working told me that this was Julio's second arrest for selling drugs.

As far as I know, Julio did not notice me. But that encounter, however brief, made a lasting impression. It bothered me to think that after only two years our lives could have taken such different directions.

---

[1] The names of the author's childhood friends have been changed.

[2] The Leadership Development Summer Institute is a collaboration between Prep and Coro. Twenty-four Prep and PREP 9 sophomores and juniors are allocated spaces in this nine-week introduction to public policy and to the various sectors that interact to keep New York City functioning.

Julio was not the only bright student in our class to run into trouble. During the six years that I was attending Columbia and Oxford, another childhood friend, Pedro, generally considered the "nerdiest" kid in our class, was serving a prison sentence for armed robbery. Another friend, Jose, had joined Pedro and his companions in many of the robberies that they had committed, but he was lucky enough to have opted out before the night Pedro was caught.

Exposure to this kind of unfulfilled potential has fueled my academic and career interest in urban poverty and social and economic inequality. In particular, I have often used these experiences as a reference point for understanding the relative roles of individual and structural factors in preventing individuals from escaping poverty. When I first saw Julio at the courthouse, I thought of our divergent outcomes primarily in terms of the different decisions that each of us had made. Julio seemed to have rejected education as a means of social and economic advancement, while I had embraced it and made it a priority. I also felt guilty. I regretted that I hadn't done more to discourage him from cutting class to get high in the school stairwells or from getting into fights with other students; at the same time, I recalled my own decisions to join Prep and to work hard at Choate.

In the years since then, however, with greater exposure to these issues, I have come to understand that the explanation for our divergent paths is far more complex, with many more nuances, than I had at first realized.

BEFORE LEAVING THE UNITED STATES to spend the spring semester of my junior year in college in Zimbabwe, I applied for a Truman Scholarship.[3] In my response to one of the application questions, I referred briefly to seeing Julio and to the factors that I thought accounted for the different directions our lives had taken. I listed a mix of factors including my personal motivation, support from my family and external supports such as Prep. But this response was necessarily brief.

[3] The Truman Scholarship provides $30,000 annually to 75–80 college juniors who wish to attend graduate school in preparation for careers in public service.

While in Zimbabwe, I was selected as a finalist and invited to interview for the scholarship at Oxford University. I booked a direct flight on Air Zimbabwe, scheduled to arrive in London the day before my interview. I would have enough time, I thought, to attend a dinner for the finalists and meet with my friend Jon, who had won a Truman Scholarship two years earlier and had agreed to help me prepare for the interview. Despite this careful planning, my plane's departure was delayed two and a half hours. We did make a landing at our scheduled arrival time—but in Cyprus! After much confusion and whispering, it was revealed that the airplane, or car pool, had been rerouted to Cyprus in order to accommodate passengers whose flight had been canceled two days earlier. I was sure that I would miss my interview, thereby losing my chance to win $30,000 as well as the money I had spent on the flight and on a new suit for the interview. Fortunately, however, our plane did make it to London, arriving at Heathrow at 11 P.M.

Four hours later, after further confusion about bus schedules, I arrived at the bus station in Oxford, where Jon met me. At that point I wanted to do nothing more than to sleep, but instead we spent an hour catching up and going over possible interview questions. The questions that Jon asked were mostly routine, and he thought my answers were adequate, especially considering the time of night and my distressing journey. However, I was not satisfied with my answer to one question that Jon asked and that he was convinced someone on the panel would raise as well. He asked me to elaborate on what differences I thought had led to my relative success compared to Julio, who at a young age had demonstrated comparable academic potential. I remember mulling for a while over differences, but not being able to give a coherent response.

Sure enough, a member of the interview panel asked the same sort of question the following morning. She asked how I made the atypical progression from public schools in the South Bronx to Choate and Columbia, and what policies I would recommend to help others from a similar background gain comparable opportunities. In response, I elaborated on factors similar to those I had mentioned in my scholarship application, including the support of my family and my own ambition.

My parents, particularly my mother, consistently prioritized the education of their children. Going to school, and doing well in school, was never a choice: it was an obligation. Before I was actually mature enough to appreciate the value of doing well in school, I did so because I feared punishment by my parents for doing otherwise. Eventually, I came to believe independently that devoting myself to success in school would generate desirable opportunities afterward.

It helped that I grew up with six siblings who followed a similar academic path. Growing up, we all walked to school together in the morning. And in the afternoon, when we weren't at PAL, an after-school program, we sat around the dining table doing our homework together. It didn't take much thinking for me to go on to high school and college, as I had four older brothers who had done it before me, including one who was also in Prep and had gone to Choate.

However, although I emphasized the role of family and personal initiative in helping me to "make it," I focused on structural factors in considering ways to improve opportunities for inner-city youth on a larger scale. I argued that broad intervention by the public sector to improve local schools and job markets in these areas is necessary for increasing opportunity. By contrast, inadequate educational and economic opportunity discourage initiative, and for Julio, Jose and Pedro they had made illegal activity more attractive. From this perspective, their decisions to sell drugs or engage in other criminal activities appear rational economic, albeit risky, ones: these activities had the potential to bring greater rewards than graduating from a low-performing school and competing in a low-wage job market. A conversation with Jose about Pedro's arrest made clear that the rewards from this kind of activity are not only material. In a context in which legal economic opportunities are consistently limited, illegal activity can also bring social affirmation from peers, especially for those like Pedro who face ridicule for being considered nerds.

In response to my answer, another panelist asked me specifically about the role that Prep had played in my transition out of the world I had once shared with Julio. He clearly thought Prep had been an essential element. In fact, he was right. Prep had introduced me to the possibility of going to an elite private school and had made the transition feasible through academic and social preparation. I had been doing well in junior high school at the time, but I was not working anywhere near as hard as I had to work for my Prep classes. My grades in the Preparatory Component of PREP 9 were lower than at my junior high school, mostly B's and C's, but the course content and the level of rigor prepared me well for the Choate curriculum. In Prep, I read many of the same works, such as *Macbeth, Catcher in the Rye* and *Their Eyes Were Watching God,* that were later part of my Choate curriculum. I also got early exposure to subjects such as algebra that were not taught in my junior high school. I learned algebra, in particular, very slowly and only with the help of weekly tutorials and regular phone conversations with Ms. Anderson, our math teacher. But I eventually got it, and in fact, during one of many slow days in my eighth-grade math class, my teacher asked me to give the class a mini algebra lesson.

Through Prep, I also established a network of friends in boarding school who were experiencing a similar transition to a new environment. This social network, combined with prior exposure to boarding school life gleaned from talks with older PREP 9 students who served as our advisors during the two summer sessions, further eased my transition to Choate. It is undoubtedly difficult to fully prepare young students for a transition to a new social environment, but in general the Prep students had an easier time adjusting academically and socially than minority students from inner cities who had not had similar preparation.

In essence, I agreed with the panelist that Prep had been critical in my successful transition to Choate and, in turn, in securing the opportunities I have enjoyed since. But I also expressed my concern that there are many more bright students in inner-city schools like my junior high than there are places in programs like Prep and at schools like Choate. And for many in low-performing inner-city schools, academic potential is stunted at a far younger age than junior high. Thus, a more sustainable large-scale strategy would focus on improving the capacity of public schools to close this gap at all levels and adequately prepare students for higher education and to compete for good jobs.

IT WAS AT CHOATE that I had gained initial exposure to the disparity in educational and economic opportunity that existed between my peers there and those in the South Bronx. I used my four years at Columbia to further explore this gap as well as public policies aimed at reducing it. For the most part, these experiences supported the views on poverty, inequality and lack of opportunity that I eventually expressed in my Truman interview.

Through several courses in particular, I studied the historical and political factors that created pockets of poverty and neglect in American inner cities, most notably housing discrimination via the private and public sector, industrial change and the "flight" of the middle class from these areas. For my undergraduate thesis, I researched the effect of inadequate school funding on the performance of students in underfunded public schools. I also did independent research on the effectiveness of New York City's "workfare" program, which required welfare recipients to do menial jobs at city agencies in exchange for their benefits. I spent the following summer working at the New York City Parks Department, the largest worksite for participants in the workfare program. While I was there, I did research to support the development of a more elaborate job training and placement program than the one required by city law. I also periodically taught the program's job training courses to program participants.

This latter opportunity for direct interaction confirmed my view that perceived defects in the character or motivation of the individual was an incorrect focus for policy aimed at reducing poverty. The majority of program participants much preferred work to welfare. Many were already working either sporadically or part-time, but were not earning enough to forgo public assistance. Those not working were limited in their ability to pursue employment due to a range of barriers to employment, including a lack of access to services such as transportation and child care, or limited education, work experience and employment skills. It was clear that bad decisions by some of the program participants had contributed to their present circumstances. This was arguably most apparent among those who faced difficulty securing employment as a result of past criminal convictions or substance abuse. However, even the origins and impacts of these detrimental decisions cannot be separated from the social and economic context in which they had been made.

Assessing my perspective on poverty and inequality during my latter college years, I began to give primacy to the role of structural factors both in creating poverty and as the appropriate focus for policy aimed at reducing it. I also began to realize, however, that the effect of structural factors cannot be completely separated from other influences such as family and individual decisions. These latter factors can help individuals overcome poverty or exacerbate its effects, but they often operate in a context in which adverse structural factors have already limited opportunity and made poverty entrenched.

I EXPECTED THAT SPENDING TWO YEARS at Oxford would give me a break from working on and thinking intensely about poverty and social policy in the United States. At first glance, Oxford seemed like an ideal place to take this break. The university, composed of some 30 colleges, in many ways resembles the setting of a fairy tale. In fact, much of the Harry Potter films was set at Christ Church, one of the university's more prominent colleges. And each of the colleges, at least the older ones, is marked by imposing, medieval-looking buildings and lush, meticulously manicured lawns.

But nearly as prominent as the aesthetic aspects of Oxford is the elitism that the university represents and perpetuates, and it was only a short while before my thoughts were again dominated by my interest in poverty and inequality. The pyramid of educational opportunity in England is similar to, though possibly narrower than that of the United States, and spaces at the top universities are filled disproportionately by wealthy white students from private schools or high-performing public schools. One need not travel far outside the university to be reminded of its exclusiveness. Like many American cities that are home to prominent universities, Oxford has a large, visible homeless population. Located only a few miles east of the university is Blackbird Leys, one of the most notorious housing projects in England.

Research for my master's in economic and social history offered me the opportunity to explore ways in which poverty and inequality played out in England compared to the United States. I wrote my thesis on 20th-century English welfare policy, focusing on attempts to induce public assistance recipients to work as a condition of benefit receipt. Such requirements were similar to American "workfare" programs and were often justified in the same way. Supporters of these programs generally believed that getting the poor off the dole required implementing policies that change individual behavior and improve the motivation of the poor rather than policies that addressed the structural factors that produce and concentrate poverty.

A welcome complement, and distraction, to my studies were frequent conversations with friends at Oxford who were concerned with similar issues. Particularly compelling was the life story of one English friend, which seemed laden with issues of race, class, poverty, inequality and delinquency, and provided me with another reference point for comparing the influence of individual and structural factors in helping individuals to escape poverty.

Dave is of mixed Irish and St. Lucian heritage. He was raised in a mostly white working-class neighborhood in London where he was forced to confront racism in the form of verbal and physical abuse from neighbors. He found his fists to be most effective in dealing with these confrontations. At 16, uninterested in and uncompelled by his studies, he left school. That same year, unable to cope with a difficult and often abusive relationship with his father, he also left home. Dave spent the next 15 or so years finding a range of ways, sometimes illegal ones, to earn a living. At 30, a series of disturbing personal events sparked a desire to change the course of his life. He enrolled in an adult education course in which he took high school and undergraduate equivalency courses. Among the external readers of a research paper he wrote for one course was an Oxford

University professor who was impressed by his work. The professor encouraged him to apply to Oxford, and at age 32 he enrolled as an undergraduate!

Dave's experiences, especially going to Oxford after having traveled a path that seemed to be heading anywhere but college, generated in him a deep interest in poverty and inequality. Our overlapping interests made for many long conversations, mostly while sitting on the steps of the Bodleian, the majestic, pillared main library in the center of Oxford. Despite being separated by 15 years and the Atlantic Ocean, our perspectives on these issues were similar. Many who become familiar with Dave's life use it as a testament to what individuals, particularly those facing barriers to success, can achieve by simply trying harder. Dave, however, rejects this interpretation and, like me, sees the improvement of public education and economic opportunity as the necessary focus for alleviating poverty and inequality on a large scale. Today, our conversations are mostly focused on figuring out what kind of work we can do to address these problems and discouraging each other from becoming cynical.

Overall, it was refreshing to encounter a like-minded comrade so far from home. My conversations with Dave have affirmed my commitment to working to reduce poverty and inequality. Becoming familiar with his story also added a sense of urgency to my efforts. Like Julio, Jose and Pedro, Dave exemplifies the kind of potential that can be lost when adequate opportunities are absent. I'm hoping that my future work will bring the impact of programs like Prep to scale in order to prevent wasted potential and instead allow bright minds to flourish.

YAHONNES CLEARY *is a member of PREP 9's Contingent V. Born in Lynn, Massachusetts, he was four years old when he moved to the Bronx, where he grew up. Yahonnes graduated from Choate Rosemary Hall in 1996 and received a B.A. in political science, summa cum laude, from Columbia University in 2000. He was also awarded a Class Prize and elected to Phi Beta Kappa. Yahonnes is the recipient of a Congressional Black Caucus Scholarship for academic excellence and community service (1997–2000), a Harry S. Truman Scholarship for outstanding leadership potential and a commitment to public service, and a Marshall Scholarship from the British government for academic excellence and leadership potential. The Marshall Scholarship enabled him to attend Balliol College, Oxford University, where he earned a master's degree in economic and social history in 2002. He anticipates using his Truman Scholarship toward law school or a doctoral program in public policy, following his current two-year appointment as program associate in the Economic Development Unit of the Ford Foundation. As an undergraduate, Yahonnes served for four years as a volunteer in the office of Congressman Charles B. Rangel, mediating between constituents and various government agencies, interned at the City of New York Parks and Recreation Department as a participant in the Government Scholars Program and at New York University's Institute for Education and Social Policy, served as a team leader and volunteer coordinator for Columbia University's Community Impact Project, and interned in the office of Mayor Anthony Williams of Washington, D.C. During the summer of 2001, he was a research assistant at the Fiscal Policy Institute and a volunteer at Project Enterprise, a micro-credit organization based in Harlem.*

WHY IS IT OKAY TO KILL COCKROACHES BUT NOT MINKS?[1]

by MANUELA ARCINIEGAS

I LOOKED AT HIM COMPLETELY PUZZLED because he seemed so different! I really only saw black and Latino people in the four-square blocks I called my universe in the Hunts Point section of the South Bronx. He was honey-brown all over. His hair hung softly down to his cheekbones. The most majestic feature of his tall, slender frame was what I considered his crown—his nose, broken. He was the epitome of cool, always relaxed, and incredibly confident, so much so that he could be sarcastic and good-natured at the same time.

"You're weird," I said in my most convinced voice.

"Thank you," he said as he slyly prepared a retort. He was four years older than me, and it made me proud to be his 11-year-old contender.

"Eww. You want to be weird?" I said in my Dominican accent.

"Weird, my little friend, is a compliment. It's like calling me unique. It means I'm not like anybody else. Special. Just like you!"

Now, wait a minute, I thought. He can't get away with name-calling by slipping it into a compliment. I'd been weird ever since I got to this country. My accent always threw people a little off, and

[1] This title is a quote from Mr. Adam Bresnick, the author's Prep for Prep literature teacher, in the fall of 1992.

so did my stylish mismatching of rags from the secondhand store. Part of the reason for my being in Prep was so my family and I wouldn't be so different anymore. "With a good education . . ." Daddy would say. Prep seemed like the key to all doors, even to undoing my weirdness.

But Himi[2] was so confident and proud when he claimed the title "weird" that I had a life-orienting moment of realization. Right then, I knew I wanted to go to the same independent school that he attended. Something in my gut told me, FIELDSTON. I wanted to go to his school, to be weird just like him, and maybe, one glorious day, we could be weird together . . . It was an opportunity to embrace myself in a new place, maybe it would fit my attitude better, maybe I could open up a little more, make more friends than I had made in public school, maybe even find a boyfriend!

Determination will get me there. Work. Dream. Work harder. Dream bigger.

As it turned out, none of this was so far off from what actually happened. Himi continued being unique, and I ended up attending The Fieldston School and became even weirder while I was there, at least according to my little sister:

"You sound like a white girl, Manny. And look at your jeans all ripped up and grimy on the bottom. What's going on with that? Dominican girls wouldn't get caught dead on the street looking like that."

At Fieldston I was making up "strange dances," interpretive modern dances, and my mom would come to see them. She wasn't very old, but one time, when she came to see a particular dance I had made up about our mother-daughter relationship, she showed up missing four or five major teeth from the top row—right in the front where everybody could see the empty space. I was hoping no one else would catch her smiling during the "coffee dance."

My friend Anika at Fieldston had smooth black skin and a soft-spoken sassy nature. In my dance, Anika played Mami, and I was

---

2 Himayat Khan, whose family came to the United States from Bangladesh, was an advisor that summer. He is currently a senior analyst at DnB Skandia Asset Management, covering global technology and telecommunications equities.

played by an eighth-grader who was so excited to be dancing modern and hanging out with high school girls. Her eyes were huge, just like mine, only hers were blue and mine are coffee brown. Mami didn't say she understood my dance, although she liked the way Anika twirled her coffee cup into three barrel turns and gave birth to little Manuela while standing up.

My 10th-grade history teacher, Ms. Reiko Hillyer, *did* understand my dance. She was also a Fieldston grad, although she had never been in Prep. She was another powerful sister with a B.S. from Yale, just like my Prep advisor, Jemina Bernard. Reiko taught me U.S. history, and I swear I don't remember ever having worked so hard in a class. She really did expect us to remember everything we read and talked about. I would hear her voice become filled with emotion every time we talked about World War II and the Japanese-American internment camps. Her mother was Japanese, and I admired Reiko for being one of the few people at Fieldston who assumed a connection to people of her ethnicity as if by an umbilical cord. When I saw her, I saw the faces of her family members, others like her, shadows of people, alive and dead, standing like an army behind her. Secretly I hoped that my own ancestors and familiars would stand next to me in class, that the other students would see them, too, and not just the one Dominican girl in their class. I felt relieved when I saw her accompanied. I started walking and talking and thinking and communicating with my own shadow army behind me. I started listening to what they needed and wanted, and thinking how I could go about accomplishing some of this, given that I was attending this great school and all, about to inherit some invisible "power" or privilege.

Reiko made me proud to be one tree with a trillion roots buried in the ground. She reminded me that this privilege wasn't only mine. She was such a bad-ass teacher, schooling us brats about what had happened to her people, what the government had done to them, and why most everyone else had just stood by and watched it all happen. She asked us questions as though we were the ones who had committed all of the atrocities we learned about in class. She was pushing us to think about what we would do if we ever found ourselves in the same situation.

Reiko's teaching style reminded me of the Aspects of Leadership[3] modules that Prep students did on four-day retreats. We'd go to some little house in the country, in upstate New York, and Diahann Billings, an Aspects facilitator (and also a Prep alumna), would ask a roomful of Prep students what they would do in difficult situations when they were the leaders and in a position to mediate certain conflicts. We were the "golden children," expected to give real thought to these questions and plot out what we would do about social injustice or the lack of equality of educational opportunity "when we grew up."

Our armies—our relatives, friends and community members from our respective, mostly low-income neighborhoods in New York City—were alive and vibrant with the expectation that we would help find answers to these questions.

WHEN DO WE INTERFERE to stop an injustice from being done to someone else? I felt like I was interfering for myself every day, and for my family. My people were the same brown-skinned kids running around in my project building while I went off to college. I had to check myself on my desire to separate from them and from my family's reality. I used to feel headaches coiling my brain tightly whenever I'd come home for vacations, thinking, "Oh yeah, I'm going to Harvard, but my family is moving on down to the projects." My family couldn't afford their old apartment anymore, while here I was all involved in after-school sports and the Dance Company, when maybe I should have been working to help Mami pay the bills, or hanging out with the folks who were my family's new neighbors, so that it didn't feel so stressful, dangerous or different whenever I came home. I felt too separated from my own folks, my own neighbors.

"*No, mi hija*, your job is school. Do a good job there. My job is to look after you kids, and I'm doing the best I can." So whenever I complained about being too sleepy to finish that paper at midnight,

---

[3] See page 367 for a description of the course called Aspects of Leadership, consisting of 11 modules (each three or four days long). Prep's high school students are required to complete at least seven of the modules.

or too frustrated at filling out financial aid forms all by myself because Mami didn't speak or read English, I sucked it up. Mami was always excited to fall back into her, "When I was your age, I only had two dresses. I would wash them every night to feel like I had a selection."

She wasn't angry because she was poor, but I was. I remember that one of the hardest things for me to do was to keep studying, working, doing my best (twice as well as the best non-Prep student, damn it). That was the secret rule, that I had to prove myself to be much smarter and more "on point" in order to be deemed just as good, in order to "get ahead," ahead to where I thought I was supposed to be. But where was that?

I am right here, right now.

AND SO TODAY IS THE DAY I was Prep for Prepping for. I have earned my Harvard degree, and I have a strong sense of what I'm supposed to do with this life I've been given. I work at the Active Element Foundation, which funnels money to the grassroots nonprofit organizations that other young people are leading in order to bring an end to violence, injustice and oppression in low-income communities or communities of color in the United States. I am gaining firsthand experience working with community organizers and activists, learning the things I could never learn in a classroom, even at Harvard. Someday, I know, I will return to school in order to put what I am learning now into a broader context and in order to position myself to be a more effective advocate for the committed young people I am meeting each day and coming to respect so greatly.

Prep knew that there were kids like me, kids who were taking our talents, responsibilities and mission in life very seriously. I was lucky to become part of Prep at just the right time, because Prep became the first of the many door-openers for me that gave me the chance to explore myself, to strengthen my intellect and to affirm my own humanity in a way that's constantly negated for most young people of color. If you are told beginning when you are very young that your humanity is less deserving than someone else's, and if you are treated in ways that confirm and reinforce this message by the schools you attend, by the books you get to read, by seeing most of your peers stuck in the same low-wage jobs that were held by the adults you knew when you were growing up, then you start to believe it, and even worse, you begin to treat others in the same way you've been treated. Strong parenting and great teachers like Ms. Gailes-Yemmer, my magnificent fifth-grade teacher, cannot single-handedly undo the damage of these messages that many young people are bombarded with in low-income schools and neighborhoods.

Prep did *not* do that to me. Instead, it affirmed me and the importance of carrying out my life's work (as shown to me by my Creator) in the best way I was capable of doing.

Because of Prep, I have been fortunate to meet people who instilled in me the importance of treating others as well as I had been treated, and of affirming other people's humanity. I have learned to respect the beauty, creativity and uniqueness of each person, the sacredness of life and our common origins. We are different, each of us, but we are also the same, each deserving our moments and opportunities to be "weird," to flourish in our own mental galaxy, to be given the paintbrush if being a painter is our life's calling, but to be and to live and to work in such a way that each of us respects and enables others to realize the magic that throbs alive in them, too.

There are young people in this country of all colors and sizes, people younger than my 23 years, who are doing what is courageous and what is needed. Despite the incredibly tough odds they face, they are organizing their communities, working toward effecting long-term positive change. They are pooling their personal and community's power in order to defy conditions and situations that cry out for change, and to overcome the lack of power they've been handed as their lot in life. Unlike me, they did not need to travel outside their communities in order to affirm each other's humanity. Among other things, these community organizers are fighting power plants that pollute their neighborhoods, thereby practicing environmental racism. Why is it, for example, that two neighborhoods in New York City accommodate more than half of the entire city's garbage?[4]

[4] The source of this data is the New York City Environmental Justice Alliance.

As a Prep student, I was given access to some of the best educational institutions in the country. I have gained access to knowledge, friends, networks, people and power that was not the likely outcome considering my background. There are very few people in this country, people of color with immigrant and/or low-income origins, who have been given the same access to power and the same long-term support that have enabled most Prep students to realize their own personal worth. As a Prep alumna, I believe I have a responsibility to funnel this very power back into the spaces where the traditionally disempowered are trapped. This obligation comes not out of pity, or the Good Samaritan syndrome, but out of duty and necessity.

I view the work I do, the career I will build, as an act of love, a conscious initiation into the weird club of which every single individual in this world, often unconsciously, is already a member. I want to dance, sing, read, write, plot and actually live the many ways in which I can affirm someone else's humanity, daily.

MANUELA ARCINIEGAS *is a member of Contingent XIV. Born in Florida, she spent most of her early childhood in the Dominican Republic and came to New York when she was six. She graduated from The Fieldston School in 1997 and received a B.A. in government, cum laude, from Harvard University in 2001. While at Harvard, she was named a Stride Rite Community Service Scholar, served as project manager for Harvard Corps Campus-Wide Service Day and was co-director of Expressions Multicultural Dance Company. Since graduation, Manuela has worked as an organizer for the Campaign for Police Reform sponsored by Youth Ministries for Peace and Justice, a Bronx-based organization, and for the New York City Environmental Justice Alliance. She is currently the coordinator for the Environmental Justice Youth Initiative sponsored by the Active Element Foundation, a Harlem-based national not-for-profit, and a community organizer for Sustainable South Bronx, which implements sustainable development projects informed by the needs of the community and the values of environmental justice.*

THREE MOMENTS IN THE LIFE . . .

by KRISTEN CLARKE

i.

THE STREETS OF DOWNTOWN JOHANNESBURG were extremely congested that fall morning as people pushed their way to work, to school or to the market in the daily hustle of what we call life. Some were heading to the taxi stand where women with large bags and baskets of fruits, vegetables, soaps and other goods squeezed in with men on their way to the diamond mines for a long day of hard labor. The taxis were made to seat about 13 people, not including the driver; however, I had yet to see one holding less than twice that number. I squeezed into the last inch of available space, which was somewhere between a woman's large lap and the space between the seat edge and the taxi door. The taxi wars were particularly heated during this time as drivers competed in a turf war to control certain routes that spanned the city limits. Like much of the economic life for Black South Africans, the taxi industry was unregulated, and individual drivers set prices and determined passenger routes. As real economic opportunity lay beyond the reach of so many South Africans, the resulting competition within the taxi industry was fierce.

I was heading 15 kilometers north to Soweto, also known as Tin City because of the sunlight that brightly reflects off the tin shacks so prevalent in the country's shantytowns. Soweto, perhaps the most infamous of South Africa's townships, is one of the key political, cultural and social centers in the country. With a booming population of two million, Soweto is the site where all Black South Africans have converged: Xhosa and Zulu, ANC and Inkhata, Christian and Muslim, traditional and nontraditional alike. Soweto was also the site of a large student uprising in 1976 that inspired similar demonstrations and protests around the country and ultimately created a climate ripe for the demise of the apartheid system. During the uprising, students protested the use of Afrikaans, the language of the white minority, as the official medium of educational instruction, and voiced their objection to the Bantu education system that had been set in place to keep Black South Africans complacent and in a position of inferiority. Many locals who can still recall the incident claim that as many as 200 protesters were killed that day and hundreds more injured. Hector Peterson, the first student killed, is commemorated by memorials and street signs throughout Soweto.

Riding the taxis during this time was somewhat like playing a game of Russian roulette. It was never quite clear which taxi would be hit, when, or by whom. Nonetheless, the taxis were the most cost-efficient and the fastest way of getting in and around the area.

I arrived in Soweto to meet a friend who had invited me to spend the evening at her home. She was about five feet tall and weighed a mere 110 pounds. Weeks before my visit, she had shared with me a very personal and tragic story about being raped a few years earlier during her final year of high school. She told me that a group of boys forced her into a dark stairwell at the top of the school, where they raped her one by one. A sense of personal shame about the incident prevented her from reporting it to school authorities or friends. Perhaps more compelling, a sense of justice constrained her from reporting it to the police. She still recalls the dark years of the apartheid era, which she described as a never-ending rape with people shot by the police, jailed without reason and silenced without recourse.

Although the apartheid era had ended in a formal sense, it was very much alive in function. As we walked through the dark streets of Soweto toward her house, my friend pointed to a white police officer in an armored vehicle who was widely known to have shot dead a number of people during the Soweto uprising. Perhaps because he had confessed his crimes to the Truth and Reconciliation Commission, he continued to enjoy the privilege of carrying a gun and policing Soweto streets, just one of many unsettling contradictions that characterized the post-apartheid era. Though eager to have them punished, my friend was not comfortable placing her rapists in the hands of white police officers known to have actively and willingly carried out the oppressive policies of the apartheid era.

Justice, my friend concluded, had to come from the streets, and she had committed her life to this principle in both theory and practice. She ran an organization aimed at doling out a civil form of vigilante justice by taking reports of crimes from residents and responding to them with immediacy and force. The goal was not an eye for an eye, a tooth for a tooth, but rather to provide the accused an opportunity to proclaim and prove their innocence, or to confess their guilt, agree to a suitable form of physical or financial punishment and determine a way to make the victim whole. Although she never brought her own rapists to justice, dealing with the rapists of others had made her whole again and had given her life a desperately needed sense of purpose and meaning that had been sucked away from her during the apartheid era.

After a modest dinner at her house, we went to sleep to the sounds of kwaito music, which gives the streets of Soweto their life. I tremendously admired my friend's strength, spirit and will, and have often tried to translate her views on justice and equality into the work that I do on a day-to-day basis. Indeed, dealing with injustice and inequality may require a kind of innovative spirit and commitment to community much like that which characterized the work of my Xhosa compatriot. I slept a deep sleep that night with the weight of inequality and injustice on my mind.

ii.

NOTHING BEATS THE SMELL OF SWEET, RIPE PLANTAINS, salt fish and dumplings first thing in the morning. I looked out the window and saw that the streets were still flooded. The tropical storms that summer were fierce all throughout the island. Over in Mandeville, things were particularly bad; the streets were not paved and there was no proper drainage system. A few taxi drivers on motorcycles braved the waters. I watched several motorcycles go by with both driver and passenger drenched virtually up to their laps in muddy water. A handful of donkey-drawn carts made their way down the street carrying fish from the bay.

I pulled myself out of bed, joined my uncle and cousins, and devoured an enormous traditional Jamaican breakfast. My uncle shared stories about my mother when she was little and told me about my extended family, which stretched from West Moreland to Sav-La-Mar. The Robinson family, of which I am a descendant, was an extremely large family on this side of the island, and chances were that when I met people who shared this surname, they were likely my extended kin. I learned about the commercialization that stretched out from Montego Bay and has had both a positive and negative impact on native islanders. While many of my cousins worked at the hotels and resorts that lined the beaches, real economic benefits from the tourism industry had yet to spill over into parts of the island like West Moreland, Mandeville and Sav-La-Mar that needed it the most. While the tourist areas had proven immensely popular vacation spots for people from all over the world, Jamaica itself remained a poverty-stricken country with high levels of unemployment and crime, sporadic political violence and increasing rates of HIV infection. Many towns remained without sufficient infrastructure, which explained the flooded streets outside my uncle's doorstep.

Earlier I had had the opportunity to spend time with relatives from the paternal side of my family. My great-aunt lived in a small house perched atop a hill that looked down into a wide ditch. The marked graves of my paternal grandmother and grandfather were located on the slope of the hill. I asked about the ditch, which appeared somewhat out of place given the predominant landscape of the area; apparently, it had been dug about two decades before by industrial companies that were looking for bauxite—one of Jamaica's greatest natural resources. I learned that the land had been taken from my family, who had received extremely modest compensation for it, in order to fulfill this company's quest for wealth. It was a dark period for those who lived in the neighborhood, characterized by loud, piercing drilling and smoky clouds of bauxite dust that hung permanently in the air. Increasing numbers of people in the neighborhood developed coughs and illnesses, and sudden deaths became rather commonplace. My family did not remain immune.

Though in Jamaica for only two weeks, I had the opportunity to learn a lifetime's worth of history about my family on both my mother's and father's side. The strong work ethic that I had witnessed growing up in Brooklyn had its roots in a strong, proud line. Oftentimes I have wondered what makes some people decide to hold to their roots on the island and others decide to pack their bags and re-create their lives in a foreign place. My mother had made the choice almost three decades ago to start her life anew in Brooklyn in order to provide her children with access to the kind of educational opportunity that she had never had while growing up in Jamaica. In a sense, the purpose for which she immigrated to the United States has been accomplished and her goals realized. She has seen me thrive at Choate Rosemary Hall, receive an extraordinary undergraduate education at Harvard University and earn a law degree from Columbia Law School.

Two college friends were also in Jamaica that summer. One day, after enjoying downtown Montego Bay and its beaches, we purchased tickets for Reggae SunFest, one of the biggest dance hall events of the year. SunFest was a concert like no other, and the music was rich in themes of culture, pride and history. The green, yellow and black of Jamaica's flag could be seen everywhere. Vendors sold everything from rice and peas and jerk chicken to sugarcane and akee, the national fruit of Jamaica.

That year's biggest headliner was Buju Banton. The energy that filled the concert space when Banton took the stage was tremendous. In almost total unison, thousands of concertgoers flickered a flame atop their lighters, jumped up to the rhythmic sound and sang the chorus of "Murderer." I obliged the crowd and joined in, and then seriously questioned whether I would even bother boarding my flight back to JFK less than a week later. Indeed, this was the concert that would never end, and the music continued far into the early morning hours. The sun was just beginning to rise, and it was time to catch a few hours of sleep before the next evening's concert would begin.

iii.

I GOT OFF THE PLANE IN JACKSON, MISSISSIPPI, and headed due west toward Louisiana. The stretch of highway between Jackson and the Louisiana border is a scenic expanse of endless green that is rich with an unsettling history of both slavery and war. Jackson was one of the central organizing locations for a number of critical events during the civil rights movement. Home to hundreds of churches and a politically mobilized African-American citizenry, Jackson saw its Black population rally against the police-led killing of Medgar Evers. Jackson also was home to Fannie Lou Hamer, who committed her life to the struggle for voting rights and equal access to the political process. Jackson, however, also served as home to vicious Ku Klux Klan chapters responsible for countless church bombings, lynchings and other acts of violence that remained at a height throughout the Jim Crow era and during the course of the civil rights movement.

Forty miles into my drive, I passed the city of Vicksburg, which is located almost adjacent to the Louisiana border. One of the biggest commercial landmarks in the area is the Vicksburg Shopping Outlets. I made a quick pit stop to purchase a Bible from one of the religious stores that lined the strip. Religious stores and bookshops are common in this region, and one can't help but feel a mixture of strong emotions while driving through it. During the Civil War, Vicksburg was taken by Ulysses S. Grant, thereby giving the North complete control of the Mississippi River and all of its traffic. This was a significant turning point in the war, but it left Vicksburg's white residents so resentful that the Fourth of July was not even celebrated in the city until as late as 1940. Shortly after the end of the war, Hiram Revels had become the first Black elected to the Mississippi State Legislature and, three years later, the first Black to sit in the U.S. Senate. Revels' term lasted only one short year, however, and soon thereafter came the end of Reconstruction and the beginning of the dark and violent Jim Crow era in which Blacks throughout the South experienced total disenfranchisement. Vicksburg, like most Southern cities, used fear, violence and intimidation to render its recently freed Black citizens politically powerless and poor.

A few miles farther on, I passed the colorful casino strip that marks the end of Mississippi's border. Its lots were filled with cars from states as far away as Arkansas and Tennessee and as close as Louisiana. A casino feels so out of place in this particular area, as the Mississippi Delta region arguably remains one of the poorest parts of the country.

I crossed the Mississippi River and headed into Louisiana where the landscape becomes almost immediately devoid of any signs of commercialization. An occasional gas station strip or diner would appear along the way, separated from any other such manifestation of contemporary America's response to the needs of travelers by cotton plantations that stretched for miles and miles. It was "cotton-pickin' season," as the locals like to say, and large balls of raw cotton blew up alongside the highway as I drove by. I imagined the fields only decades earlier filled with hunched-over African-American bodies picking those pieces of raw cotton. Now the fields were almost empty of any human presence except for the occasional man-operated machinery. The need for human labor on the plantations had finally been replaced by large mechanical cotton pickers, which now took care of both the picking and the fertilizing. Enormous rectangular beds of machine-picked cotton stood alongside farmhouses, ready to be picked up by commercial trucks that rolled heavily down the highway.

The fact that I had never seen a cotton field before was somewhat hard to digest for some of the older Black folks in the region who had never left this part of the state. Cotton was just about the only industry there, and for many Blacks who had lived through Jim

Crow and sharecropping, cotton was the centerpiece of their personal, political and economic existence. For just about every African-American in northeastern Louisiana, cotton was also a symbol of pain, suffering and deprivation. I heard stories about schools closing down during the early part of winter, as late as the 1970s, so that students could go out in the fields to strip them bare of the raw white balls. Before the advent of the more modern machines, some of the cotton remained on the plant even after the machines had supposedly picked the cotton, and plantation owners wanted the fields stripped clean. Indeed, cotton was deemed more valuable than an education.

The sight of trailer parks is not uncommon alongside the highway. For the poor, a trailer provides basic shelter at a fraction of the price of a freestanding home. I pulled alongside one park where I noticed a yellow school bus that had been creatively converted into a home. An air-conditioning unit protruded from its back and foil paper lined its many windows, affording its residents privacy. A few footsteps away was an outhouse that was used as a bathroom by many residents of the trailer park. Just across the road was another large cotton plantation where many of the park's residents likely labored. Apparently, this particular plantation owner was paying his workers so little that they could not even afford what most Americans would consider the minimum in terms of standard living conditions. Although sharecropping in a formal sense had ended, the relationship between African-Americans and whites had remained almost unaltered, still characterized by the almost total dependence of African-Americans.

I soon reached my destination, where I hoped to address several issues concerning voter intimidation. My office had received complaints that voters in the area were being subjected to crude forms of harassment, that police had plans to be outside patrolling polling places and that the local district attorney was filing unsubstantiated allegations of voter fraud against minority voters—all in a coordinated effort to stifle the African-American vote. Indeed, a number of hotly contested races were on the upcoming ballot, contests in which long-term white incumbents were being challenged by Blacks looking to change the political status quo. I had heard stories about many plantation owners not allowing their workers time to vote on Election Day. And I had heard other stories about wealthy white candidates using small cash handouts to buy votes. Perhaps most disturbing, however, were the stories about local white officials abusing their positions of power in order to keep African-Americans disfranchised and politically powerless. My job was to make sure that the laws were being enforced fairly, neutrally and equally. Federal oversight of elections often was needed to make sure that this was the case and that the political process remained open to everyone.

iv.

AS A CIVIL RIGHTS ATTORNEY TODAY, my work has taken me to some of the poorest parts of the Deep South, to some of the most hostile areas in the Midwest and to some of the most blatantly racist areas that I have come to call home in the Northeast. I have had the opportunity to examine the African-American quest for the American Dream in various parts of the country, and it appears that for many this dream remains impossible to achieve. Equal access to educational opportunity is the key to the persisting struggle for equality and freedom in this country. A citizenry that is educated is also positioned to exercise political power and is emboldened to challenge the status quo.

As a graduate of Columbia Law School, I was well positioned to secure a high-paying job as a corporate attorney and earn a comfortable six-figure salary. I have opted instead for a career as a civil rights attorney so that I can challenge injustice and inequality at its core. Today, the American Dream has yet to be realized by large numbers of African-Americans whose lives are still impacted by racial inequality and lack of access to opportunity. How to make the privileges and benefits of our country's economic strength and democratic system of government more equally and fairly distributed remains one of America's great challenges in this new century.

As a young student at Choate Rosemary Hall, I observed the stark contrast between privilege and poverty simply by contrasting my experience in Wallingford, Connecticut, with my life back in Brooklyn. I had learned the meaning of struggle and poverty at an extremely young age, and I appreciated the opportunity to think and analyze in an environment devoid of these distractions. Yet guilt often weighed heavily on my conscience because I was only one person, and I was leaving behind a brother, a sister and many friends who did not and could not enjoy the same privileges that had become available to me. As an undergraduate at Harvard, I had the opportunity to sharpen and hone my intellectual ability and consider the multiple ways in which I might use my educational access to the benefit of others. While in law school at Columbia, I discovered numerous ways to use the legal skills I acquired to benefit residents of the underprivileged areas of Harlem that surrounded the school.

Today, African-Americans face a range of seemingly insurmountable challenges including unemployment, lack of access to educational opportunity, and severe political and economic inequality. Indeed, racial hierarchies, a reactionary judiciary and legislature, defiant police officers and increasing racial hostility in public dialogues taking place around our country often make it seem that these challenges cannot be overcome. It is within this context that I now seek to use my law degree as a tool to promote principles of racial justice, fairness and equality.

What gives me pause at times is the realization that this struggle is one that is global in scope, extending from South Africa to Jamaica, from northeastern Louisiana to Brooklyn. However, the mere possibility that my work might bring us one step closer to the goal of political and social equality provides me with the patience, hope and energy that drive me every day.

KRISTEN CLARKE *is a member of PREP 9's Contingent II. Born and raised in Brooklyn, she graduated from Choate Rosemary Hall in 1993, received an A.B. in government and Afro-American studies, cum laude, from Harvard University in 1997 and earned a J.D. from Columbia University School of Law in 2000. As an undergraduate, she served as president of the Harvard-Radcliffe Black Students Association and was the recipient of an Andrew Mellon Foundation Grant. At Columbia, she served as a staff editor of the* Human Rights Law Review *and as editor in chief of the* National Black Law Journal. *Kristen also served as director of the Community Lawyering Project, was a teaching assistant to Dr. Manning Marable and was named a Harlan Fiske Stone Scholar and a Human Rights Fellow. In addition, she was awarded the Jane Marks Murphy Prize for Excellence in Clinical Work. During the summers, she clerked for the NAACP Legal Defense Fund, Inc., and was a summer associate at the law firm of Davis Polk & Wardwell.*

Kristen joined the U.S. Department of Justice through the Attorney General's Honors Program and currently serves as a trial attorney in the Civil Rights Division. Among other activities, she handles litigation concerning a statewide redistricting plan for the Louisiana House of Representatives. She also coordinates federal observer coverage of elections throughout the country, spearheads investigatio ns into allegations of voting rights violations, conducts administrative review of various state, county, city and school board redistricting plans, and drafts pleadings and memoranda in connection with litigation arising under the Voting Rights Act of 1965. Finally, Kristen is the founder and director of her own 501(c)(3) nonprofit organization, the African American Coalition Against AIDS, which promotes public education and prevention-oriented activities pertaining to HIV/AIDS.

INTERVENTIONS WITH POWER

by ANTHONY E. WRIGHT

THOUSANDS OF MILES FROM MY BEGINNINGS in the Bronx—literally and figuratively—I now live on the outskirts of an agricultural outpost in California. On my street corner in this college town of Davis, I can look and see nothing but flat farmland of green and gold extending past the curvature of the earth. The view is limitless.

Two decades ago, my view was from the playground at P.S. 61, a classic brick-and-concrete edifice from which I graduated elementary school. The building is located on Charlotte Street in the South Bronx, nationally famous as a symbol of urban blight and as a backdrop for two presidents of the United States to announce campaign plans to address the issue. As flat as farmland but with no signs of growth or life, the scene through the chain-link fence from the elevated playground was of what seemed like eight square blocks of abandoned lots, littered and ringed by a perimeter of burned-out buildings and dilapidated projects in the distance.

I've visited that school playground recently, and the view has changed. From those abandoned lots has sprung a community of single-family ranch homes, graffiti-free, complete with lawns, driveways and other suburban staples that signify safety rather than inner-city insecurity.

How did the view change? The transformation is remarkable, a testament to the power of intervention. Margaret Mead once said, "Never doubt that a small group of thoughtful, committed citizens can change the world. Indeed, it's the only thing that ever has." Since my youth on that playground, I have witnessed the work of dedicated people who have won improvements in housing and community reinvestment, who have helped create changes in the Bronx and other distressed neighborhoods. I have worked with them and others to force change on a range of issues. Yet I continue to be awestruck at the power of intervention by the individual, and also by a whole community. More than the actual subject matter of my academic experiences, it's a lesson I have continued to learn.

I AM MULLING OVER whether to make the trip to attend my 10th-year college reunion. Has it really been a decade since I lived in a dorm and crammed for an exam? I miss the classic New England college campus in the fall, stunning with the transformation of lush green grass to glistening white snow. The changing colors of red and yellow leaves on oak and maple trees nicely frame the brick dorms and classroom buildings, and give a radiance to the rolling hills in the distance.

I recently received another fund-raising appeal from my alma mater, which spotlighted, among other selling points, the school's commitment to financial aid: "Since its founding, Amherst has remained one of the few truly need-blind colleges in the nation; students are admitted without regard to financial needs, and each admitted student is guaranteed financial aid equal to financial need." While the college's commitment is real, I am amused, since I remember when the administration almost abandoned its need-blind admissions policy. And it took the concerted initiative of many, directed at the powers that be, to prevent what would have been a disastrous abandonment of an important principle for the college and for education in general.

The spring of my sophomore year at Amherst, I read in the student newspaper about the administration's proposal for the college to move away from its historic commitment to admitting students without considering their financial status and from its guarantee that all admitted students with demonstrated need would get financial aid commensurate with that need. Budget cuts were being proposed for many areas of the college's operation, but the administration was particularly concerned with the fast rise of the financial aid budget. The projected deficit in the financial aid budget alone was expected to grow to $520,000 in the next year. Of the limited number of elite colleges that even had the resources to have need-blind admissions, many—including Brown, Columbia, Smith and Wesleyan—had already abandoned the policy or were actively considering doing so.

While the news was disturbing to many of my friends and colleagues, it was at first unclear what to do. Students for Educational Equality, a campus organization whose members tutored children in nearby Holyoke, circulated a petition. Student government leaders sounded the appropriate notes. Serving as co-chair of La Causa, the Latino student group, I reached out to the heads of the Black Students Union and the Asian Students Association, who served with me as partners in the Cross-Cultural Committee. Through this larger umbrella, I worked to organize a coalition of a dozen other student organizations, representing international and transfer students, and other constituencies. We worked on the petition drive, helping to gather over a thousand signatures—more than two-thirds of the student body—to express students' alarm and discontent.

This wasn't the first or last time that I would get involved in a campaign on an issue of political or social concern, but the focus around educational opportunity was personal. I was acutely aware that elite schools were gateways—and gatekeepers—to future success. I benefited from scholarships at both Riverdale Country School and Amherst, and would not even have known about such schools had it not been for my participation in Prep for Prep. Since fifth grade, I had been afforded a series of extraordinary educational opportunities, but early on it had become clear to me that I was the exception, able to take advantage of a program open to a select number of children. In college, I had little interest in again being an exception. Given that 95 percent of the American population would require financial aid in order to attend an expensive school like Amherst, it seemed unfair that the college would restrict the number of matriculants who required some degree of financial aid to 40 or 45 percent of an entering class.

We used the summer to research the background of the financial aid policy and to see how other campuses were handling this issue. With the beginning of the new year in the fall, I organized 15 key campus leaders from the coalition's organizations to meet with college president Peter Pouncey, a classics professor with shocking white hair, horn-rimmed glasses, an appropriate British accent and a matching sense of arrogance and humor. He termed me and the other co-chair of the coalition, Lisa Grumet of Students for Educational Equality, as the "financial aid jolly jumpers."

We pressed for details of the college budget. We urged a public process to discuss the proposed changes in admissions and financial aid. As part of the effort, we organized a campus-wide forum that I moderated with the president and the director of admissions. We kept the campus updated on developments through frequent mailings, weekly letters to the editor and announcements in the dining hall.

Not getting anywhere with the administration, however, we went to the only remaining power that had the authority to reverse the decision. When the board of trustees came to visit the campus for a regularly scheduled meeting, we used that as an opportunity for intervention. We organized students from all across the campus to hang banners from their dorm windows, emblazoned with slogans like "Keep Amherst #1: Save Need-Blind," "If We Aren't Blind, We Won't See Color" and my favorite, "Class Shouldn't Matter in Class."

We actively publicized and organized students to attend the October meeting with the trustees, turning what had been intended as a casual and obscure pizza reception into a contentious town hall meeting with over 200 students asking about financial aid policy. Students asked tough questions of the trustees as a whole and also expressed their views individually to selected members of the board, which included the chair, Thomas Wyman, former head of the CBS network. This was an intervention directed at the hearts and minds of those who held power. Mr. Wyman seemed surprised by the tension of the forum, although we had to imagine that it was not new to him, having read in news accounts of his recent participation in corporate board meetings rife with intrigue. The forum got the notice of not only the local media, but also the *New York Times* "Campus Life" section on Sunday.

Only a few days later, a change in policy was announced. The board reversed its direction, deciding to maintain a need-blind admissions policy by making some across-the-board reductions, tweaking financial aid packages and spreading the deficit over two years. The decision was reported in the following Sunday's *Times.* While reluctant to credit the change of policy to the activities of the coalition, President Pouncey was quoted as saying, "The force of concern shown by students" at the forum with the trustees "may have prompted a kind of gentleness of response." The reaction by the mass of students at the forum, it was reported, "impressed on them the immediacy of concern."

Hence the paradox of politics. There are countless examples of how an individual can make a difference. And yet, absent the power of position or wealth, for us it ultimately required the mobilization of many: a thousand-plus signatures, hundreds to attend a meeting, multiple organizations acting in coalition, and so on. An individual makes all the difference, but it doesn't make a difference if that individual stands alone.

Early on, I was moved and inspired by Henry David Thoreau's essay *Civil Disobedience,* yet he would seem to disagree. "I know this well," wrote Thoreau, "that if one thousand, if one hundred, if ten men whom I could name—if ten honest men only—aye, if one honest man, in this State of Massachusetts, ceasing to hold slaves, were actually to withdraw from this copartnership, and be locked up in the county jail therefore, it would be the abolition of slavery in America." I loved the passion and power of the piece, and of this passage particularly, which called for individual action based on conscience.

MY PARTICIPATION IN POLITICS today is in a different state and involves different issues. Leaning out the window of my office, I can see right across the street the state capitol of California, complete with a majestic dome and a new white paint job, and ringed by a park green with grass and palm trees. While working at my computer, I keep tabs on a closed-circuit television, awaiting a final vote on a piece of legislation that would assist patients in getting timely access to care when dealing with their HMOs. From my air-conditioned office, well equipped to withstand Sacramento's triple-digit-degree summers, I witness the state assembly quickly take up and pass this bill, one of over 50 that will be considered this one afternoon. I continue to make plans for an upcoming press conference and to work on an e-mail to update colleagues all around California on the latest developments regarding crucial details of the state's $100 billion budget that looms over the assembly's deliberations.

I serve now as executive director of Health Access California, the statewide consumer group working toward affordable, quality health care for all. This umbrella coalition includes 200 organizations representing seniors, immigrants, communities of color, people of faith, working families, children, labor and other constituencies that care about health care.

It's hard to describe my work to my parents, to my friends and sometimes even to my wife. They've given up on getting what they regard as a clear, comprehensible answer to the commonly asked question "What does he do?" Sometimes, it's easier to talk about the substance of my work, about the victories my organization has had passing a statewide HMO Patients' Bill of Rights, or expanding health insurance programs for children and low-income working families. In a previous job as program director of New Jersey Citizen Action, I could describe campaigns that scuttled a billion-dollar insurance merger that would have endangered public assets and prevented a utility company's attempt to double basic telephone rates. If the question is about the day-to-day experience of my work, it is easier to focus on a specific aspect or two: building and maintaining a coalition, lobbying policy-makers, researching and advocating policy issues, or running a campaign to get media attention on an issue.

Ultimately, any one answer is insufficient, but at least these activities convey the notion that we are attempting social change through the means of intervention at our disposal.

A decade ago, I helped organize a college coalition that worked to prevent a decision that would have gutted a principle and policy of educational equity because of a half-million-dollar deficit. This past year, I helped staff a statewide coalition that successfully worked to prevent severe state budget cuts in health care, a crisis precipitated by a $24 billion deficit. Under the proposed budget cuts, hundreds of thousands of California families would have been denied or delayed medically necessary health care.

Leafing through old college papers about the need-blind campaign provides not only nostalgia but surprise at how the principles and tactics that worked on a student issue on a small New England campus are relevant in working on a major issue in the nation's largest state. The fundamental strategies and tactics are the same, including coalition building, mass turnout, creative protest, concerted research and media attention. Part of my job now is to build a broad and deep coalition with the political power to see the vision of affordable, quality health care for all become a reality. As much as I take Margaret Mead's maxim and Henry David Thoreau's writings to heart, there is an important addendum: No small group can change the world by itself, but even one individual can help mobilize enough people and institutions into a powerful enough force to make a world of change.

JUST AS AN INDIVIDUAL CAN INFLUENCE THE MANY, the many can influence an individual. I am indebted to many people for helping me along this path, through these multiple vistas. First and foremost are my parents, who sacrificed for my success; they instilled in me several important values, including a work ethic. Examining my career in political and community organizing, it is amazing how much I learned as a Prep for Prep student. The most important parts of this education were not even in the syllabus.

Every Wednesday afternoon in sixth grade, I would take the subway from P.S. 61 downtown to attend Prep for Prep classes at

Trinity School. Riding the train on the elevated tracks over the Bronx, a fellow classmate and I would see our imposing red-brick schoolhouse fade into the distance over the abandoned lots and then, as the various neighborhoods went by, bustling and vibrant thoroughfares, with people milling in and out of bodegas and drugstores, hair salons and shops. Then the train would go underground and eventually I would emerge in Manhattan, to navigate the streets of the Upper West Side in order to arrive for Prep classes by four o'clock.

Such public transportation served as a vehicle for social mobility, taking me to Prep and then afterwards to Riverdale Country School, which I attended for six years. On these trips around the city, I saw firsthand the inequality and disparities that wonderfully and disgracefully coexist in New York. While both my home and my high school were in the Bronx, they could have been in different worlds. My commute to Riverdale Country School by public bus took an hour and a half each way, snaking through the various streets, through rows of multiple-story projects, past the Bronx Zoo, onto the Fordham Road commercial center of discount stores, alongside Van Cortlandt Park and finally up to the mansions of Riverdale. The trip to school was an education in and of itself.

"Is it not a man's duty, as a matter of course, to devote himself to the eradication of any, even the most enormous wrong?" asks Thoreau in a passage I can still recite from memory. With my placement by Prep into an exclusive private school, I was presented with both the problem and the means to a solution. I developed my own perspective on the inequalities of society, and my education provided me with both the desire and the ability to envision how to make change.

Beyond providing educational opportunity, Prep was a living example of social change disguised as a scholarship program. One of its earliest brochures talked about diversifying private schools by identifying and preparing academically motivated and exceptionally bright minority students, while at the same time giving such students an opportunity they deserved but might not otherwise get—the opportunity to obtain a quality education. After placement, "graduates are closely monitored and provided with continuing counseling, tutoring if and when necessary, the support of a transition peer group, and the help of an advocate, until success in prep school appears secure." While the program always stressed follow-up, its ambition appeared to be limited to making sure the children did well in their new schools.

When I entered Prep in the program's fifth year, a good portion of the program's infrastructure was already in place: the use of Trinity School, the curriculum, the schedule, the advisor groups. Yet, as the program was reshaped and continually augmented, we joked that we were guinea pigs. But we were guinea pigs also in a much more significant way, part of a radical social experiment that gave its students a "double consciousness" not unlike what W.E.B. Du Bois described in *The Souls of Black Folk* a century ago. Between the social and class dislocation created by placement in private school, and my own mixed-ethnic Ecuadorean, Chinese and Irish background, I had a profound sense of adolescent cultural confusion. But with that came a critique of race, class and culture, and ultimately a clarity of purpose.

Just as our individual ambitions grew, so did those of Prep. Today's brochure focuses primarily on the concept of "leadership development" and the 14-month academic program is now only one of many "components." Over the years the program has expanded to include a wide array of leadership development projects for its high school students as well as professional advancement and other opportunities and services for the program's college undergraduates. As the goals of the program have grown, the expectations of its graduates have as well. Our responsibility is no longer simply to get into New York's elite independent schools and do well there. "America needs the kind of leaders that Prep for Prep students have the potential to become," the more recent brochure declares.

I witnessed some of this evolution in my years as a student, project participant, volunteer and alumnus. I benefited from just the beginnings of what was to become a highly structured leadership development program at Prep. The program did assist me, for example, in getting a White House internship right after college in

Vice President Al Gore's office during the first year of the Clinton presidency.[1] Well before then, however, I had already decided to focus my career on the notion of public service. More important than the actual curriculum during those initial 14 months, or the various opportunities that Prep made available to me, Prep gave me a firsthand example of, and insight into, the nonprofit ethic that I strive to maintain today.

Embodying the program was Gary Simons, a workaholic perfectionist who seemed to live in Prep's offices at all hours, directing traffic in the hallways, churning out memos and directives of considerable length, totally dedicated to his vision, down to each specific detail. Students recognized a similar drive in each of our teachers, most of whom taught at Prep after their full-time jobs at other schools and institutions, and in each member of Prep's own full-time staff. As the founder and director, Gary Simons proved the value of individual action, but also showed how it only worked because he had managed to build another type of coalition, to get literally thousands of others to buy into the vision: teachers, staff members, funders, public and private school educators and administrators, not to mention the students themselves and their parents. At an early age, I understood that work could be more than just a job; it could be a mission.

As a high school junior I was among the editors of *The Telegraph,* Prep's newsletter, and it was then that I first heard Gary Simons describe an even broader vision while making a triangle with his fingers. "If society is structured like a pyramid, with only a few leaders at the top, then Prep's mission is to find and develop the best talent from the bottom of the pyramid to take many of those leadership roles. Not only would such leaders be able to represent those at the bottom of the pyramid, but they also would be able to help change the shape of the pyramid—to change society by making it more equitable in the first place." This took Du Bois' notion of giving the

[1] During each year of the Clinton presidency, at least 6 and sometimes as many as 15 Prep undergraduates obtained positions as White House interns. Since these are unpaid positions and the students needed to contribute summer earnings as part of their college financial aid packages for the following year, Prep provided each intern with a stipend and also provided living accommodations in Washington, D.C. Interns worked in a wide range of departments.

"key to knowledge" to the "Talented Tenth" a step further, not just to lead society, but to change it. And Prep showed by example that it was possible, that by taking constructive action, believing in the possibilities for a solution and working toward it, a problem can be addressed. While the program was not perfect, and the broader issues of educational inequality continued to need to be worked on, it was a more powerful approach than cynicism and inaction or unchanneled anger.

My career has focused on working for social change, organizing through nonprofit advocacy organizations in Washington, D.C., New Jersey and California. As program director for New Jersey Citizen Action, I sent my organizers to the Midwest Academy, which sponsors a weeklong training session on direct action. Perhaps taking some issue with Thoreau, the Academy reminds consumer groups like those for which I have worked, that we don't win because we are right on the issue, or as a matter of conscience, but through the strategic understanding of power relations and how to intervene to make change. The Academy teaches that the goal of political organizing is not just to win victories, but to develop leaders and build strong institutions for future efforts. It puts forth three fundamental goals of organizing: 1) to win concrete improvements in people's lives, 2) to make people aware of their own power, and 3) to alter the relations of power.

Long before it officially acknowledged its "leadership development" mission in 1988, Prep was already an agency for organizing. Not only was I a beneficiary of access to a first-rate education that provided concrete improvements in my life circumstances; I was also given a sense of my own power, and a mission.

As an individual, I am acutely aware of the potential and the limits of my power. As an organizer, however, I don't see any limits. I just see a vision of what needs to be done.

ANTHONY E. WRIGHT *is a member of Contingent V. Born and raised in the Bronx, he graduated from Riverdale Country Day School in 1989 and received a B.A., magna cum laude, in both English and sociology from Amherst College in 1993. At Amherst, he was awarded the Charles Hamilton Houston Fellowship and the Donald S. Pitkin Prize in Sociology. During the summer of 1993 Anthony interned at the White House in the Office of the Vice President, and in the fall he interned at* The Nation *magazine. For the following two years, he served as coordinator of The Future of Media Project for the Center for Media Education in Washington, D.C., managing all aspects of an advocacy, research, organizing and public education initiative focusing on "information highway" policy issues on behalf of consumers and the public interest. In September 1996, he joined the staff of New Jersey Citizen Action, the state's largest consumer watchdog coalition, as its main organizer for the Campaign for Patients' Rights, and from April 1997 to June 2001 served as program director, winning HMO Patient Protections, defeating for-profit takeovers of Blue Cross Blue Shield and dramatically expanding health coverage for low and moderate-income families. For this work, he was awarded an Equal Justice Medal by Legal Services of New Jersey. In July 2001, he became director of organizing for Health Access California and in early 2002 was named its executive director with responsibility for the overall management of this state umbrella health care consumer coalition, made up of 200 member organizations.*

EPILOGUE

WHEN I PAINTED *BE THE DREAM* 25 YEARS AGO, there was no way I could have imagined the size and scope that Prep for Prep would attain, nor the strength that over 1,700 alumni and over 1,000 students would draw from our membership in the Prep Community. I was going on 12, and I knew nothing of how organizations were founded, sustained and developed. What I did understand were the fears and hopes of a Puerto Rican boy growing up in a housing project in the South Bronx. As the youngest of four children in a low-income family, it seemed to me that everything that mattered resulted from forces beyond one's own control. Yet in the midst of an area dominated by the vicious winds of hopelessness, a special teacher operating a special classroom gave me the strength to see and step toward a better tomorrow. A newfound love for learning inspired me to believe that a young man *could* determine his own future, even if that kid was from the South Bronx.

Little did any of us know back in 1978 that our decisions and actions would have a ripple effect on nearly 3,000 children and families within the following 25 years. The power of Prep as an intervention is as strong today as it was a quarter-century ago, but now the outer limits of its influence seem never-ending, for each Prep student and alumnus touches the lives of countless others and Prep for Prep itself stands as a model of what is possible. As a student and artist who was present at the launch of this local restoration of the American dream, I feel blessed to be a part of Prep for Prep's story. To me, it is as if the figures in my painting have come alive many hundred-fold.

As I think back to my life before sixth grade, I grow embarrassed —and at the same time proud—of the audacity of the *Be the Dream* mural. With three older siblings, I had familiar footsteps to follow in and no reason to expect my path in life to be any different from theirs. The empty lots and abandoned churches that surrounded my school emanated pessimism, a voice that seemed to whisper to us that we wouldn't amount to much as adults. My entire experience in public school up to that point had convinced me that life had little to do with one's individual efforts and everything to do with the impersonal institutions and forces that made decisions for and about poor children. I don't think I was capable of putting those feelings into words like these, but the message was received and felt nonetheless.

My parents had come to New York in the late 1950s in search of work and better opportunities for their children. Back home in Yabucoa, Puerto Rico, my father had discontinued his education after the eighth grade, while my mother had left school after the fifth grade to raise her younger siblings. When I was born, my family moved to a three-bedroom apartment in the Forest Houses, where our building was one of a dozen red-brick monsters perched on a hill on Tinton Avenue and 163rd Street. Burned-out tenements and abandoned courthouses lined the 15 blocks between the Forest Houses and the nearest landmark, Yankee Stadium. A friend from my parents' hometown helped my father get a job in the kitchen of a Bronx nursing home, where he worked for over 30 years. My mother never really learned much English and remained a full-time wife and mother.

Although our apartment felt like a safe haven (always warm with the smell of Puerto Rican rice and beans), my perhaps unusually keen observation skills made me realize at a very early age that we lived in a very dangerous neighborhood. Stories of local stabbings or muggings were rarely in the local papers, *The Daily News* and *El Diario.* Instead, my mother would bring the stories home with the avocados collected at the local supermarket. Occasionally, my older brother, Jimmy, and I would find trails of blood in the stairwells of our building when we made our weekly run to the bodega for the Sunday paper and Italian bread. His friends always had a detailed version of the events of the previous night, but Jimmy and I would usually go our way without wanting to know or dwell on it too much. It was the only way to respond, I learned. Quiet resignation mixed with some dash of fear was the normal response to violence in the projects.

Bored by being trapped in my apartment most days, I longed to start school and experience it for myself. It represented a coming of age and a part of growing up. Whenever my two older brothers or my sister, Carmen, talked to my parents about their schools, I would listen intently, hoping to catch details of what the future had in store for me. I could not understand why my siblings seemed so nonchalant and unexcited about school.

While I enjoyed prekindergarten and the start of school, I soon realized that each day had a meaningless redundancy to it. More and more, as I moved up the grades, teachers focused on trying to minimize behavioral disturbances and just maintain order. The constant potential of physical confrontations between students, and occasionally between a student and a teacher, kept everyone in a state of tension, especially the frequently appearing substitute teachers. Rarely was any real intellectual challenge offered to us. The most rigorous assignments were three to five pages in the boring, out-of-date textbooks known as our "readers." I soon realized that I could complete these reading assignments during the commercial breaks of one of my favorite afternoon television shows. The great irony was that while teachers fussed about the distribution and collection of these readers at the beginning and end of the academic year, they never really held us accountable for actually doing the reading assignments on all the nights in between. Nor did I ever hear any student express concern about not meeting the teacher's expectations with regard to these assignments.

In my memories of public school, one image keeps reappearing. More than any single event, it was the daily end-of-day routine that seemed to permeate most of my elementary school experience: the rushed herding of students to the building's exits as close to the earliest possible interpretation of three P.M. This dash was accompanied by the loud stamping or punching of time cards by teachers in the main office. Each teacher had to punch out, and they all made sure it was the absolute last thing they did before rushing to their parked cars. The daily herding had the tempo of a fire drill. Perhaps it offered the lessened probability of witnessing a brawl or being approached by an angry parent whose child had been expelled. Whatever the reason for this daily routine, it left me with a prevailing feeling of rejection that would only seep into my consciousness much later.

It was in the last year at my elementary school that I did far more learning than in all the preceding years. My school was called The Eagle School, but not until I stepped into Mr. Simons' classroom did I feel that I could fly. Within a few months, my sense of achievement led me to look at my situation very differently. Finishing entire paperbacks in rapid fire and being held strictly accountable each day for the contents of the previous night's reading was doing something that six months before I would have thought absolutely impossible. It was almost as if I could take those paperbacks, pile them up, take a step up and climb over the invisible walls that encircled my neighborhood. Empowered by my achievements, with my imagination fueled by the readings in history and literature, I could imagine new horizons far beyond the South Bronx. It was a vantage point made possible by books, a teacher's high expectations, a consistent structure and the message that the individual *does* matter.

It was with such thoughts racing through my mind that I painted *Be the Dream.* The image of a boy holding the world in his hands was so laughably literal. The bubbles of possibilities around him, a technique borrowed from comic books to convey what a character was thinking, was not something I would ever use again once I began actual art lessons that fall. But who the heck did I think I was to have the temerity to believe that one's own efforts in school could actually lead to the fulfillment of one's dreams—in the poorest congressional district in the country!

As an art project, I loved doing the mural. It was on a scale I had never attempted before. The size of the brown butcher-block paper allowed me to make the characters almost life-size. It was my personal Sistine Chapel.

Only three blocks away from my school, *Fort Apache, The Bronx* was filmed. Paul Newman starred in it. Some friends and I heard that young people were getting two or three hundred dollars to serve as "extras." We trotted over for our payday, but when we got there, we learned that there was only one spot left and we had to pick a number to see which one of us would get selected. I lost that draw and missed out on being in the movie. It was probably a blessing, however, because the film depicted the local residents as savages who only cared about drugs. We should have known when they handed out bottles made of sugar to be thrown at the actors who were dressed in police riot gear. One extra broke a fake baseball bat over an officer's back. In another scene, someone was thrown off a rooftop.

The time was certainly ripe for a cadre of young leaders who would have the courage and the means to begin challenging such stereotypes. Little did I know that the new program Mr. Simons had started would develop just such leaders.

During that first Prep summer, Elaine Richards, the director of admissions of The Calhoun School, where I was to matriculate in the fall, visited our classes. Much to my surprise, she requested that at the end of the summer my mural adorn a wall at her school. *Be the Dream* was transported from Trinity School down to Calhoun and hung outside Calhoun's admissions office. At first, it didn't occur to me that the message would resonate at my new school as much as it had at Prep, since on the surface my new classmates seemed to have everything they could possibly want. I did not mind that the admissions office had incredible traffic, which would probably mean occasional accidental tears in the mural since Calhoun had tight passageways in its administration area. I was just proud to know that a wider audience would be enjoying my work.

Wanting an environment where I could focus on academics and avoid neighborhood distractions, I matriculated at The Hotchkiss School for ninth grade. As Prep's first student to attend boarding school, I wanted to represent Prep in the best light possible. Hotchkiss offered me so many opportunities to develop as a person that I wanted to take full advantage of them all. Much as I had done in Mr. Simons' class years before, I dedicated myself to my studies. Each vocabulary word I did not recognize was one I would look up. Each rewrite that I was allowed to do for a slightly higher grade, I did. What I lacked in natural eloquence, I tried to make up for with hard work and determination. Attending Hotchkiss allowed me to meet an incredible group of people during a key developmental point of my life. I enjoyed it tremendously.

And it was during those years at Hotchkiss that the old dictum "From those to whom much has been given, much is expected" became comprehensible and important to me. It was part of what Mr. Simons was preaching at Prep, and it was Prep as well as Hotchkiss that would soon offer me many opportunities to contribute. I knew that I didn't leave the Bronx to go to Hotchkiss, but instead I was bringing the Bronx with me. Being one of only two Puerto Rican students at Hotchkiss, I felt my viewpoints could add value to the Hotchkiss Experience for my fellow students. Boarding school allowed us to learn from one another, and we had to make the most of it.

One day, a fellow student said to me, "You're one of the good Puerto Ricans because you actually study."

"You just haven't met enough of us yet," I replied.

Rather than wrestle with stereotypes he had picked up from some late-night movie like the one filmed in my neighborhood, I determined to participate fully in the life of the school and by doing so attempt to change such stereotypes one person at a time. As teammates, for example, striving toward a common goal together made us see commonalities among us first and differences second. Classmates whose parents were leaders in various industries were equals with me in wrestling practice or in class, and we respected one another.

At the end of my junior year, the faculty selected me to be a dormitory proctor and my peers on the varsity wrestling team elected me their captain. No longer was I that Puerto Rican kid from the Bronx. Instead, I had become a respected artist, athlete and member of the school community who happened also to be proud of his Puerto Rican heritage. I could even take the stage and "break-dance" at school socials, sharing a bit of inner-city culture.

Back home for the summers, I was given the chance to serve as an advisor at Prep. Each summer, strengthened by my Hotchkiss Experience, I returned to Prep like a soldier trained in new leadership strategies. Working with children who were literally following in my own footsteps proved to be intensely satisfying.

At the end of Summer Session 1984, Gary Simons said to me, "Get yourself ready, because next year we're going to entirely restructure the way advisors work with and communicate with the faculty and administration. We need an organized summer advisory *system,* and you're going to be its head. It *has* to be an all-Prep corps." It was the kind of announcement I had gotten used to, like when a coach or mentor tells you that you're going to have to step up and do something for the larger good. And so the following summer, as a newly minted Hotchkiss graduate, I served as the first head of our Summer Advisory System, having chosen 16 (in later years 24) of Prep's high school students to replace the former mostly non-Prep corps. I returned each of my Princeton summers to build on that first summer's work.

In 1989 Gary informed me that the board of trustees had passed a new mission statement and that a position as coordinator of leadership development activities was being created. Would I consider taking a crack at it? Six months later, I was director of Leadership Development, a newly established component of Prep, responsible for the high school juniors and seniors and charged with developing projects that would nurture their leadership potential.

I can still remember calling board members for leads on possible placements and the excitement of launching the Summer Jobs Bank. I can remember the initial meetings with the folks at Coro and the excitement of our first collaborative nine-week Leadership Development Summer Institute, which introduced selected Prep students to the world of public policy. Those first LDSI participants were charged with the responsibility of starting a student-run project, and I remember working with young student leaders like Robyn Young, Corey Modeste and Makonnen Payne to launch a child advocacy organization, Students Advocating for Young Children (SAYC), which continues today. I remember working with Tony Allen to create the Local Government Summer Internships Project to allow students to build on their LDSI experience. I remember the start of our now long-standing partnership with the U.S. Experiment in International Living, which over the years has enabled hundreds of Prep students to serve as ambassadors to at least two dozen countries on six continents, changing the world one friendship at a time. Prep students have become citizens of the world and have been making a difference all over the globe.

I remember when Gary and I began discussing in 1993 how our students were being given access to many experiences that developed their leadership skills and their aspirations, yet we had no structured forum to allow them to examine the meaning of leadership. Out of those discussions came Gary's determination to create Aspects of Leadership, the one leadership development project in which all Prep students are now required to participate. It has been particularly fulfilling to be one of the facilitators (teachers) of Aspects modules and to press students to explore the challenges of ethical and effective leadership. Hearing our students discuss the kind of leaders *they* hope to become is among the most inspiring experiences one can imagine.

In 1996 I said to Gary that with seven contingents of college graduates, I thought the time had come for an annual alumni giving campaign. Having offered to chair this effort, I remember the satisfaction of recruiting fellow alumni to serve on the AGC

Committee. When I think of those individuals who responded to my calls, I am still astounded at the level of commitment they brought to the project; it makes it clearer to me how the organization could have come this far. I continue to be flabbergasted by the unwavering support of people like Pamela Gee, Steve Del Villar, Robyn Young, Karen Young, Jerry Bright, Oba Davis, Bo Tan, Claudia Cruz, Elbert Garcia, Jemina Bernard, Pang Lee and Diahann Billings-Burford, among many others, who not only were generous financially but gave many hundreds of hours to calling fellow alumni over the six years I chaired the AGC.

Few things have been as rewarding as reconnecting with fellow alumni and hearing from them how they felt Prep had played a key role in enabling them to get where they were in their lives. In the course of hundreds and hundreds of solicitation calls each year, we would often discuss the impact the organization and people in it had had on their lives.

Far more important to me than the chance to develop and launch projects have been the many wonderful friendships I have developed with alumni, many of whom I've known since they were children and others whom I am still getting to know. So many of us share close bonds forged by similar journeys. I have had the chance to get to know so many extraordinary individuals, I can't imagine how Gary could even decide whom to ask to contribute to this book. There could easily have been hundreds of other, equally compelling stories.

Reading the stories in this book made me laugh and cry, but mostly they made me nostalgic and proud. I can still remember sitting with Charles Guerrero to reorganize his loose-leaf binder, something akin to a daily ritual his first summer at Prep; it's incredibly rewarding now to see current Prep and PREP 9 juniors and seniors have the joyous experience of working with him as Prep's director of College Guidance. Similarly, it is a joy to work with Joseph Ayala, who has brought his incredible commitment to Prep's younger students to his various roles at Prep, as advisor, interviewer, Research Skills teacher, Aspects facilitator, and for the past four years director of Leadership Development Counseling. I remember the shock I experienced when visiting Pang Lee at the hospital and my anxiety that his having become the victim of random violence might derail his college plans. I will never forget Elbert Garcia's overly respectful nods to various prominent advisors, when Elbert himself was still a "grad." One could already see a desire in his eyes to make his mark. I have numerous memories of Diahann Billings-Burford, including the time we appeared together on *CBS This Morning* (along with Jessica Zayas) to represent Prep live nationwide. And years later I enjoyed training Diahann, when she agreed to join my component as a college counselor. Her strong analytical skills made me realize that she really wasn't going to need all that much training; she was a natural. I remember Kevin Otero's disappointment that he had not been encouraged to apply to Yale and his determination to persist and pursue that dream with a little encouragement from me. His appreciation and his ongoing commitment to being the best he can be is a testament to Prep and fills me with pride to have played even a small part in his development and that of other equally exceptional young people. And I remember many years ago sitting down with Karen Young so Gary and I could explain why we believed she should succeed me as head of the Summer Advisory System, and I remember our conversation last year when I asked Karen to pick up the reins from me and chair the 7th Annual Alumni Giving Campaign.

For many years at Prep for Prep's annual orientation for newly admitted students and their parents, I've urged parents to get behind their children when the going gets tough. For many years, I talked with students and parents at these orientation meetings and individually during the summer about what it means to have the opportunity to become an educated person and what it means to earn membership in Prep for Prep.

I have been extremely lucky to have seen Prep develop from its very beginning, to have seen someone's dream and vision become a vibrant reality. For 25 years, I have believed fervently in this dream. I always will.

Frankie Cruz
January 15, 2003
New York City

FRANKIE CRUZ *is a member of Contingent I. Born and raised in the Bronx, Frankie graduated from The Hotchkiss School in 1985 and received a B.A. in politics from Princeton University in 1989. At Princeton, he served for three years as a minority student recruitment coordinator, working with the Admissions Office to interest more Latino students in applying to Princeton. Throughout his undergraduate years, he spent each summer at Prep, serving as the first head of the Summer Advisory System.*

Following graduation from college, Frankie joined Prep's full-time staff and, over the next seven years, built the now multifaceted Leadership Development Component from scratch. His commitment to the many other young people following in his own footsteps was recognized by his alma mater when in 1993 he was among the first few recipients of the Hotchkiss Alumni Association's Community Service Award. In 1995 he launched and for six years chaired Prep's Annual Alumni Giving Campaign, which achieved a 71 percent participation rate (among Prep's college graduates) during each of those years. In 1996 he became the first Prep for Prep alumnus to be elected to Prep's board of trustees.

Also in 1996, Frankie began a two-year hiatus from Prep in order to explore politics in the Bronx, first working as special assistant to Assemblyman Roberto Ramirez, who was then chairman of the Bronx Democratic Party. Coming to believe that people of low-income communities were too often not receiving appropriate representation, and particularly chagrined at how the 79th assembly district in which he had grown up was being represented, in 1998 he challenged nine-term incumbent Assemblywoman Gloria Davis. While he succeeded in turning back a determined effort to prevent his getting on the ballot, Ms. Davis nevertheless won the primary. Following the election, Frankie responded to entreaties that he return to Prep, where he currently serves as deputy executive director for Leadership Development.

IN THE WORDS OF YOUNG CHILDREN

DAMALI DRISKELL, whose autobiographical vignette accompanied the introduction to this book, also delivered the commencement speech for the contingent that completed the Preparatory Component in August of 2002. Her words, and the words of other equally eloquent 11- and 12-year-olds, have moved everyone involved with Prep for Prep over the last 25 years.

While students do a great deal of writing at Prep, there are a few special occasions on which a boy or girl comes to the podium and speaks from the heart. It seems only fitting to end this book with some of those expressions of excellence, integrity, commitment and, perhaps most of all, courage.

SPEECH DELIVERED AT COMMENCEMENT

SEPTEMBER 7, 2002

by DAMALI DRISKELL, *Age 12*

ON JUNE 28, 2001, I waited outside my house for a school bus to pick me up. It was going to be a hot summer day. Kids were off to their last day of public school, celebrating the end of the school year. But while that meant the end for them, that day was only the beginning for me and 154 other students like me.

I was very nervous that day. If that wasn't bad enough, the bus was running late. I waited for 15 minutes. Then 20 minutes. I was in a panic. Finally, the bus picked me up, half an hour behind schedule, and in a burst of speed I was raced off to the unknown.

After hours in sweltering classrooms, I returned home, stunned by what I had just experienced. I would have sat down to analyze the situation further, but I had a lot of homework to do. That was my first day of Prep for Prep, about 14 months ago.

Since then, I feel that I have grown and learned a lot about myself. I am more open to new ideas, people and opinions.

When I look back, I see that I got more from Prep for Prep than the obvious—the better educational opportunity and the prestigious private school placement. Prep has changed how I make

---

Damali is currently a seventh-grader at Trinity School.

decisions and execute tasks. In retrospect, I feel that the 14 long, hard, exhausting months we as a contingent endured was a small price to pay for the help, advice and opportunity we will receive from Prep and our independent school communities.

Through Prep for Prep, I revealed and expressed more of my inner self. Assignments that I completed exposed more about my personality and tastes. For example, I had an assignment in which we had to write a piece about one of the books that we had read. I chose to write a piece concerning the novel *Fahrenheit 451*. I realized that I like books that focus in on one strong main character and have an interesting plot line. Coming from a very large family like mine, with two sisters and three brothers, I understand why I enjoyed a book that focused on only one person.

Through this, I learned that either consciously or unconsciously I make decisions related to my work, based on my surroundings and lifestyle. I like when things I do or know relate to me. Coincidence cannot account for the fact that I make choices that reflect situations in my life. I naturally pick the option that most affects me.

In a similar situation, I wrote about education for a PIMAS essay assignment. PIMAS is one of our second-summer courses, in which we explore problems and issues in modern American society. Education plays a significant role in all our lives. While we are rightfully grateful for our new educational opportunities, we cannot forget the public school system where many of our brothers and sisters are enrolled. We, Contingent XXIV members, have to convince our independent school communities to support improvements in New York City's public schools.

I have always had a problem with time management, and attending public school while taking Prep classes on Saturdays and Wednesdays from September through June complicated the demands on my time. Prep taught me to prioritize the most important assignments to be tackled. Did I do my math homework first because I liked it or because it was easiest? I had to choose between watching some TV after dinner, like I usually would do, and finishing my homework. I decided, using my better judgment, to do my work.

I spent many late nights finishing homework and appreciated every hour of sleep I got. I eventually learned how to budget my time and get my work done. Now, if I have a block of time available, I use it more efficiently than I would have in the past.

Prep's motto is Excellence, Integrity, Commitment and Courage. A vital part of this motto, Integrity, influences my thinking, especially when weighing different options. I look at the situation and consider what is the right thing to do. What would I do if someone were watching me? If I did the same act that I would have done under close scrutiny, then it was probably the right choice. Integrity, as it relates to myself and other people, along with common sense, helped me over the 14 months. It is a standard by which to live and work.

Prep for Prep has and will continue to affect my life in numerous ways. When I receive my certificate this afternoon, I will be doubly proud because I will receive it from my elder sister, Soyini, a Contingent XX member, who will begin her junior year at Packer Collegiate Institute this fall. The Prep family is now an integral part of the Driskell family.

As I look back, I see that I've changed significantly over the last 14 months. I've changed in how I see things that I may have overlooked in the past, in how I act and execute decisions. Prep for Prep strives to build and develop leadership qualities in minority youth. We have all faced trials as individuals and as a contingent for 14 long months.

Contingent XXIV will forever be linked to the World Trade Center tragedy. Our first summer ended as the towers fell. Today's ceremony is five days before the first anniversary of this horrible event. September 11 opened our eyes to the flaws in society that we, as future leaders, must strive to improve. New York must be rebuilt, and all of the Prep graduates must be leaders in that process.

To my fellow members of Contingent XXIV, though we will all go our separate ways and continue to work hard in our private schools, the bonds that have made us a community will remain.

I would like to thank the teachers and staff that kept us motivated and moving forward. I would like to thank my friends who gave me support and advice when I needed it. Your competitive spirit forced me to do better.

And I would especially like to thank my parents and all the Contingent XXIV parents who applauded, guided, assisted and inspired us through our journey. They picked us up at 6:30 P.M. on Wednesdays during the school year and woke us up each day at 6:30 A.M. for two summers in a row. I express my gratitude. We could not have made it alone.

Thank you and good evening.

SPEECH DELIVERED AT COMMENCEMENT

SEPTEMBER 6, 1997

by JOANNE CACERES, *Age 11*

GOOD AFTERNOON. Most of us join Prep to get a better education. But what does having a better education mean? Fourteen months ago, the answer would not have been so clear to me as it is now. A better education should make you more aware and teach you to reflect on things. It should also teach students to make connections between what they are learning and the world around them. Knowledge is not only knowing facts, but understanding their significance. During the past 14 months, I have acquired what I believe is a better education.

The Preparatory Component of Prep has made me more intellectually aware. In Prep, I did not just learn Newton's Three Laws of Motion; it was taken a step further. In class, we did various activities to prove to ourselves these laws. Mr. Taylor, my science teacher during the school year and the second summer, especially comes to mind, because he was always willing to show and tell us *why* so we would understand instead of memorize the material.

In fact, every teacher I've had at Prep has helped me in some way. Ms. Greenebaum really helped me become a better student. With

Joanne Caceres is currently completing her senior year at Horace Mann School and in December 2002 was admitted to Princeton University under its Early Decision Plan.

her everlasting wisdom and open ear, she taught me important skills, like being a more active participant in class and taking intellectual risks. She also taught me to read between the lines. *To Kill a Mockingbird* is not just about Scout and Boo Radley; it is about the savage inequalities in the South. Ms. Greenebaum, as well as other teachers, taught me to learn from my own mistakes and to aim not only for high grades, but for a greater understanding. Through my literature classes I have learned the power of creativity and felt the completeness one gets from finishing a book.

It seems the more you know, the more there is to learn. Each answer seems only to raise new questions. This is pretty amazing. I could learn for centuries and still have lots more to know.

Something I didn't expect from reading books was that they would help me learn so much about myself. I found myself crying for Boo Radley. "How would I feel if I were him?" While reading *Lord of the Flies,* I would wonder, "Would I be a Ralph, a Jack, a Simon, a Piggy, or just another follower?" and "Has my good side overpowered the bad, or am I just a balance of both?" Reading and discussing the books in class helped me realize how little I had known about myself and how much I was beginning to learn.

I learned not only from books and teachers, but also from advisors and peers. Janelle James, my advisor both summers, would take the time every day to find a special quotation for us to analyze during unit period. Janelle's quotations not only taught me life-lessons, but further proved to me that an entire group can disagree with you on a topic and still be your friends.

While the fact that I was not the only one to go through the 14 months was surely very comforting, there were many times when I might have slacked off if not for the help of my family. My dad was always willing to transport me from place to place. My sister was a rope that I could always cling to for support. My little brother's naive smile could transform me from a monster to a princess. And lastly, there was my mom, who was always there to talk, philosophize or just give me a hug. The 14-month Preparatory Component helped me realize how much my family means to me.

At Prep, I began to recognize the feelings I was experiencing, both good and bad, which were greater in intensity than ever before. My emotions have been like a box of crayons; before Prep, it contained only eight different colors, but with time and creativity these eight basic colors have mellowed and intensified into 96 different shades. Thus, because of the many experiences I've had over the last year, there are now many tones of sadness, like frustration, stress, defeat and disappointment, and many tones of happiness, like control, comfort, triumph and joy.

By being more personally aware, I am also becoming socially aware in terms of understanding society at large. For example, PIMAS, a course about problems and issues in modern American society, has shown me what happens when problems are not addressed. Poverty is one of America's biggest social problems. The country does not understand its welfare recipients. This is why various programs have failed. It seems to be something politicians today do not care about. Maybe the future will be different with us around.

The greatest skill a "better education" can teach you is how to make connections. Because of my time at Prep, I can now make connections between math and science, *Animal Farm* and *Lord of the Flies,* and the most important connection, the past to the present.

A "better education" is one that takes facts a step further. Something in every lesson should make you reflect on yourself. The past 14 months with Prep have done this and more for me. I thank Prep for all it has done for me, and all that it has allowed *me* to do for myself.

BREAKING DOWN A WALL

SEPTEMBER 8, 2001

by GRACE JIANG, *Age 12*

MY MEMORIES OF WHEN I WAS EIGHT consist mostly of a wall, spotless and sinister, trapping me in the small room my family of three lived in. When my family first came to New York, immigrants, we lived by the dime. To save money, we shared a small three-room apartment (originally two, one room then divided in half) with two other people; one bathroom, one kitchen and five occupants. Mainly immigrants and laborers occupied the building, called College Hall because some of the renters went to Brooklyn College nearby. My father juggled driving a delivery van in the day and college at night. My mother worked 12-hour days as a waitress. I was left in the room to watch TV with a neighbor baby-sitting me on the day my father had night school. Like Jose's grandmother in the film *Sugar Cane Alley,*[1] my parents did not want me to mix with the other children in the building. They believed that we would one

When a contingent has completed the 14-month Preparatory Component, the children are invited to enter the *Be the Dream* Essay Contest. Each child is asked to explain what *Be the Dream* means to him or her, and the winning essay is recited by its author at Commencement. Grace is currently an eighth-grader at Poly Prep Country Day School in Brooklyn.

[1] A contingent watches and discusses this film during its four-day trip at the end of the second summer of the Preparatory Component. The film, directed by Euzhan Palcy, depicts life in Martinique in the 1930s and focuses on one boy, Jose, who escaped a life working in the sugarcane fields by winning a scholarship to the island's elite school.

day move away from the building, and those kids would put the wrong ideas in my head. And so, I watched the wall for hours every Wednesday night, and each time I saw it, it seemed more intimidating.

As I assimilated with the kids in my public school, I learned about my classmates' ambitions: Julio was to be a lawyer, Jessica a nurse for her brother, Jeffrey a doctor. I dreamed of a wide range of jobs, from firefighter to freight train engineer. But every time I daydreamed about the wonderful life I would have as a scientist or such, there was always that forbidding wall, staring back at me, mocking.

Reality seeped in more as I got older, until I was a serious fifth-grader, cynical at times. Those old daydreams I dismissed, because I knew that there was no way Julio's family would be able to afford law school, or Jeffrey's family medical school. I never thought about independent school, or actually attending one; it was as distant as the lands of Siberia. Not even when I was in Prep, at first, did I picture myself as the "rags to riches" girl from all those fairy tales, although it did happen quite often in New York City. The mural *Be the Dream,* when I first heard of it, was just another Prep principle that I had to follow, a mere relic of Prep 20 years ago.

After the 14 months at Prep, however, the mural *Be the Dream* finally began to make sense. The boy in the painting reminds me of myself when I was that little girl in P.S. 152. I thought I held the world in my hands, all paths open. Although I had discarded the research scientist fantasies long ago, I now once again feel hope for the future, that despite my background I will still have a chance at a successful life. Prep must have broken the invisible barriers for the boy who painted the mural, Frankie Cruz, just as it pushed them down for me.

Another strong memory I have is of the day when we moved out of the grimy apartment. My father brought down that wall with a hammer. I felt free for the first time. Freedom and opportunity are what *Be the Dream* represents to me, the freedom to do what you want with your life. I live the dream right now, thanks to others. And as I cross over to independent school, I won't forget my past, nor will I take my future for granted.

HISTORY, MISSION & PHILOSOPHY OF PREP FOR PREP

by Gary Simons

At first, Prep consisted of a talent search to identify eligible candidates and to select those we believed would benefit the most by membership in Prep; a 14-month intensive, academically rigorous Preparatory Component (two seven-week summer sessions with classes Monday through Friday, as well as classes on Wednesday afternoons and all day Saturday during the intervening school year); a multistep placement process through which students and families learned about different schools, made choices and went through the application process to those schools; and post-placement counseling to ensure that the transition to independent school went as smoothly as possible and to intervene and assist with any problems that did occur.

In 1987 we launched PREP 9, an internal replication of Prep with two critical differences: the students were admitted at the end of seventh grade (as opposed to the end of fifth or occasionally sixth grade), and the students were to be placed in leading boarding schools (as opposed to day independent schools in New York City and the metropolitan area). PREP 9 provided a second entry point for students who warranted admission but were somehow missed two years earlier, either because their elementary schools did not participate in the nomination process or because their families did not respond to our literature and notices about parent meetings.

In 1988-89 a committee of board and staff members developed a new Mission Statement for the program. The original mission spoke of helping particularly able and motivated young people from minority group backgrounds to access a first-rate education and thereby enhance their professional and life prospects. The new Mission Statement added to this by declaring that Prep's long-term goal was to nurture and develop the leadership potential of particularly able and motivated students from groups that are grossly underrepresented in the leadership pool from which most segments of American society draw their leaders. As tensions that derive from the differences and inequalities of opportunity among us continue to tear at the fabric of life in our nation, the need for capable, credible leaders committed to the common good becomes ever more apparent. By increasing the number of such individuals in the nation's leadership pool, Prep for Prep seeks to impact indirectly on a set of interrelated problems that threaten to rend our society.

Prep's efforts are premised on the belief that all segments of the American population must see that their best and brightest are represented in the leadership of our country's major institutions and in all critical sectors of society. Absent our country's ability to continue to make progress in this regard, it will become increasingly difficult to appeal to "the common good" or to the fundamental widely shared political values that hold our society together. Given the increasing ethnic, racial and religious diversity that now characterizes the American people, increasing the pool of well-educated, credentialed, committed leaders from underrepresented groups becomes more of an imperative with each passing day.

Following the adoption of the new Mission Statement, Post-Placement Counseling & Activities was divided into two separate components, with the 11th- and 12th-graders constituting the new Leadership Development Component. New projects were gradually established, all of which shared the general purposes of enhancing the self-confidence of our students, emboldening their aspirations and enabling them to become more aware of life's possibilities. As time went on, many of the offerings of the Leadership Development Component were made available to our 10th-graders as well.

In 1994 Aspects of Leadership was added to the LDC's offerings in order to provide a structured forum in which our students could consider the meaning of leadership and its importance. The overall intent of Aspects is to help our students understand the kind of leadership that increasingly will be needed in a pluralistic and diverse society premised on democratic principles. Aspects takes the position that we must understand and hold on to some common values and some shared concept of what "America" is and could be. Aspects does not gloss over the tremendous problems we have in our society, yet it stands squarely on the conviction that a continuing disintegration of the concept of "America" will hold us back from narrowing the gap between the rhetoric of American ideals and the reality of the situation for many of our people.

Eleven three- and four-day modules are organized into three strands: Attributes & Tasks of Leaders, Ethics of Leadership, and Leadership in the Context of American Politics. Each module consists of readings, videos, role plays, simulations and discussions. Debates, poetry, mini-projects and videotaping of student sessions are among the other techniques used. John Gardner's *On Leadership* serves as a starting point, especially as he sets forth the attributes and tasks of leaders in late-20th-century America and the key political values underlying our society. Aspects of Leadership presents issues that too often are viewed as either/or dimensions but that we cannot afford to view in this way. Among such issues are the perennial debate between individual rights and the common good, the tension between our emphasis on individual achievement and responsibility versus the development of a social conscience, and the need for leadership that is both ethical *and* effective.

The new Mission Statement and the expanded programming that followed its adoption arose from three sources. First of all, in explaining to our students the long-term goals of the program, in discussing openly with them the obstacles youngsters from minority group backgrounds frequently face and need to overcome, and in our general approach to students and what we expected from them, "leadership"—while not singled out and labeled as such—had always been part of the ethos of the program. Secondly, in 1985, the

Summer Advisory System, a critical element of the Preparatory Component, ceased hiring high school or college students who had *not* been part of the program. When the Summer Advisory System became an all-Prep corps, the difference was extraordinary. The advisors' commitment to assisting the younger children who were literally following in their own footsteps gave the Preparatory Component a spirit, a sense of community and a joyousness that greatly enhanced the experience while also allowing selected high school and college students to hone their own leadership skills. A third consideration was the fact that so many Prep students had emerged as leaders in their various independent schools. Far from being the "second-class citizens" that critics often feared they would become, large numbers of Prep students had become heads of student government, captains of teams, leaders and often initiators of various clubs and student organizations.

When we considered these developments against a backdrop of daily news articles that so often made evident the danger of fragmentation in our society, the difficulties encountered in trying to get different communities to work together as one larger Community, it became clear to us that Prep students represented an invaluable national resource. Their backgrounds, their success in adjusting to a new school culture and coming to understand the workings of the broader society, and the energy and sense of purpose so many of our students exhibited rendered them a source of potential leaders who would be able to bridge the gaps and chasms in our society that are a common element of many seemingly separate societal problems. We began therefore to describe Prep for Prep as "a long-term investment strategy" to develop such leaders.

I have referenced the Summer Advisory System as having played a key role in the clarifying of Prep's broader mission. Let me add that the Summer Advisory System is also a central element in Prep's culture, and readers will find that relationships between advisors and advisees will be referenced in several of the stories in this book. The Summer Advisory System can be thought of as the infrastructure of the Summer Session. Advisors see their advisees individually each day in "pull-out" meetings (which happen during each child's

Writing Conference Period, so students do *not* miss any actual instructional time); they meet with them as a group during the daily Unit Period and eat lunch with their Unit; and they share information among themselves about one another's advisees, since each advisor also spends part of his or her busy day as a teacher's assistant. Advisors, in fact, are the program's "eyes and ears," our first line of defense in quickly getting to know more than 200 new students and thereby responding more effectively to different students' varying problems and needs. Advisors also instill Prep's values in the new students and draw them into the Prep Community. Adjustment to Prep would be a far more daunting task for new students were it not for the enormous help and support they receive from their advisors. As a result, the bonds between many advisors and advisees are very strong.

As programming expanded for the older high school students, so that students attending different schools saw each other more frequently, an unintended but highly significant result was the strengthening of Prep as an "adolescent community," one in which "peer pressure" became a positive as students urged each other to take advantage of opportunities and to avoid risks and temptations that could jeopardize all the things for which they had been working. That sense of a forward-looking, achievement-oriented adolescent community is now one of the key dynamics of the program.

The strong sense of a Prep Community also laid the groundwork for extending the trajectory of Prep's operations into the undergraduate years. Many of our students are the first in their families to attend college, and even those who have a parent or sibling who has attended college rarely have close family members who have attented the nation's most demanding and most selective universities. As the sense of a Prep Community grew stronger among the high school students, there developed an expectation that the organization would maintain contact with its college students and graduates and would orchestrate means by which alumni remained in contact with each other. Doing so also enabled Prep more effectively to assist those alumni who did encounter problems in college. For these reasons, we overcame our earlier fear of being charged with "big brother forever looking over our shoulders" syndrome, and in recent years have devoted increasing resources to build up the Network for Undergraduate Affairs & Professional Advancement.

Despite continued growth in the number of students served and the scope and complexity of the program, the key philosophical, pedagogical and ideological elements that give Prep its ethos, its energy, its spirit, have been there from the beginning. For those seeking to understand Prep, it is probably of more importance to focus on these elements than on the details of how the program is structured.

At orientation for each new contingent of students, I repeat an old mantra: "*You've* got to want it! *You've* got to do it!" I say this in the context of first having explained the many sources of help at Prep and having urged students to be honest and seek out help when it is needed. Yet it is made clear from day one that nothing at Prep is proffered on a silver platter. Membership, in fact, is earned. Accountability is a basic fact of daily life for each student during the 14-month Preparatory Component, and it informs our approach to working with our students throughout high school and college. Our Preparatory Component is often referred to as an academic boot camp, but the sense of accomplishment one feels in the air and hears in the student speeches at Commencement is tangible.

Over the years, many alums, even those with advanced degrees, have told me that Prep for Prep is still the hardest thing they have ever done. I take such statements with a grain of salt, realizing that part of what makes the Preparatory Component so hard is that the students confront its demands at such a young age. In addition, for most of them, it was the *first* really hard thing they had done. Nevertheless, these so often repeated statements are important to an understanding of Prep's influence on its students. Success at Prep requires conscious choices, commitment and stamina. An enormous amount of maturing occurs over those 14 months, and the awareness of having succeeded at something very difficult *does* make a difference in how a child sees his or her future place in the world.

Prep has always urged its students to set goals, to aim high, to strive to be the best that each of them could be. We have sometimes been called "elitist," but having personally conducted the talent search during Prep's first eight years, having aggressively sought out able students in East Harlem, East New York, the South Bronx and Bedford-Stuyvesant (among many, many other neighborhoods, as the Program has grown), it is hard for me to take seriously the charge of elitism.

In Prep's earlier years, we talked a lot about "challenging the stereotypes" that often are held of black or Latino youngsters. We have less reason to emphasize this nowadays, because with so many Prep students in leadership positions at their independent schools, and the vast majority of our alumni attending or having graduated from the nation's leading colleges and universities, each new contingent knows it has a tradition of excellence to maintain. Obviously we have always emphasized the value of making sacrifices (in terms of free time and other activities) at an early age in order to have greater options later in life, options that have the potential to provide intellectual satisfaction and a sense of accomplishment in life. Simply put, working hard at Prep and in independent school is expected and applauded. A veteran foundation program officer who spent an entire summer morning visiting Prep classes remarked that what she saw was the oddest combination of extremely rigorous academic demands and obvious care and attention to each individual child that she had ever observed.

From the very beginning, we have talked about "giving back" and "making a difference," and we have asked our students to think of their own academic success in a larger context. Education empowers people. Leadership positions enable individuals to push for change in our society. It is the rare Prep student who is unaware that much needs changing in our society in order to close the gap between the rhetoric of our loftiest ideals and the realities confronting so many of our people. Most of our students see the problems each day in their neighborhoods.

Early in Prep's development, we took as our motto "Excellence, Integrity, Commitment and Courage." Advisors and counselors talk to children about these concepts. Each child is asked at one point during his or her first summer at Prep to attempt a personal definition of each of these words. While an emphasis on such concepts may not seem "cool," at Prep it sounds legitimate and is taken seriously.

While Prep provides a forum for discussion of problems that students might encounter in making the transition to predominantly white and predominantly affluent independent schools; and while Prep provides opportunities throughout high school for students to talk with counselors about incidents or encounters that have occurred that disturb them; and while Prep does *not* paint a picture of America as a Pollyanna Land devoid of any lingering racism or discrimination; nevertheless we have emphasized day in and day out that opportunity *does* exist—that the emboldened aspirations of our students are legitimate. I have often said to the parents of prospective applicants, "If you do not believe your child's hard work will pay off, if you believe that the deck is so stacked against him or her in ways that will undermine the goals and dreams that we will encourage, then Prep is *not* a good place for you to send your child. Your child will be caught between two different worldviews, and only confusion can result from that. What your child hears from us at Prep is what your child needs also to hear from you, as parents, at home. He *can* make it! She *can* make it! Aim high! Go for it!"

We have always said to our students that when they matriculate at independent school, if all they do is go to classes and compile a strong academic record, the ticket will not be worth its cost in time and energy. We urge them to become involved in their new school communities. It is not unusual to hear that a Prep seventh-grader, enrolled in his school for barely a month, has been elected president of his class. We want our students to know they can be members and leaders of communities with a small "c" and *also* of the larger Community.

What ties it all together can perhaps best be explained by Prep's frequent reference to the poem *Invictus* by William Ernest Henley. The last two lines of the poem declare: "I am the master of my fate; I am the captain of my soul." In fact, we have a course called Invictus in which, among other things, students consider the extent to which this statement is true. Clearly, each of us faces developments in our lives that we cannot control. How we respond to these setbacks, however, can often make a real difference. And to the extent that an individual believes that overall she or he can determine the general parameters of his or her adult life, the more likely it is that the individual will assume responsibility, set goals and work toward them. To the extent an individual believes he or she is a victim of society's inequities, and that victimhood becomes an important component of the individual's identity, there is little incentive to try one's best, to go the extra mile. At Prep, although we do not operate with blinders on or see the world through rose-tinted glasses, we have little patience with those who want to engage in an ongoing dialogue about victimization.

Thus Prep emphasizes the importance of individual effort, initiative and determination, while at the same time stressing the importance of community. Both are crucial, and we see them as mutually reinforcing rather than as opposing perspectives.

From all of the above, it is clear that Prep has a "culture" as well as an ideology and a mission. Faculty and staff members *respect* the students and convey that sentiment to them. We take the students seriously, starting when they are only 11 years old and beginning the Preparatory Component. Our message to them is that they must also take themselves seriously or they cannot expect others to do so. It is made clear to the young students that we regard what they are doing as important and laudable and that they are the central figures, the main characters, in this endeavor. While here to help, to orchestrate activities, to access opportunities, faculty and staff are in reality the *supporting* cast.

Most of us can remember a time when we truly believed that the American dream was becoming more inclusive. Civil rights laws had been passed, and the War on Poverty had made some inroads. Hosts of idealistic young people were committing themselves to careers in education and social work. The war in Vietnam was coming to an end, and we would be able to address the evident but manageable problems at home. In 2003, however, we can no longer escape the realization that something is terribly and fundamentally wrong in this country. Morning in America has come, and gone, and what has followed for a great many of our children is darkness at midday and hunger at night.

We forget at our peril Lincoln's admonition that this nation cannot long endure half slave and half free. In America today, millions of children are shackled by ignorance, imprisoned by poverty, enslaved by a lack of hope and a blighting of their spirits. Slowly and surely, as they give up their freedom, we give up ours. Each time we bolt our doors with one more security device or watch as friends ensconce themselves in yet another gated community, each time we choose another means to travel or an alternate street to cross, each time we succumb to judging a young person by the color of his skin and the supposed likelihood that his color and his intentions toward us are somehow correlated, each time we resign ourselves to conditions that should prompt rage rather than resignation—we *all* become a little less free.

Acknowledgments

All books require the combined efforts of a lot of people, but *Be the Dream* represents a collaborative effort of unusual proportions. There are a great many people whose contributions must be acknowledged, and there are a great many others I would include if space allowed. The 35 alumni who have shared their personal experiences, feelings, beliefs and hopes have been true collaborators at every stage of the long process of producing this book. Their willingness to give of themselves has been extraordinary. Quite apart from the time devoted to writing their stories, each of them has had to bear with our numerous requests and questions. I am grateful for their efforts and encouragement and patience over these many months, proud of this mosaic of a book we have created and thrilled that they have succeeded in telling Prep's story

Peter Workman understood why Prep's story must be told; without him, this book would not have come to pass. Susan Bolotin volunteered to edit the book; I am grateful for her suggestions and patience, and for bringing Lynn Strong to the project. Lynn's manuscript editing was always impeccably wise and sensitive. In addition, I want to thank Paul Hanson for his elegant interior design, and Paul Gamarello for the handsome cover design, as well as Philip Hoffhines, Wayne Kirn and Barbara Peragine, who all worked under tight deadlines and did a superb job nonetheless. I am also grateful to Elisabeth Scharlatt and Algonquin Books of Chapel Hill for seeing the book through the publishing process. And a special thanks goes to the Banta Book Group for donating the printing of the first edition of *Be the Dream.*

A very special note of gratitude goes to Marian Wright Edelman, president of the Children's Defense Fund and the nation's foremost champion of children, for gracing this book with her commentary. Mrs. Edelman's involvement in this project is a great honor.

Numerous people helped bring the book to the attention of important writers and public figures; I thank each of them. Three individuals, however, deserve special thanks for providing invaluable cheerleading and unrelenting support that sustained me through the many rough spots: Jill Iscol, Robin Lester and Keith Meacham. On the homefront, Kate DeMello assisted me every step of the way with unyielding good cheer and fast turnaround of work that allowed deadlines to be met. She also helped me greatly in maintaining communication with all those collaborating in the writing of this book.

Finally, I want to thank Anne Gilchrist Gleacher, the president of our board of trustees, for her warm reception to my idea for this book. It was Annie who first suggested that the book might interest a much wider audience than we initially thought. Her faith in the project helped enormously to fuel my own efforts.

Prep for Prep Participating Schools

The Allen-Stevenson School, Manhattan

Bank Street School for Children, Manhattan

Berkeley-Carroll School, Brooklyn

The Brearley School, Manhattan

Brooklyn Friends School, Brooklyn

Browning School, Manhattan

The Buckley School, Manhattan

The Calhoun School, Manhattan

Canterbury School, New Milford, Connecticut

The Chapin School, Manhattan

Choate Rosemary Hall, Wallingford, Connecticut

Collegiate School, Manhattan

Columbia Preparatory School, Manhattan

Convent of the Sacred Heart, Manhattan

The Dalton School, Manhattan

Deerfield Academy, Deerfield, Massachusetts

Eaglebrook School, Deerfield, Massachusetts

Fay School, Southborough, Massachusetts

The Fieldston School, Riverdale, New York

Friends Seminary, Manhattan

Grace Church School, Manhattan

Groton School, Groton, Massachusetts

Hackley School, Tarrytown, New York

The Hewitt School, Manhattan

The Hill School, Pottstown, Pennsylvania

Horace Mann School, Riverdale, New York

The Hotchkiss School, Lakeville, Connecticut

Kent School, Kent, Connecticut

The Kew Forest School, Forest Hills, New York

The Lawrenceville School, Lawrenceville, New Jersey

Little Red School House and Elisabeth Irwin High School, Manhattan

Manhattan Country School, Manhattan

Marymount School of New York, Manhattan

Middlesex School, Concord, Massachusetts

Milton Academy, Milton, Massachusetts

Miss Porter's School, Farmington, Connecticut

Nightingale-Bamford School, Manhattan

Packer Collegiate Institute, Brooklyn, New York

Phillips Academy Andover, Andover, Massachusetts

Phillips Exeter Academy, Exeter, New Hampshire

Poly Prep Country Day School, Brooklyn, New York

Riverdale Country School, Riverdale, New York

Rye Country Day School, Rye, New York

Saint Ann's School, Brooklyn, New York

Saint David's School, Manhattan

Spence School, Manhattan

St. Andrew's School, Middletown, Delaware

St. Bernard's School, Manhattan

St. Luke's School, Manhattan

St. Mark's School, Southborough, Massachusetts

Staten Island Academy, Staten Island, New York

Tabor Academy, Marion, Massachusetts

The Taft School, Watertown, Connecticut

The Town School, Manhattan

The Trevor Day School, Manhattan

Trinity School, Manhattan

Village Community School, Manhattan

Westminster School, Simsbury, Connecticut

This list includes only those schools at which at least three Prep/PREP 9 students are currently enrolled or that have consistently committed places for Prep/PREP 9 students.

About the Editor

Gary Simons founded Prep for Prep in 1978 and served as executive director until June 30, 2002. During those years, he turned a 25-student program into one with over 2,600 students and alumni. Mr. Simons, now vice chairman of Prep for Prep, is currently focusing on ways that the organization can serve a larger number of deserving young people, while developing an updated curriculum that can be offered to students beyond Prep's own ranks.

Mr. Simons earned a B.A., cum laude, in history from Harpur College (now SUNY Binghamton) and a masters degree in psychology from Teachers College, Columbia University. While at Teachers College, he was appointed a fellow in the Graduate Leadership Education Project in Gifted Education; it was as a Fellow, and under the guise of fieldwork (and the auspices of Teachers College), that he launched Prep for Prep.

While at Teachers College, Mr. Simons continued to teach full-time at P.S. 140 in the South Bronx. During a 12-year period, he taught each of the elementary grades.

(continued from front of book)

"*Be the Dream* tells the story of the power of believing in our young people and offering them the education they need. It highlights the transformative potential in high expectations, academic rigor, student support and family commitment. The compelling and inspirational stories in *Be the Dream* illustrate the way in which developing each child's potential can effect societal change. *Be the Dream* should be read by everyone who genuinely cares about working toward a more just America."

—Pearl Kane, Associate Professor of Education,
Teachers College, Columbia University;
Director, Klingenstein Center for Independent School Education

"The principle at the heart of the Prep for Prep experience—'education can transform lives'—comes to life in the eloquent accounts of Prep alumni. Through the engaging and utterly inspiring stories in *Be the Dream,* familiar phrases like 'striving to do your best' and 'reaching for your dreams' take on real power. As one Prep veteran says, 'This is what Prep has always been about—breaking stereotypes, defying expectations and demanding excellence at all levels. Prep matters, and Prep works.' *Be the Dream* perfectly captures this spirit."

—Edward J. Shanahan, Headmaster, Choate Rosemary Hall

"As a corporate citizen, Goldman Sachs views Prep as one of the most effective efforts now underway to ensure that the leadership pipeline available to business, government, academia and *all* important sectors of American society includes a far larger number of well-educated, highly motivated young people from segments of our American population that continue to be underrepresented in that critical leadership pool."

—Henry M. Paulson, Jr., Chairman & CEO, Goldman Sachs

"*Be the Dream* chronicles the personal stories and accomplishments of the young people of Prep for Prep. It speaks to their personal struggles, life-turning moments, and victories. Prep for Prep gave these remarkable students a field of opportunity and a road map for their journey to higher education. A dozen Prep graduates have come to study at MIT. For example, Pang Lee, MIT Class of '97, arrived from Prep and expanded the sense of community and common purpose of our entire campus. I celebrate the positive impact of Prep in the lives of the students it prepares, the institutions they attend, and the work of the nation and world their leadership makes possible."

—Charles M. Vest, President, Massachusetts Institute of Technology

"Since 1628, Collegiate School has been an educational enterprise committed to New York City's brightest and most aspiring boys. Thankfully we have always been a place insistent that worthy boys should have access to this opportunity regardless of their families' means. For the past 25 of our 375 years, we have had in Prep for Prep the most catalytic partner imaginable in helping us, and other like-minded schools, reach our laudable goal of inspiring and training young people in order that they might go on to lead and serve. Over the years, 69 students we have shared have gone on to laudable undergraduate experiences and forged impressive adult lives; currently, 35 Prep for Prep students are enrolled at Collegiate. Rarely in a community does an attractive idea, however compelling, have the powerful impact that Prep for Prep has had on the students who have been part of the program. And that says nothing about the rest of us, students and faculty, whose own lives have been dramatically affected by schools that are palpably more dynamic, just and interesting than they would have been were it not for this fruitful partnership."

—Kerry Brennan, Headmaster, Collegiate School

"Harvard has benefited enormously from the amazing work Prep for Prep has done over the years with the 72 Prep for Prep alumni already with Harvard degrees and the 43 more currently here. Throughout my career, I have cited Prep for Prep as one of the country's most important programs in identifying and developing promising students from all backgrounds. If we could replicate Prep for Prep around the country, America would be in a much better position to make full use of its talented young people."

—William R. Fitzsimmons,
Dean of Admissions and Financial Aid, Harvard College

"There are tremendously talented students in our inner cities, and Prep for Prep has given many of them a chance to show what they are capable of achieving. I've seen firsthand over many years the great work this organization is doing. It has helped to develop today's student into tomorrow's leader."

—Kenneth I. Chenault, Chairman & CEO,
American Express Company